Teaching Children

about

Jesus

Dr. Charles R. Vogan Jr.

ISBN 978-0-6151-3931-9

Ravenbrook Publishers

A subsidiary of

Shenandoah Bible Ministries

www.shenbible.org

Contents

Introduction 1
How to use this book 7

Section One: Difficulties

  Difficulties In Teaching About Jesus 12

Section Two: Jesus and Children

  Who Is Jesus? 38
  What Do Children Need From Us? 94
  Jesus And Children's Needs 138

Section Three: Teaching from the Gospels

  The Gospels 172
  Sample Stories 202
  The Wider Scope 219

Section Four: Results

  Teaching Children: Results 254

Conclusion 269

APPENDICES:

  The prophecies concerning Christ
  Types of Christ
  The Old in the New
  Christ in Ephesians
  The Tree of the Knowledge of Good and Evil

Introduction

Almost every creature on earth teaches its young, and humans are no exception. And we have much to teach our young! Life is so complex, dangers are so prevalent, knowledge is growing at an enormous rate, and circumstances are moving so swiftly in our society that it has become mandatory that our children learn as much as they can, as quickly as they can, and as well as they can, before they step out into the world on their own. There has never been such an extensive educational system as ours, and there has also never been the need for one as we now have.

The reason we teach our children is because we love them. We want them to have a better chance to make it in the world than we had; at the very least we don't want them to enter life disadvantaged and have no chance to make a success of themselves. We don't want to see them under the burden of poverty and ignorance; we want them to find jobs and families, fit into society well, and provide for themselves and find happiness in their work.

A more far-reaching concern that we have is that the world isn't stopping for anybody, and it will soon be our children's turn to take their places at the helm of life, and our time to retire from the job. The nation will soon turn to them for decisions: politics, education, science, social services, business, entertainment – all these areas and more will be their responsibility. Will they be ready? Will they have the necessary knowledge to carry on and do a good job? What is more important, will they have the same *values* that we have and be just as interested as we are in working for the goals that really count? Or will they change the program, and the rules, and undo all that we have worked so hard to achieve?

This is why we train our children. We want to pass along the torch for the race that we are all in, the same race that our own fathers ran. We hope and pray that our children will see the same vision that we have, will share the same hopes and fears, will build on our efforts and reach for the goals that we've been working for. They are, in a very real sense, a part of us and an extension of us.

If what we have been working for is good, then we had better hope that our children catch the same spirit! If our country was built on tyranny, selfishness, materialism, self-pride, destruction and hurt, ignorance and false propaganda, then it would be better for the whole thing to end with us! It would be better that our children change the way things are instead of prolong them. On the other side of the coin, if we have put together a system that is worth keeping and building upon, and our children tear it all down and replace it with a wicked society, then it would have been better if they had never been born to us. Our name will go down in infamy as having bred a generation of tyrants and self-serving pleasure seekers. So we *both* are responsible in this matter: we are responsible to lead our children in the way they should go, and they are responsible to learn and build on the foundation that we laid in them.

Nowhere is this more true than in the Church of Christ. The situation that the Church faces in this world is becoming more desperate with the passing of each generation: in a hundred years the Church has passed from a position of power and respect to the bottom of the social scale. Almost nobody takes the Church seriously any more. A pastor often has the same respect from the community as a dishonest car salesman. Very few people see the need for morality; and because of our modern science and medical advances we often don't have to suffer from the results of immorality like past generations have had to do – those negative results tended to keep people in line. So whenever the Church has something to say to our generation, it's an uphill battle to even be heard.

We have fearsome battles to fight on every front. In spite of the increase of knowledge and wealth and leisure time, our country's problems are getting more difficult to solve, and it's obvious that the experts' answers aren't solving a thing in spite of their modern tools and skills. And the Church, which ought to have the right answers – at least by the testimony of her own Scriptures – is split into a thousand warring divisions inside her own ranks over just about every issue in Christian doctrine. If we ever needed a generation with some answers, and that quickly, we need it now.

Which brings us to the subject of this study. The task that the Lord has given us to do is to teach our children about himself. The only solution for our distressed and torn world is to learn about the Life of God, the Light of God, the Wisdom of God, the Word of God – Jesus Christ. By God's infinite mercy he has put everything that man could ever need for this life and the next in his Son, and made him available to us. All we have to do is "take and eat" – it's that simple – and we will live. *We* have the answer that the world is looking for! Jesus heals the hurts, repairs the damage, enlightens the ignorant, and does what all of our social and physical sciences can't do for us. His promises have always worked and will continue to work for every generation that turns to him for help.

So we must tell our children about this powerful answer to life's problems, and let them share in the power of the Son of God. If we have seen for ourselves that Christ is our only hope, and that he truly is all that we will ever need, then it won't be hard to convince ourselves that it's Jesus that we want to pass on to our children, not this world's riches or secondary issues that divide Christians.

We have to be careful how we do this because our children are depending on us! We have to give a profound understanding of Christ to our children so that they will know how to use the resources of Christ to handle the immense problems that they will face in the world. We will have to show them from our experiences that Jesus *does* hear prayer and save his people, so that they will not lose hope. We will have to think this through very carefully so that we will know *what* to say to them, *how* to say it, what to steer them toward, what values to have and what to put aside – in every way being careful to give them wisdom on how to *trust in Jesus*. We will have to show them that all this Christianity business really does work – by proving it from our own lives and testifying how God worked with us.

Does all this sound as if it's over our heads? It does to me! I'm afraid that our track record hasn't been so good! If the world got to be in such bad shape during our lifetimes, what in the world are we going to tell our children? "Do as I say, not as I do!" Where is the wisdom that we will pass on to them? Are our lives such a testimony that our children will be impressed, take notice and imitate us?

Perhaps a more penetrating question is this: Do we ourselves really understand Jesus, the message of God's Gospel, in a way that changes life? That's not always an easy question to answer. You would think that a mature Christian would know enough about Jesus to take advantage of the good things in him – but unfortunately that's not always the case! We often haven't been trained well ourselves, and to tell the truth we haven't studied the Lord and his works enough to tell others much about him. Remember, the depth of the riches in Christ is far more than man can conceive; if it wasn't for the Spirit of God helping us we wouldn't be able to understand him in any way at all, let alone find salvation in him. And once we've begun the Christian life, learning about Christ is like taking college courses – it's a never-ending process, and you can go as deeply as you like without getting to the bottom. Unless you have been spending much time every day studying about Christ, the little you know about him probably isn't good enough for your children. They need more than we often have.

Furthermore, with just a little bit of study we find unexpected ways to apply the knowledge of Christ to everyday problems; more joy and overcoming and freedom comes with more study. If we study him at all then our lives would change! Unfortunately we all start out ignorant of the riches in Christ, and without a clue on how to use those riches. It's too bad that few people move on to become experts in him.

The point, then, of being a Christian is to *know Christ*:

> I pray that out of his glorious riches he may strengthen you with power through his Spirit in your inner being, so that Christ may dwell in your hearts through faith. And I pray that you, being rooted and established in love, may have power, together with all the saints, to grasp how wide and long and high and deep is the love of Christ, and to know this love that surpasses knowledge – that you may be filled to the measure of all the fullness of God. (Ephesians 3:16-19)

If we know him like this, then we have something to say to our children; if not, then it will be no surprise if they fail at life in the same ways that we have failed.

Some of us feel the failure more than others. We know that our knowledge of the Son of God is pretty shallow – or at least we can't seem to get our thoughts together well enough to tell the simple Gospel to little children. If we need proof of that, we need only to look at the state of our spiritual walk with him. It's quite possible that we will fail to testify of the Lord's great salvation to our own sons and daughters. That would be a tragedy that could have been easily avoided. What we have to do first is get a hold of what Jesus is – his person and work – and why he is so important to all of us; then we must tell our children about him, in all the ways that the Spirit gives us power and opportunity to do so.

We train them for many things in life; but the one thing that we simply have to give them is an opportunity to see the Lord of Glory in the same way that we have seen him. If we are successful in this, then they will "rise up and call us blessed." They will have the chance to make their world worth living in, since they will have available to them the only real solution to man's problems.

How To Use This Book ...

You can read the entire book through, in order to get the whole picture from beginning to end; or you can use it as a reference for different aspects of teaching children about Jesus. I had to back up and give a big panorama of the field in order to do justice to the theme. For example, there are reasons why teaching children about Jesus is difficult and we simply have to face them if we want to get on past them. And we have to find out the core truth about Jesus if we want to teach others about him. So there is a logical progression of ideas, and if you want to get the entire overview then you can just read from the beginning.

On the other hand, you can look up a topic that you may need help in as you teach:

> *If you find that you are having difficulties teaching children about Jesus*, turn to **Chapter One – Difficulties In Teaching About Jesus**. You may find that your problem isn't so unique after all – there *are* problems in doing this.

> *To learn more about who Jesus is*, turn to **Chapter Two – Who Is Jesus?** He is a vast subject, and it's important to get firmly in hand the truth about him if we hope to teach the truth.

In *Chapter Three* – **What Do Children Need From Us?** – you will find some *surprising things that children need from you the teacher.* If you want to really help them, get ready to add some spiritual depth to your toolkit.

In *Chapter Four* – **Jesus and Children's Needs** – you will find *what Jesus can do for children,* especially at this age.

Chapter Five – **The Gospels** – discusses how to approach the four books that present the story of Jesus. *You will learn their characteristics* that make learning the important things about Jesus easier.

There are **Sample Stories** in *Chapter Six* from the Gospels of Matthew and Mark; you can follow the story and the analysis for an example of how to present the Gospel to children.

In **The Wider Scope** – *Chapter Seven* – you will find a discussion on *what you can learn about Jesus from the rest of the Bible:* the Old Testament and the Epistles of the apostles.

In *Chapter Eight* – **Teaching Children: Results** – I discuss how to get results when you teach children about Jesus, and what results to expect from them.

The **Appendices** give much information about Christ that you can find in Prophecies, Types, Old Testament quotes in the New Testament, and how Paul uses the doctrine of Christ in his letter to the Ephesians. Use these resources, as you prepare your lessons on the stories of Christ in the Gospels, to add necessary depth to the picture of Christ that you present to the children.

I also discuss in **The Tree of the Knowledge of Good and Evil** the subject of the fundamental sin in man's heart (from Genesis 3) which adults do all the time and which children curiously lack when it comes to spiritual matters. Keep this in mind when you take advantage of the open door of the opportunity of a young mind.

Section One:

Difficulties

Many people are surprised that they run into problems when they try to teach about Jesus, especially to children. They shouldn't be – for many reasons this is a difficult thing to do.

Difficulties In Teaching About Jesus

You would think that teaching about Jesus is probably the simplest thing to do in the work of the Church. We all remember, if we grew up in the Church, the devoted women who taught the children's Sunday School classes – teaching us the Bible stories of the Gospels, and the Christian songs that were so full of Jesus the friend of children. We remember Vacation Bible School that often focused on the Gospel stories. What we don't know much about are the Old Testament and Paul's letters, probably because our teachers (and pastors!) didn't themselves know much about them. So when someone wants to "start at the beginning," they will inevitably turn to the stories about Jesus.

The thing is that we run into problems here every time. There is something about the story of Jesus that seems simple on the outside, but when we open it up for study we are faced with all sorts of difficulties, mysteries, unexplainable statements, contradictions – we very quickly get in over our heads. What happened to the simple Gospel? Why is it that the more we study him and the longer we follow him, the more complicated this Christianity business becomes? What happened to the good old days when all we did was "believe in Jesus and be saved!"

If we have so much of a problem figuring him out, then it's no surprise that our children get mixed up when we teach about him. Try asking them sometime (if you are ready to see the real results of your teaching!) what they got out of your lesson. You are probably going to hear everything except what you thought you told them! Somehow the foggy ideas in our own heads got lost in the communication process, and the children end up knowing far less than what we wanted to teach them.

Why is it so difficult to teach children about Jesus? I think that there are many reasons for this, some real and some imaginary:

> **Difficulty #1:** *Children aren't impressed with eternal matters.* Their little minds are more impressed with the "here and now," the next meal and the toy in their hands. They understand Daddy's love and anger; they don't really know about God's. They are more concerned with making their friends like them, and not so much with an invisible God's opinion of them. And living forever? That concept doesn't hit them as it does us adults, because *we* know all about sickness and death – in other words, the possibility of not living forever – and so we fear death; whereas a child can't conceive of not living forever!
>
> There are many wonderful things about the Gospel that we would just love to tell children, but we feel sure that it would be wasted on them. When we have found such joy and reasons to be thankful in the things of Christ, and what our Father has done for our salvation, we want to share it with others; but what if someone doesn't understand our excitement? What if they don't even understand the issue? That's how a child too often responds to our lessons: he or she just doesn't see the point of what we are excited about. They don't understand why such a thing is even

important. It has no application to their lives, no place to fit into their limited circumstances.

And there are some solemn truths about God and sin and judgment that we are concerned to tell others about, because we want to warn them of the dangers in the world and the punishment for sin. But what if they don't see what's so bad about the things we condemn? What if they don't understand the evil? Does it make sense to tell a child not to murder when he has no inclination to murder – when he doesn't even know what murder is? There are many sins that adults are all too familiar with, which Jesus talked about in the Gospels, which the Epistles warn us about and give us remedies for, which are completely lost on children. So, if you can't put the fear of God in their hearts, how are you going to show them the precious value of the remedy for sin in Jesus?

The things of God are wonderfully deep; someone can dig there forever, it seems, and just get bigger and more complex and wide-ranging views and understanding of the Truth. But are children capable of seeing the depth of God's wisdom? Aren't we limited by *their* limitations when we teach them? Don't we have to keep things on a very simple, almost superficial level if we want children to get *something* out of the story of Jesus?

Difficulty #2: *The moralisms just aren't satisfying.* Teachers almost always use the stories of Jesus to teach moralisms. By "moralism" I mean telling the student to do what the people in the story did, or not to do what they did. It comes from an age-old teaching device that parents have always used with their children: "The moral of the story is, Johnny, that you mustn't lie" because someone in the story got in trouble for lying.

This works for a while, but it's a particularly unsatisfying way of looking at the stories of Jesus. If the only thing that you can see in story after story is that "you must believe in Jesus, Johnny" then Johnny is going to get bored with the point. He knows already that he must believe in Jesus! What he doesn't know is *why*.

Some of the more popular moralisms that teachers focus on in their lessons are "believe in Jesus," "trust in Jesus," "follow Jesus," "obey Jesus," and "tell others about Jesus." These kinds of lessons will work for a while because they appeal to human nature: we want to be doing something, especially something that will make God pleased with us. And children are great when it comes to activities! But after a long time of doing, some of the more discerning students are going to start asking, "Wait a minute – we are all marching around, and it's been fun; but who are we following? What are we doing this for?" Then is when you will have to come up with something better than moralisms. A person needs more of a reason for doing something that demands his time and energy and interest than just a "You ought to do this" – he needs to see the goal that he's headed for.

The reason we often drop into teaching moralisms is because we don't see anything more than that in the story ourselves. We will look at this problem further in a minute.

Difficulty #3: *The stories don't hang together well.* The Gospel stories are short snippets from the life of Jesus, almost like a picture album of his life. Pictures are still-life snapshots of a point in time and aren't very useful for getting the flow of the whole story. When the evangelists wrote their accounts, they included stories that they had either seen for themselves or heard from eyewitnesses. The result is a collage of little "story-ettes" that you could almost rearrange in any order and they would make just as much sense.

So it's difficult to put together a story line of the life of Christ. Some authors have attempted to do that very thing: they have collated the accounts from all four Gospels and attempted to create a single story of his life. But the same problem is still there, in their attempt at a "Life," because the individual stories just don't fit together with each other. First he does this miracle, with its special lesson; then he does that miracle, with a separate lesson; then he goes over there and teaches this point; then he comes back and does another miracle with a separate lesson. There doesn't seem to be any historical time-line, no thread that we can follow from "introduction" through "buildup" and on to "climax" like other books.

We like to see logical connections because we are heirs of the Greeks. Our scientific outlook makes us look for sense in the arrangement, and connections where there are none, and conclusions that often prove to be false (because Christ's culture was completely different from ours). We don't like his teaching style, so we rearrange and make lists and form theologies to try to make sense of the scattered stories. Of course, our discontent with the form in which the Truth of Christ comes to us gets conveyed to the children, because they watch us struggle with rearranging it and twisting it into a more comfortable form. I think we lost something vital in the process, though; the Gospel writers – and Jesus himself – were wise in how they passed these things on to us. There's something in the way these stories were presented to us that we are missing.

Difficulty #4: *Lessons tend to focus on his teachings instead of him.* If you have a Bible with the words of Jesus in red, you will see that much if not most of the Gospels is the teachings of Christ – the words he spoke. Now there's nothing wrong with listening to what Jesus says; he wants us to do that! It's just that there's more going on here than meets the eye. We can very easily miss seeing him even when we listen to him teach us, and then everything comes out all wrong.

The hero of the Gospel stories is Jesus, not anybody else. The Gospels only make sense if we focus on *him* as we read. We have to ask ourselves some questions: Who is this who is talking? Why do I need to know this about him? What is this story teaching me about him? Is there something about him that this story shows me that I can depend on and use for my life? Why can nobody else make this statement?

After all, if we were only after moral and ethical systems then there are many other religions and philosophies in the world to satisfy us. What we want to see in the Gospels is *Jesus Christ*. There is no other place in the world to see him. We must train ourselves to think deeper and reach out and touch him in these stories. Unfortunately, that isn't easy to do; it's much easier to do what the rest of the world does with the teachings of Jesus – they isolate them from the Master who first spoke them, as if they can ignore him so easily, and build ethical systems completely devoid of the presence of God.

To explain what I mean, let's take an example. Jesus said in Matthew 5:17-20 that the Law was extremely important to God, and that we must have a righteousness that was greater than the Pharisees themselves had. If you just focus on what he is saying you may tend to drift into thinking about the Law, and how good you must be, and how carefully one must fulfill the Law. In other words, we end up looking at ourselves and how we are going to do what Jesus says to do.

But look at the entire passage for a minute and see the bigger picture. Jesus is a King, and here he is telling us how his kingdom will be set up. The Beatitudes are the conditions for entering his kingdom – they are not the ways that people would have thought! His people will be perfect (not like the superficial Pharisees!) which is something that *he* must do for them; he will not tolerate imperfection even in the smallest detail. Then he goes on to describe just how extensive and fine-tuned our obedience must be by showing the spiritual side of the Ten Commandments; do you appreciate now what he must do to our souls to make us perfect "even as our Heavenly Father is perfect?"

We could go on, but I hope you get the point: you'll miss out on so much of the dynamics of what is going on in this story if you focus on simply the words of Christ without backing up and seeing Who is saying these words, and in what context. In this example, especially, it makes a world of difference who says these words! The Pharisees also demanded perfect living by the Law. But they went about it in entirely the wrong way, and the kingdom of God never did come to the Jews while Pharisees led the nation. Jesus, however, has a better plan – and a much better chance – for bringing in the kingdom of righteousness.

Difficulty #5: *We don't understand this material ourselves!* It's very difficult (perhaps impossible?) to teach something we don't understand very well. And if we don't understand the mystery of God in Christ, it's no wonder that we have a hard time teaching this mystery to the children!

There's a saying about teachers: they must know at least ten times more about the subject than what they intend to say about it, if they hope to do a good job at teaching. Do you know ten times as much about Jesus and his life and work than what you will tell your children? Or do you hope they don't ask you any questions about him as you struggle with very simple ideas yourself?

Probably we all get caught thinking that the Gospel stories are simple to understand, so we don't spend much time studying them when preparing to teach. After all, what can be so difficult about turning a few loaves of bread into enough food to feed thousands of people? It's just a miracle, right? You just tell them what happened and tell them to trust Jesus who will take care of them too.

Is that all there is to this story? Let's look at it and dig down deeper than the surface:

1) *Man has his ways of solving a problem, and God has his ways. They are never the same! You can count on that. Jesus contradicted their common sense solution and said that something else is needed instead of earning enough money to feed everyone. What was it?*

2) ***Who*** *did Jesus say must feed the crowd?*

3) *What of this world does God need to do his work? Have we seen this before in the Bible?*

4) *How did Jesus make that little bit of bread stretch out for thousands of people? What was the process used? Does the rest of the Bible help us understand this process?*

5) *What role did the disciples play in this story? Would they do this kind of thing again?*

6) *What was Jesus teaching the disciples?*

7) *Which one of Jesus' many names does this story reflect?*

8) *Which characteristic of God does this story show? Is there a Scripture that predicts that Jesus would do this kind of thing?*

This is just for starters! There are many other things that we can get out of this story, if we spend enough time on it and compare Scripture with Scripture. The point is that most of us would have rushed into teaching this story without doing enough study to find out what the passage is really teaching about Christ. (*Answers are at the end of the chapter!*)

It's such a shame to just skim the surface of the Gospel stories without digging in; you may be able to fill in an hour lesson with moralisms and such things, but there won't be a deeply satisfying knowledge of Christ if you do. So, because we often don't know what a story teaches about Christ, we can hardly expect to know what to tell our students.

Difficulty #6: *Children have their own special problems.* Children, after all, are just starting out in life and they are still trying to put together what the world is all about. They are living on a different level – emotionally, physically, and mentally – than an adult lives on. We just can't use the same lessons with them that we would use with grown-ups! They like action, they need constant discipline, they need to see the point in pictures, they often don't understand the spiritual point involved, they need approval and fear rejection from their elders, and a host of other characteristics. In fact, their little minds often take surprising turns that we don't know how to deal with because of their completely different viewpoint on life; you've probably had a child ask a question that didn't relate to the lesson at all, or wasn't realistic, and wondered why they asked that.

This is why there are thousands of books out right now about child psychology – everyone has always recognized the differences between the child mind and the adult mind, and there is no shortage of suggestions and ideas for the teacher to help him reach the children where they live. The only problem is that, in spite of all the helps, it's still difficult teaching these deep truths to children who just don't get the point!

This has led many people to believe that there is simply a list of things that children will understand and another list of things that they won't understand. So teachers will teach certain subjects and not others; why spend time trying to make a child grasp what he can't understand anyway? If some subjects only get clear after a certain age in one's development, why not leave those things till later and work on things that they *are* capable of getting now?

Difficulty #7: *Jesus doesn't seem to fit in with the rest of the Bible.* What I mean is this: the Old Testament has its own flavor, and the Gospels have their own flavor, and the Epistles have theirs.

It seems that each section stands apart from the other two, and when we need to teach about Jesus, why use anything but the Gospels? The Gospels seem particularly unique and stand apart from anything else in the Bible. For that reason, however, we can't seem to fit Jesus in with the Jewish Old Testament because he challenges their way of doing things so much, and we can't seem to fit him in with the New Testament Church because he's still so Jewish and we are Gentiles. So here we are, stuck: we just don't know how to handle these stories about Christ and fit it in with the rest of the Bible.

Modern unbelievers have really capitalized on this division. They have accused the apostles of changing Christ's message (they say, to contradict Paul, that Christ came *only* to give us simple moral lessons and to reform the Jewish religion) and creating a new thing, the Christian Church, to help the Faith spread to the Gentiles. In fact, they counsel us to forget the stories of Jesus; they aren't accurate anyway, they tell us, because the apostles have changed so much in them to better suit what the young Church needed. I don't mean to shake your faith with this stuff – I would hate for you to be convinced by their perverted arguments! The problem is that these liberals (I call them unbelievers) have already done a startlingly efficient job at destroying most of the faith that the twentieth century Church once had. Their poisonous heresies have probably already touched your life in some way, if you have had anything to do with modern mainline denominations.

The result is that we can't get any profit out of reading the Gospels – we feel that we constantly have to go to the Epistles for spiritual uplifting. That part of the Bible makes more sense to us! Even our sermons and Sunday School lessons tend to gravitate to other parts of the Bible, instead of the Gospels, for their teaching material. This is probably because we are heirs of the Greeks in our way of life and in the way we think (Jesus was very Hebrew) and Paul appeals to us more. Jesus seems remote from us moderns.

What has made the problem even worse is that the modern Church is very much different from the early Church, so much so that you probably wouldn't recognize a church meeting if you were transported through time to the days of Pentecost. How do I know that? Because many Christians say that the Bible's simple way of doing church would be unworkable in our setting! Our modern ways of hired professionals in the pulpit, church buildings and programs costing hundreds of thousands of dollars, youth ministries, and many other cultural add-ons have made the "simple" Jesus remote, almost unreal and impractical for us now.

Difficulty #8: *The Gospels aren't as easy to understand as they first appear.* We made some reference to this before; the unfortunate thing about the Gospels is that we think at first that they will be the easiest part of the Bible to understand, when really they prove to be the hardest part.

You probably know that many people counsel young Christians to start reading the

Gospel of John – mainly because it glorifies Christ so magnificently and yet uses the simplest words and phrases to do it. But John's Gospel is probably the most difficult of the four! If there was a philosopher among the Gospel writers it had to have been John; true to the trade of philosophy, he uses common words and ideas to express things that this world struggles to understand: the root issues of human existence and depravity, the profound mysteries of God's characteristics, and the startlingly rich feast of spiritual solutions in Christ. The waters in the Gospel of John are as deep as you care to wade into.

So are the other Gospels difficult in many places. Unless we are satisfied with just teaching superficial moralisms, the lessons in these stories usually escape us. What is the point, Jesus? we ask over and over again. Just like the crowds that he taught, we also are confused by the parables and mysterious language. We don't understand Jesus' relationship with the Law, nor the necessity of some of the miracles, nor how a physical healing was OK in that day and not good enough in ours, nor the reason the Lord was so insistent on going to the Jews and not to the Gentiles, and on and on. In fact, we don't have to get far into a lesson until a sharp little boy or girl can bring us to a mystified and embarrassed standstill with a question that we have no answer for.

It seems, if we boil down all the above problems, that there are basically two areas we are weak in: 1) there are things about Jesus (and his Word!) that we ourselves don't understand very well; and 2) we don't know how to get the children to understand the material that is more on the level of adults (which is most of the Bible!). But I have a feeling that these problems are *our* fault, not problems in themselves. If we don't know much about Jesus, it's because we haven't been studying about him as we ought to be. And if we don't know how to bring this material down to a child's level, it's probably because we don't understand it as well as we thought, and we also don't understand the spiritual needs of children.

Now if you don't get a good grip on who Jesus is, and the special needs of the children, and how to put Jesus in front of them in such a way that they understand him and can learn to live with him, there are going to be serious results.

> ***Jesus won't have a face.*** If you don't show the children who Jesus is, they won't be familiar with him. They will know all the words of Jesus, and how the prophets predicted his coming, and how much Paul appreciates him – that is, they can quote Scripture all day long! – but they wouldn't be able to recognize Christ on the street if they saw him!
>
> That seems like a strange way to put it but unfortunately it's true and it's very important. Jesus still lives – our doctrine teaches us this, and our hopes depend on it – and he's working right this minute in our world, in our very lives. Both the unbeliever and the believer need to recognize this. The sad thing is that Jesus can be working under our noses and we don't know it! We don't recognize his handiwork, or know his special ways, or know the sound of *his* voice when he speaks (in and under the words of men and circumstances). Even though our lives are daily in his hands, we fail to see him daily. Even though

he is leading us to the goals he has for us, we don't see his path nor his cross as he walks on ahead. In other words, Jesus has no face for us – we don't know him nearly so well as we think we do.

It's so providential that cameras weren't invented in Jesus' day. If there were a genuine photograph of Christ, all Christians would worship it and millions would make the annual pilgrimage to gaze on it. Because of the picture we would all miss the real point: that we can see the face of Christ in the Gospels themselves, not in a photo, and he gets clearer and clearer to us as we study his story. It's a shame, then, when we don't understand what we read there because we will therefore never know what he looks like.

Jesus will be a strange person to them. Christ takes some getting used to! His own people couldn't get along with him because of his strange ways and strict views; certainly Gentiles like us are going to have even more difficulties getting used to him. What, then, do you think a generation of children will do with him who have never heard of him, who have never studied anything about him? Worse yet, what will children do if they've been taught the wrong things about Jesus? For a good example of this, just turn to the Moslem world: they teach their children that Jesus was an impostor, and the good Muslim spits on the ground and curses at the name of Jesus Christ. Is our generation headed for the same kind of response?

If Jesus isn't well understood – and I want to emphasize the idea of *well understood* – he will be pretty much useless to a society except as a convenient swear word. He is either everything we need or he has nothing that we need! Either we look to him, or we must look elsewhere. He will be a massive disappointment to a people looking for answers if his claims don't turn out to be true. There is a real dilemma here about Christ that surrounds nobody else in history: his claims put him in a position of either delivering on those fantastic claims or else nobody will ever take him seriously anymore.

That makes our job of teaching about him all the more difficult. These children are not stupid: either Jesus is real, either he is someone we can benefit from, or he's just a fairy tale and of no use to anybody. If you can't show them a real Christ who speaks to our generation just as powerfully as he spoke in the Gospels to the Jews, then Jesus will remain a cultural misfit, a famous figure from history long ago, a Jewish fanatic, and someone that doesn't belong in our day. They will see no reason to turn to him with their problems; they will think Jesus to be a strange place to turn for answers to their modern problems, and they just won't be inclined to do such a foolish and unreasonable thing.

Though they hear, they will not understand.
Remember that Jesus said that the people listening to him will not understand his teachings!

> This is why I speak to them in parables: though seeing, they do not see; though hearing, they do not hear or understand. In them is fulfilled the prophecy of Isaiah: "You will be

ever hearing but never understanding;
you will be ever seeing but never
perceiving. For this people's heart
has become callused; they hardly
hear with their ears, and they have
closed their eyes. Otherwise they
might see with their eyes, hear with
their ears, understand with their
hearts and turn, and I would heal
them." (Matthew 13:13-15)

It's a sobering thought that there's
something peculiarly mystifying and perplexing
about the Gospel of Christ. It's entirely possible –
even probable – that someone hearing it will miss
the point! Far from being easy to understand and
clear to see, the message of Jesus will only find an
understanding heart in someone who has "eyes to
see and ears to hear" – a spiritual awakening that
makes a person able to see and hear spiritual truth.
Otherwise a person will never see his glory. This
is what he meant in John 3 when he talked with
Nicodemus.

Although God calls teachers to take the
message of the Gospel to the next generation of
children, we can't assume that *all* teaching about
Christ finds its mark in ready hearts. If it's a
mystery to the teacher, it will probably be a
mystery to the children too! And even when we
have understood the Gospel ourselves, we can't
always guarantee that we will be able to tell it in
simple terms to students. And even if we get past
those hurdles, it often happens that children have
hearts like hardened paths, thorny ground, stony

ground, and it will just go in one ear and out the other. (Matthew 13:1-23)

As if things weren't already difficult, there's an additional problem: we could do a poor job at teaching – that is, not understanding the Scripture ourselves, not preparing our hearts to teach, not coming under the point of the lesson ourselves, not taking every care to make it plain and simple to the children, not focusing their attention on the important points of the passage – which of course will end up with them not learning about Christ. The result may be that *they* become hardened to the stories of Christ. It didn't mean anything to them the first time around, so they quit listening to them from then on! So we become responsible for their closed minds.

There will be no connection with the rest of the Bible. The message about Christ is linked tightly with the rest of the Bible. You can't understand him without also understanding the Old Testament, and you shouldn't teach the Old Testament without seeing Christ in it everywhere. Furthermore, the Epistles *depend* on the Gospel stories, more than you can possibly imagine. They don't stand on their own! You will surely misinterpret the Epistles if you haven't done your homework in the Gospels first. The point is that understanding Jesus and teaching about him in a true way will make the entire Bible your resource material; you will find enlightening things about him all over the Bible. But if you don't understand him, and if you don't offer him in his fullness, the Bible won't prove to be very useful to you in your teaching.

I know that sounds strange, to say that the Bible won't be useful to you as you teach from it! But too many teachers have found this to be true. They can't see any more than superficial "lessons" in the stories about Christ. That means they don't understand the prophets who spoke and taught about him; they don't understand the Law that made his coming necessary; they don't understand the nation of Israel who are his people; they don't understand the purpose of David and Joseph and Abraham and other types of Christ. They miss out on all the vast teaching material on Christ that the Old Testament has for us.

What they put in its place is their own opinions, values, and customs – whatever we modern Americans think that life should be like. They make this strange Jesus conform to our world, our likings, our needs, our standards, instead of being the work of the Biblical God. The stories of Jesus become a way to tell the children their own message instead of God's message – this is inevitable when someone doesn't understand Christ! What is scary about this thought is that we all do it, to some degree or another, until we finally come to a perfect knowledge of the Son of God (which will only be in Heaven!)

You won't be letting Jesus speak for himself. Teachers are so eager to do the talking that often they don't stand back and let the Master speak for himself. He does have a way of getting into someone's soul, you know, that is beyond our limited skills! For some reason we forget that too easily. Instead of stepping back and letting him whisper his powerful Word in a student's heart, we step in front of him – thinking that the spiritual point won't "take" unless we do – and steal the show away from him with a display of our own abilities and wisdom.

This comes from not appreciating the fact that Jesus can do well enough without our pitiful efforts. He has condescended to use us in his work in the Church, but he doesn't *need* us, you know! We pour words all over people like water out of a pitcher, but none of that can get into the soul. Jesus, however, can take the least significant, off-hand remark that we didn't intend anything by and literally pierce someone's heart through with it. Without our knowing it, and without our help, he ministers to people through his Word. Besides, only he can speak to someone in a way that will really help them – if we didn't believe that, why teach about him?

But when we get carried away with our own glory, we push Jesus' message aside and fill up the hour with ourselves instead. The children get to see plenty of us, but nothing of Jesus! They learn to fear us, but they don't have any fear of the Lord. They love us, but they feel no affection at all for the Lover of men's souls. In other words, if we don't open the door to our class and let Jesus himself come among us and minister to us all, it's no wonder that children get the idea that Jesus is, for all practical purposes, *dead* and not able to speak to us today.

It takes a great deal of faith for a teacher to let Jesus speak for himself in a lesson. It also takes a great deal of training, understanding and skill to do that. Not that a seminary or university will give you the necessary skill – it won't – but the Lord himself must train you in his ways and how to help him build up his kingdom. It's primarily because of this lack of spiritually trained workers in the Church that it has been a long time since we have heard the Master's voice among us.

Answers to questions about Matthew 14:13-21

1) A *miracle* is needed. If the problem needed anything less than a miracle then the disciples' solution would have been perfectly OK. But as it typical of man's solutions, it just won't help people the way God wants to help them, and Jesus can't use those common sense solutions even if we have it all planned out how we intended to do it!

2) Jesus said that the disciples must feed the crowd. He didn't change his mind about it, either, when the disciples brought the bread to him, as you will see while the story unfolds.

3) He needs almost nothing of this world to do his work. We need lots of money, lots of people, lots of materials; he purposely uses very little to pull off a miracle. We see that in the little people he chooses to do his work (the shepherd boy David chosen to be king of Israel); the small numbers of people (the 300 men who followed Gideon to defeat the entire Moabite army); the paltry materials (five smooth stones to bring down Goliath).

4) We don't know how he did it – that's the point! His miracles are scientifically unexplainable; we can't duplicate them. He is God, we are only creatures who depend on him to do what we can't do for ourselves. If a scientist were there with all the instruments in the world, he couldn't have begun to explain how Jesus did it; even if Jesus himself explained it to us, we wouldn't see it. This is the *Creator* at work, who speaks and things come into existence.

5) The disciples, notice, took the bread from Jesus and gave it to the people. It was their hands that carried the bread of Jesus to the crowd. This is the basic function of any who will minister to Jesus' sheep. One extremely important way they did this in future years was to take the words of Christ and deliver them *as is* to the rest of the Church throughout history – in the New Testament. Modern critics who accuse the disciples of changing, deleting, or adding to the words of Christ don't understand this story of the feeding of the 5000.

6) Jesus was teaching the disciples that the crowd will not be fed by anything less than the miracles of Christ – whatever comes from his hands – and they are to carry *all* of that to them. It was a graphic lesson on the impossibility of the job for ordinary man, and the ease when Christ does it, and the role of the disciples as bearers of the miracles of Christ to the people.

7) The Manna from Heaven. Didn't the Lord feed his people with miraculous bread when they were wandering in the desert, away from any other source of food? Jesus is obviously the same source of bread that the Israelites had.

8) God feeds his people. He always does; he shows his interest in their well-being when he feeds them. The Scripture that predicts that God himself will feed his people is in Psalm 145:

The eyes of all look to you, and you give them their food at the proper time. (Psalm 145:15)

Because Jesus is the Son of God, he too shares this characteristic of his Father.

Section Two:

Jesus and Children

In order to teach children about Jesus, we must first know ...

⇨ *who Jesus is* – not an easy task, by any means, because of his amazing fullness and importance!

⇨ and the *spiritual needs* of children.

Who is Jesus?

The point about being a Christian is that we focus our attention on *Jesus*, "the author and perfecter of our faith." (Hebrews 12:2) Jesus is all that we hope for, all that God has done for us, all that holds the world at bay and protects us from our enemies. A person can be ignorant of everything else in the world and yet *have it all* by understanding and holding on to Jesus. I cannot emphasize this point enough. Churches too often focus on every subject *except* Jesus, as if we can stay healthy spiritually on any other kind of bread. If people want to learn about psychology or philosophy or science or politics or economics, they can do that better in schools than in the Church. What they won't get anywhere else, however, and what the Church *must* train us all to become experts in, is the subject of Jesus. After all, Jesus is inexhaustible; we can study him for the rest of our lives and never run out of new material! It's not as if any of us has a complete knowledge of him yet.

When it comes to the role of teaching in the Church, we again must emphasize the importance of focusing on Jesus. What do we hope to pass on to the next generation except that "one thing needful" that they won't find anywhere else in the world? Spurgeon, the famous English preacher of last century, once told his ministry students to preach Christ in every sermon, from every text – and if the text didn't explicitly say anything about Christ then jump the fence to a neighboring passage and pull back something that will! What he means is not to do injustice to a particular text, but that *all* the Bible teaches us something about Christ, some passages more plainly than others, and our duty is to use the Word to enlighten our students about the Savior that it teaches about. "These are the Scriptures that testify about me." (John 5:39)

The reason we must become experts in the subject about Jesus is that we must be able to give a reason for our hope. The Jews have the Law, the Muslims have their Prophet, the Hindus and Buddhists have their philosophies, the modern heathens have their "scientific" analyses – what do we Christians have to offer against all that? Don't we have anything that's distinctive from, say, the Jews? If we simply focus on doing good, how can we say that we are Christian? The Jew will agree with everything we say! And if we claim that we have the revealed Word of God, the Bible, how will we convince the Muslim who has his Koran given by his prophet? My point is that unless we find out what *does* make us different from everyone else, we will get nowhere with our students. Unless we teach a living Messiah, the children won't be able to answer the world's challenges or resist the world's many deceits.

Spiritual hurdles

So, what we must do first is find out who Jesus is. There is the key to teaching him to children. It's not very easy at all finding out who he is! If we were teaching math or science we would have a much easier time of it, because the principles are plain to see and easily explained. The data is there for everyone to explore. But Jesus is different, much different from any other subject under the sun. What we thought would be an easy job turns out instead to perhaps the most difficult job of all! Remember that the religious experts in Jesus' day struggled to understand him; even those who supported what he was doing – in spite of the fact that they were experts in God's Law – couldn't grasp the essence of Jesus. There are some startling obstacles in our way in just learning about him, let alone teaching about him. In fact, considering the problems in the way, it's a wonder that any of us says anything at all correct about him!

Jesus is the most misunderstood man in history, and that's not an exaggeration. That's all the more remarkable since we've had 2000 years to get it straight who he really was, and for the most part we *still* haven't gotten it right. No other person in the world has been so discussed, abused and revered – millions, perhaps billions have claimed to be followers of his in one way or another, and that many more are his determined enemies. The theories about what he actually did during his short stay on earth are both numerous and contradictory; everything that has been said about him can't possibly be right, because so much of it doesn't agree.

Why is it so hard to put a finger on him? What is it about Jesus that mystifies wise men? What reasons account for all the confusion about him? I hope you realize that we ourselves, though we claim to be his disciples, also struggle to understand him. Being a Christian doesn't automatically clear up all the mystery of Christ for us! I think we know all too well that Jesus is difficult to grasp when we sit down to teach children; in fact, because we *are* teaching children, and the lesson has to focus on simple things about Christ, it's all the more embarrassing and puzzling that we struggle against invisible barriers trying to understand who he is.

> ***The mystery of God*** – "Surely you have heard about the administration of God's grace that was given to me for you, that is, the mystery made known to me by revelation, as I have already written briefly. In reading this, then, you will be able to understand my insight into the mystery of Christ, which was not made known to men in other

generations as it has now been revealed by the Spirit to God's holy apostles and prophets." (Ephesians 3:2-5)

A mystery is a hidden secret. It's a thing that we can't know, and can't hope to know, unless the holder of the mystery chooses to reveal it to us. This describes our Lord Jesus Christ. Have you ever thought how much hidden secret material is in Jesus? Information that men have craved for thousands of years, that all their powers and investigations have failed to uncover on their own. The hidden secrets of life are in him: the reason we are here, the power behind the universe, the purpose of creation, the rhyme and reason to creation's order, the goal of mankind, the key to perfect peace and goodness, the door to eternity itself. These things have been outside the reach of the best of men, though all men have searched for them in desperation, and now they are all here among us for us to see and take hold of in Christ.

People say not to "put all your eggs in one basket." But that's exactly what God has done in putting all the answers to man's problems and needs in Christ.

But in these last days he has spoken to us by his Son, whom he appointed heir of *all things*, and through whom he made the universe. The Son is the radiance of God's glory and the exact representation of his being, sustaining *all things* by his powerful word. (Hebrews 1:2-3)

The reason God has put all the answers in Christ is because of the utter dependability of his Son, that Jesus can use all those answers to save us to the fullest extent. There will be no failure this time! Before Christ's coming, some hints of God's truth trickled out here and there in the ministry of the prophets of Israel; but now we have it all in Jesus.

The problem is that very few people see that. They are still looking in other places for their answers! They can't for the life of them see that Jesus is the end of the search, the beginning of the rest of eternity, and the encyclopedia of Heaven.

Veiled in flesh – "Since the children have flesh and blood, he too shared in their humanity." (Hebrews 2:14) This was probably the biggest stumbling block for the Jews – that God would be a man. They were always offended that this "son of a carpenter" claimed to be God's Son. The Pharisees never did see the glory of Christ, because the veil of his flesh hid that glory from them. How could a man be God? "The god of this age has blinded the minds of unbelievers, so that they cannot see the light of the gospel of the glory of Christ, who is the image of God." (2 Corinthians 4:4)

People ever since those days have had the same problem, but with a bit different twist. How could a man who *died* be the Son of God? The early Church wrangled over this issue for centuries because there were people who simply couldn't accept Jesus' humanity. And modern unbelievers, who feel that they know very well what a human being is because of their scientific and medical explorations, will readily accept that Jesus was a man like us but *not* that he was God in any way. It's much easier to accept something that we know and understand than what we don't know; Jesus, however, if he *is* the Son of God, is an unknown quantity. So we generally focus on his earthly life, the ways he helps us physically, and the good he can do for societies in general (like ethical systems and such things). We can't get past his humanity either.

Set aside his glory – "Who, being in very nature God, did not consider equality with God something to be grasped, but made himself nothing." (Philippians 2:6-7) At one time – *before* time – Jesus was a sight to behold; he had the same glory that the Father had – remember in his "priestly prayer" that he asked the Father to "glorify me in your presence with the glory I had with you before the world began." (John 17:5) God's glory, you know, is such that man can't stand to look at it, it's so powerful and radiant. It humbles the proudest creature; the angels bow before it in fearful obedience.

But when he came to live with us he put aside that glory. We simply couldn't have stood in his presence if he hadn't! What people saw instead was a humble carpenter, a poor Jew, an uneducated man from a local village that almost nobody took seriously. He didn't even have the glory of men about him! He had none of the necessary pomp and ceremony, the gold and glitter, that people surround themselves with to add importance to themselves. He simply stood before everyone stripped of all glory. One had to accept him on a purely spiritual basis – a sheer act of faith in who he said he was – and ignore the fact that he had none of the outward signs of importance that people expected him to have.

People on both sides of the issue pleaded with him to show his glory. They thought he was committing political and religious suicide by refusing to back up his claims with a little well placed self-exaltation here and there. But he consistently refused, and lost many followers as a result. People have always followed the showman, the man who can dazzle the crowd, the one who struts his stuff in front of everyone, even if he ends up empty-handed and not able to do anything for anybody. They don't like to follow a seeming failure, however.

The Servant – "Taking the very nature of a servant." (Philippians 2:7) We all would have expected a king to come to earth and set up his throne of power; but what we didn't expect was this Servant. He was a king, and he never denied being a king; but his first visit among men was to serve them, not to rule over them.

That has caused no end of consternation among men. The disciples were deeply offended when Jesus wore the clothes of a lowly slave and washed their feet. Not their Master! Not the one who was going to take Jerusalem by storm according to the prophecies! And he spent most of his waking hours trudging the dusty roads of Palestine in search of the poor, the blind, the lepers, the rejects of society – anybody who needed help. We tend to think that his ministry of miraculous healings brought him fame and honor, and he just went around showing off his stuff. But that is far from the truth. It was exhausting work: it meant daily putting off what he needed in the way of food and rest in order to help the helpless. The people he helped were unable to repay him – it wasn't as if he spent his time around the rich and influential! He was the friend of "sinners and tax collectors."

We too have a problem with his servant-hood. We are told repeatedly that he is Lord (which he is, and we don't do much with that idea either!) and that we need to obey him and honor him and lift him up before the world. But what we hear very little about is that he is God's Servant sent to help us. If he isn't straightening out our lives, and if things in our hearts aren't getting cleaned out for a change, and if we aren't beginning to find it possible to live the kind of life that God expects us to live, then Jesus simply isn't working in us. We know the housekeeper has been around when we find the rugs have been cleaned and the beds made and the dishes washed up; we know Jesus has been in our hearts when things *change* there.

The thing is that we are in desperate need of help. We don't like to admit that we need help, but this problem we have with sin is literally killing us. We simply have to set aside our pride and let someone else, who is more skillful and knowledgeable, doctor on us a while. Have you ever been in the hospital? Sometimes it's necessary for nurses to tend to your physical needs that embarrass you, that would shame you if you weren't so helpless. But it's necessary, and they don't mind doing it – they're paid to do it. Jesus doesn't mind doing some dirty work on our souls, straightening out the messes in our lives that we've gotten ourselves into, because he came to serve us in our helplessness. I think it's that aspect of Jesus' humility that most bothers proud people.

The enemy's lies – "Why is my language not clear to you? Because you are unable to hear what I say. You belong to your father, the devil, and you want to carry out your father's desire. He was a murderer from the beginning, not holding to the truth, for there is no truth in him. When he lies, he speaks his native language, for he is a liar and the father of lies." (John 8:43-44) I'm afraid that we underestimate the excellent training that we have all received at the feet of our first father. From our birth we've been drinking in the lies of the devil – through all sorts of channels, not necessarily by devil worship or anything like that. The world is full of avenues for the enemy's work among us. We have heard and seen enough "proofs" against the preciousness of Christ and the truth of God to permanently warp us; we simply can't accept at face value anything that Jesus says – something in us wants to pull away from him.

That sounds like a harsh judgment against us, but unfortunately it's more true than we realize. We've been trained in "common sense" and therefore are more than a little hesitant when we read about Jesus' miracles. We've been trained how to take care of ourselves, so we proudly resist Jesus' attempts to help us in our desperate need. We've been told how good we are, way down in there somewhere, so we don't like to hear Jesus' diagnosis of "You are unable to hear what I say!" (John 8:43)

As long as the stories of Jesus stay relatively harmless and just quaintly interesting then we have no problem with them. It's when the people around us start taking this material seriously that we panic and fall back on a system that we feel better about.

Leave family, friends, job, house, possessions – and willingly suffer persecution, starvation and rejection? No thanks! Surely we aren't all called to do such things – so let someone else do it! I can please God with a more modified Christianity, a subdued, rational lifestyle in which I can worship God on Sundays and have all my modern American luxuries the rest of the week.

And the Bible – it's all right to use it as a standard for some things in life, but surely it's going overboard to study it all the time! After all, I'll go to Heaven even if I don't know much about it.

And other Christians? It's not necessary to spend all my time around them. I have to work, don't I? It will be enough to see them at church a couple of times during the week. We modern Americans like our privacy, anyway.

These are bare-faced lies spread by the enemy himself, along with many other lies just as destructive. The reason our country is in the terrible shape that it is, and why the Church is so helpless in our generation, is because we've let ideas like these slip into our heads. If you check the teachings of Jesus you will find statements directly contrary to these ideas; he absolutely refused to let people get away with such thinking. As typical of the devil's concoctions there are elements of truth and common sense in all of it, to better deceive us; but that only makes it easier for someone to swallow them. At any rate, the point is that Jesus and his teachings go ignored while we too often have sat at the feet of the enemy of Christ.

Considering the hurdles that a teacher has to cross in order to understand the basic things of Christ – important things, things that we must understand to take advantage of what God has for us – it's a wonder that any of us know him at all! Everything and everyone seem conspired against us to keep us from knowing the truth about him. And yet, to know him means life – *abundant* life, as he put it – and not knowing him means that we will die. We have no choice but to plead for this precious knowledge at the throne of Grace.

Children are going to have the same problems with Jesus unless you are ready to help them through the difficulties. They need you to help them get past the false appearances. If you aren't prepared ahead of time, though, both of you are going to struggle to understand this mysterious man and probably not get anywhere for all your efforts.

Don't underestimate these difficulties that face us. Millions – no, billions – of people could not grasp the importance of Christ and are now lost. Jesus told us that "If you do not believe that I am the one I claim to be, you will indeed die in your sins." (John 8:24) He told Peter, who saw that he was the Christ and the Son of God, that he was truly blessed to be able to see that: "Blessed are you, Simon son of Jonah, for this was not revealed to you by man, but by my Father in Heaven." (Matthew 16:17) One or more of these barriers will come between every person and Jesus, in some way or another, just as they have been the reasons that most people before us in history could never find the life they needed in Christ.

The Father knows our severe limitations, however; he understands how impossible it is for creatures of dust (and sinners at that!) to grasp spiritual realities that are outside our reach. So he put a tool in our hands that makes the impossible possible: he gives us his Spirit. The Holy Spirit's role in making the truth about Christ plain to us is critical in the process of salvation. Without the Spirit none of us could be saved. Those who will be lost in the end have never known the touch of the Spirit in their hearts. I wish we could get into a more detailed discussion of the role of the Spirit, but we can't; it will be enough to mention here a few critical functions that he does for us:

> ***The Spirit reveals Christ.*** "He will bring glory to me by taking from what is mine and making it known to you." (John 16:14) The Spirit uncovers the veil from our eyes and enables us to see what the Pharisees couldn't see – the Son of God in all his glory. The Spirit makes each aspect of Christ's character, each type of work that he does, each precious gem that glitters with God's grace for helpless sinners plain to see. The world still can't see the point about Christ because it doesn't have the Spirit.

> ***The Spirit opens our minds and hearts.*** Since we were born spiritually dead – that is, completely unable to sense God or communicate with him, or obey him in the way he expects of us – the Spirit

first has to breathe life into our souls and make us
"alive to God in Christ Jesus." (Romans 6:11) He
gives us the ability to see God, to talk to him, and
to hear his voice. The Spirit gives us the strength
to follow Jesus when others would turn back in
despair – a spiritual strength.

The Spirit brings us his Word. To many people
the Bible is simply a book about religion, a
collection of stories, black ink on white paper in
the language of men. Evangelical Christians
believe that the Bible is much more than that,
however; to them it's the Truth of God whether
anybody believes it or not! It stands as God's
spoken Word and by that fact alone has all the
authority that it needs to condemn us or save us.
But unless the Spirit moves its truth into the heart,
it's of no spiritual benefit to us. That's what the
Spirit's work is when we hear the Word preached
or taught: "It penetrates even to dividing soul and
spirit, joints and marrow; it judges the thoughts
and attitudes of the heart." (Hebrews 4:12) Man
can never impress the Truth of God on sinners'
hearts to make them change their ways; on the
other hand, when people do change under the
teaching of the Word, you know that the Spirit is
at work.

The Spirit empowers us to take hold of Christ.
The jump from earth to Heaven is a long one! We
may want the things about Christ that we read
about, but how in the world are we going to get
any of it? Wishing doesn't make things happen,
not even in the land of miracles. If physical man
is going to walk in spiritual pastures, if the rebel of
earth will be accepted in the courts of Heaven,

then Somebody must bridge the gap for us – provide the means and the power to reach up into Heaven and take the gifts in Christ. The Spirit enables us to do what we've never been able to do before in our lives, what unbelievers can only dream about doing.

Now, through the means of the Holy Spirit, we can do what used to be impossible for any sinner to do – to both understand and take advantage of the grace of God in Christ. He's no longer a mystery to us, or a closed door. We just can't begin to appreciate the importance of this gift; without him we are lost. Whenever we teach – *every time* we teach – we simply have to ask for and trust in the Holy Spirit to go before us and open closed eyes and hearts to the realities of God's spiritual world.

Who is Jesus?

The most important question that any of us could ever ask is this: Who is Jesus? The people in his day were trying to find out the answer to that question, using Scripture and experience and common sense, and still couldn't pin down exactly who he was. Peter, however, put his finger on the answer immediately:

He asked his disciples, "Who do people say the Son of Man is?" They replied, "Some say John the Baptist; others say Elijah; and still others, Jeremiah or one of the prophets." "But what about you?" he asked. "Who do you say I am?" Simon Peter answered, "You are the Christ, the Son of the living God." Jesus replied, "Blessed are you, Simon son of Jonah, for this was not revealed to you by man, but by my Father in Heaven." (Matthew 16:13-18)

Notice two things about this passage: **First**, it seemed to be a difficult thing to figure out Jesus. Not only were most if not all the people in confusion about him, but probably his own disciples had wrong notions about him. In fact, the things that even *we* think about Christ will more than likely be wrong! **Second**, if we do know the truth about him, it won't be because we figured it out or someone else told it to us – it will be because the Father revealed it directly to us. This alone proves that children are just as capable of understanding the most important aspects of Christ as we adults are; it's God's doing, not ours, that we understand Jesus. God can just as easily make a child understand the truth as he can an adult.

What we want to do now is unpack that statement that Peter made about Christ. It seems to be a summary of everything that's in Jesus; get a hold of this and we will know what we need to know about Jesus, whether we are old or young. As you think about these things, notice how many "handles" there will be that you can grab and use in every day life; these are the kinds of things we all need to solve our problems and comfort our hearts.

Immanuel – God with us

When Jesus was born, the people remembered the old prophecy that was made about him: "The virgin will be with child and will give birth to a son, and they will call him Immanuel – which means, 'God with us.' " (Matthew 1:23) There's a tremendous amount of significance in that Name! The God that the Jews had heard about, had read about, and had hoped for had finally come down to them. Here he was! Not only was he here among us, he was one of *us* – which made him very approachable, something that the Old Testament saints didn't get to experience.

Because Jesus is God, these things are true about him:

• *He knows us.* Jesus knows us as only God can know us. "He did not need man's testimony about man, for he knew what was in a man." (John 2:25) He can see inside us and see the sin there, the hurt there, the "thoughts and attitudes of the heart." (Hebrews 4:12) He can see the needs that we have in life, in a way that nobody else can know. "The lamp of the Lord searches the spirit of a man; it searches out his inmost being." (Proverbs 20:27) His eyes are like fire, searching us through and seeing the truth about us: "His eyes were like blazing fire." (Revelation 1:14) He knows our weaknesses, and he knows the reason we stumble. "The spirit is willing, but the body is weak." (Mark 13:48)

Jesus knows our past life, detail by detail. "Come, see a man who told me everything I ever did." (John 4:29) He isn't surprised by anything about us as others are. So we know that, if he accepts us, it will be in spite of anything and everything that may be in our hearts and in our past.

Jesus knows our future, detail by detail. "Simon, Simon, Satan has asked to sift you as wheat. But I have prayed for you, Simon, that your faith may not fail. And when you have turned back, strengthen your brothers." (Luke 22:31-32) It's pretty awesome to think that Jesus knows even when we will fail him in the future, and still he accepts us. We won't surprise him even then. It's good to know that somebody knows where I'm headed – that my life isn't just chaos and chance, but it's running according to God's plan.

- *He does miracles.* It was very important to Jesus that people understood this about him. What hope would we have if we didn't have a God who does miracles? If God is as limited by problems as we are, whom do we have to turn to for help? But the Good News is that Someone has arrived with the power and wisdom of God, and now amazing things are going to start happening! The logjam of problems is going to break.

> The Spirit of the Lord is upon me, because he has anointed me to preach good news to the poor. He has sent me to proclaim freedom for the prisoners and recovery of sight for the blind, to release the oppressed, to proclaim the year of the Lord's favor. (Luke 4:18-19)

So he did what no man could do: he went all over the countryside doing miracles and amazing people with his power. When John the Baptist sent one of his disciples to Jesus to find out if he was really the Christ, Jesus returned a message: "Go back and report to John what you hear and see: The blind receive sight, the lame walk, those who have leprosy are cured, the deaf hear, the dead are raised, and the good news is preached to the poor. Blessed is the man who does not fall away on account of me." (Matthew 11:4-6)

But miracles and teaching about God were the only two things that Jesus had for people; if they didn't want these two things, he left town and looked for someone else who would want a miracle. In his home town, it says, "He did not do many miracles there because of their lack of faith." (Matthew 13:58) But in another town, "People brought all their sick to him and *begged* him to let the sick just touch the edge of his cloak, and all who touched him were healed." (Matthew 14:35-36)

A miracle, as you will find as you study the Scriptures, is something that man needs desperately but only God can do. I'm afraid our modern form of Christianity doesn't need much from God; we need to study the miracles of Jesus and ask ourselves, "Aren't these things that I need in my life? Shouldn't I be begging the Lord to come by me and touch me too?"

- *His Word is powerful.* When we want to get someone's attention we just yell louder; if that doesn't do it, we resort to some sort of physical measure to make our point. But Jesus' bare word is enough to handle the toughest problems that this world can throw at us. "He got up and rebuked the winds and the waves, and it was completely calm." (Matthew 8:26) We study how we can bring vast amounts of machinery and manpower together to handle life's challenges; but Jesus simply speaks and gets the job done immediately and in a way that leaves us speechless. When the disciples saw how his command calmed the storm, they were amazed (as we are, when we see the same thing happen!) and said "What kind of man is this?

Even the winds and the waves obey him!" (Matthew 8:27)

Remember how God first created the world? "And God *said* ..." All it took, because he *is* God, was the word of command and everything obeyed him. Even inanimate objects that we don't think of as capable of obedience jumped at his command and did his will exactly as he wished. So we shouldn't miss the point when we read about Jesus' miracles. Almost all of them were done with a word, a command, a simple call to the things in this world to do his bidding. But there's more than just a command, because we are no more able to obey him than the rocks are; furthermore, we don't often *want* to obey him because of our sin. So with the word of command comes the power to obey: the command "stretch out your hand" was followed with the healing of the arm so that the man *could* obey Jesus. (Matthew 12:13)

If you have watched Christians struggle with the truth they read in the Bible, you will know that they try to take this very seriously. The Word is powerful enough to arrest a sinner, convict him of his guilt, and send him to the throne of God pleading for mercy. There is no other power on earth that can do that, and yet the Bible has been doing that for scores of centuries. It also gives us a hope even in the middle of this world's dark nights – cheering the soul, giving a vision of future glory, and strengthening us for the tiresome battle of life. All he has to do is speak and we will know, suddenly, that we have something that will hold us up.

• *He puts us in touch with God.* What everyone needs, deep down, is to get back to God. God created us, we belong to him, and we aren't going to be happy until we are back with him. He gave us meaning to live – when he created Adam and Eve he gave them the work that they were to do and promised himself as their constant foundation. Even after man fell into sin and doomed himself to complete alienation from God, the Lord nevertheless offered himself again as a refuge, a hope against hope, that we could cling to. Without God we have nothing to live for – Paul describes this as the ultimate curse on somebody: "Remember that at that time you were separate from Christ, excluded from citizenship in Israel and foreigners to the covenants of the promise, without hope and without God in the world." (Ephesians 2:12)

That's why the coming of Christ is so exciting for us. "Anyone who has seen me has seen the Father ... The words I say to you are not just my own. Rather, it is the Father, living in me, who is doing his work." (John 14:9-10) This is why when Christ speaks to us, it hits home – it's the truth and we know it; he puts his finger on where we live inside because God himself is talking to us. When he forgives us, our guilty conscience is finally laid to rest and we *know* that we are accepted now. "Then Jesus said to her, 'Your sins are forgiven.' The other guests began to say among themselves, 'Who is this who even forgives sins?' Jesus said to the woman, 'Your faith has saved you; go in peace.' " (Luke 7:48-50) When Jesus calls a person to follow him, they know that God calls and they must follow him or lose every chance they have at eternal life and peace: "'Follow me,' he told him, and Matthew got up and followed him." (Matthew 9:9)

When Jesus speaks to us, or does something for us, it turns into a life-changing experience, something that the world is puzzled with and can't explain. People have willingly gone to the stake for what they have found in Jesus. How do you explain the presence of God to someone who can't see God? How do you explain the urgency in God's Word to someone who wants to live by other standards? Yet millions have heard that call of God in the voice of Christ, who came here close to us so that we can hear the voice of God; and millions have seen their God in the works of Christ and hope for the day when they will see him face to face. Their lives are completely changed now, since they've seen the Lord in his glory, and they are bound to follow him at whatever cost.

• ***The moment is now.*** Because Jesus is the Son of God, when he speaks we feel that we just *have* to take him seriously. There is something in his voice, his urgency, that forces us either to accept him completely or to reject him totally. There are only two things that will happen when you come under his voice: either you will bow before him and devote yourself completely to him, or you will hate him and get as far away from him as you can.

This accounts for the crowds of his day that followed him wherever he went. Can you imagine people leaving their daily work and responsibilities and spending days with him out on the mountainside – whole families, the sick, the community leaders? Can you see people doing that nowadays? They even went without food for days in order to follow him! But, on the other hand, his enemies hated him with a passion. The Pharisees plotted how to kill him – a man who worked miracles and taught the Word of God! Whatever he was and said cut deep in their souls and they swore they would get him for that.

A lot of talk that goes on in teaching and preaching nowadays isn't necessarily the Word of God. In fact, it's difficult for man to speak the words of God and get anybody roused up about it. But when the Spirit of God takes the words of man (faithful words, that is – they must at least be the truth!) and pierces the hearing heart with them, the same urgency comes upon a person that those people in Jesus' day felt. Either they must drop everything and follow him, or they wince under the barbed arrow of conviction and resist it violently. Unfortunately the latter often pick out dedicated Christians as their targets, since Jesus himself isn't very handy.

● *The only source for everything.* Another reason why Christ is so precious to us is that he, like God the Father, is the source of everything we need. It didn't take people long to see that Jesus could give them anything. Miracles flowed from him like a never-ending spring, fresh from the throne of Heaven. The sick found complete healing, the hungry got bread, the ignorant got wisdom, the lonely found friendship, the weak found strength, the laborers found work to do, and the lost found a direction to go.

The Scripture says that God owns the cattle on a thousand hills. (Psalm 50:10) He created the world, and the whole world lies at his disposal. We borrow his capital for the short time that we live, and then we must give it back to him when we die. He disposes of the world's wealth as he sees fit, to every creature, and we all must accept the lot in life that he has for us. If this is our God then it's also true of Christ himself. It's easy to see that in how he "gave gifts to men" during his ministry, as if it were all his to give – as a matter of fact, it was! Jesus himself lived a simple life free from the pursuit of worldly wealth; "Foxes have holes and birds of the air have nests, but the Son of Man has no place to lay his head." (Luke 9:58) To pay his tax he had to send Peter fishing – and the tax was in the fish's mouth! (Matthew 17:27) But in his very poverty we can see his infinite richness; who else can get whatever he needs from the simplest things of life?

The disciples knew that they had everything they needed in their Master. "Lord, to whom shall we go? You have the words of eternal life." (John 6:68) Jesus told them that "Everyone who has left houses or brothers or sisters or father or mother or children or fields for my sake will receive a hundred times as much and will inherit eternal life." (Matthew 19:29) It's easy to see this when we watch Jesus dispensing the wealth of Heaven, as he did in the Gospel stories; we can see plainly that here is someone who is in touch with the treasures of God – a limitless storehouse of treasure, freely giving it out to whoever will believe and take it.

The Savior

Jesus is also a Savior. If he were *only* God, and did nothing to help us, it would be a grim sort of knowledge to know that he was so *able* to help us and yet very *unwilling* to do so. The devils have such a grim knowledge! But to man he takes a different approach: he wants to save us. He not only wants to, he has done the things necessary to completely save his people from the impossible mess that they were in. The job was enormous and took nothing less than what the Son of God could do; no man has ever successfully done what Jesus did in a few short years. But what a salvation!

- *He canceled the Law's regulations.* Our biggest problem is what the Law of God had against us. In the Law's eyes, we were sinners from birth – Law breakers, rebels against God, irreconcilable enemies with the One who created us. We could do nothing right; everything we did smelled of rebellion and self-will. And we knew that. Something inside tells us that we can't stand before God without guilt; he surely looks upon us with disgust and anger.

  It's good news, then, that the Lord has come to address that problem first. We have nothing unless we have the Law off our backs! The Law spells doom to any and every sinner, no matter what his sin, without mercy; Jesus therefore takes the entire load of punishment off his people's back so that they have *nothing* to fear from the Law any more. They can actually stand before God clean in their hearts, with no guilty conscience, with "full assurance of faith" that God accepts them completely. We aren't used to that kind of forgiveness, but that's the kind that Jesus gets for those who believe. "As far as the east is from the west, so far has he removed our transgressions from us." (Psalm 103:12) The forgiveness we have is so complete, that as far as the Lord is concerned, we are *righteous* and no longer sinners. Though we struggle with sin, he doesn't treat us as sinners, as he once did; we are his children now, needing discipline but headed for glory, not condemnation.

Adults have problems forgetting other people's sins. Although we say we forgive them, we can't seem to forget; the pain and humiliation are just too deep to forget. We therefore have a hard time accepting the fact that God can forget – even such things as we have done against *him*, which, when you think about it, are far worse than we've ever done against another human being – and he determines never to remember or let it come between us again. The sacrifice that Jesus made for God's children is truly astounding in its effects: it surely must have been just what God wanted done to take care of our problem of sin!

• *He gave us the Spirit.* The next step of salvation is to put the principle in our hearts that will make us fit to live with God forever. If we remain sons of Adam then we can never hope to inherit anything more than this world – and all this world will be done away with at the end of time. Besides, to be forgiven of our sin is wonderful, but what will keep me from sinning again in the future?

The One who makes us citizens of a new world, with new hearts ready and willing to live for God from now on, is the Holy Spirit. This is such an important step that the Old Testament prophets told us this way ahead of time. The Israelites demonstrated how well (or how poorly, that is!) a people can follow the Law of God on their own efforts and strengths: they can't. God lamented that his people continued to anger him and rebel against him, even though they had his Law and his promises and a long history of his mercy. So, someday he would *make* these people obey him.

> I will give you a new heart and put a new spirit in you; I will remove from you your heart of stone and give you a heart of flesh. And I will put my Spirit in you and move you to follow my decrees and be careful to keep my laws. (Ezekiel 36:26-27)

Well, the time to fulfill this prophecy came when Jesus started his Church. You will remember the story of Pentecost when the Spirit of God came down in power on the followers of Jesus. The Spirit has come down in power ever since on his followers, because this is what the Church is all about. It's because we have the Spirit in our hearts that we can do God's will, and we can "understand what God has freely given us." (1 Corinthians 2:12) We can't get into a full discussion of what the Spirit does for us, but for now we can say that he 1) *enlightens us* so that we can see the things of God, and 2) *empowers us* to live the spiritual life that God expects of us. Jesus sends his Spirit to us so that we can please God in our daily walk.

• *He released us from sin.* Our relationship with God is the first essential step of salvation; the problem of the sin in our hearts has to be addressed immediately. Get right with God first, because all your future hangs on whether this is taken care of. But then move on to the reason you got into trouble with God in the first place, or else you have reason to doubt that Jesus is working with you.

Probably the most exhilarating feeling that a new-born Christian has is the realization that he doesn't *have* to sin anymore. He is free from its oppressive burden. Yes, sin is still around – we won't be free of its presence until we die and come before God in Heaven where there is no more sin. But it's a precious part of our salvation that we don't have to march to the tyrannical drumbeat of everything that offends God. "Through Christ Jesus the law of the Spirit of life set me free from the law of sin and death." (Romans 8:2) "You have been set free from sin and have become slaves to righteousness." (Romans 6:18)

Before, we had no hope – when sin rose up in our minds and hearts we had no choice but to follow its leading. We were helpless slaves to it. Now, however, our spirits have a way out. Jesus hangs a salvation rope down to us so that we can grab a hold when we find ourselves falling into the pit of sin. He is always close – the Rescuer, the Helper, the Older Brother, the Counselor, the

Door, the Light, the Bread from Heaven. We need not fail anymore like we used to.

An encouraging aspect of this is that he makes us hate what God hates. Sin may appeal to the flesh, but it doesn't appeal to our sensitive souls anymore. When we indulge in a little bit of forbidden pleasure we forget our birthright; in the light of God's Word, and often in the presence of God's people, such filth and corruption makes us feel ashamed of ourselves. Just a little bit of sin is enough to make the Christian's conscience agonize! Though we *must not sin*, sin is often a prod (though an unfortunate one) back to the righteousness of God, which alone gives life.

• *He made us alive to God.* Because of Adam's sin we have all fallen under the curse of death. Physical death is bad enough; but to be *dead to God* is truly disastrous. We can't see him, we can't hear him, we can't understand him – how in the world are we going to please a God we don't know and can never know? A sheer impossibility! But Jesus takes care of this problem beautifully by waking our souls up into the original state that Adam and Eve were created. They knew God, in their spirits, and were able to obey him and enjoy him. Now the Christian can have the same capability.

This is birth into a new world. The new believer wakes up into the realm of the Spirit, where God lives. It's true that he understands little of what he sees, like a new-born baby unable to put together the strange sights and sounds; but that will come with time as he gets used to his surroundings and learns about the Kingdom of God. "Unless a man is born again, he cannot see the Kingdom of God." (John 3:3) Paul uses the same strong picture of new birth: "Count yourselves dead to sin but alive to God in Christ Jesus." (Romans 6:11)

The signs that you are alive to God are these: you can see the Lord of Glory now, in your prayers and in the Word as you read; you now see the world from God's perspective instead of by your old opinions; you hate sin when it shows up in your heart; you understand the Word as it speaks to you about hope and faith and love; you love the children of God and want to fellowship with them instead of the children of the world. Now you may not have any of these graces in super-abundant measure, but at least the spark is there – at least you want these things, whereas before your conversion you couldn't have imagined such things. It was Jesus who made you feel like this about the things of God.

• *He fulfilled the Law's requirements.* We will never know the terrible complexity of the Law and all its demands. The Jews thought that they could do the Law and please God by it; then Jesus came along and gave them a demonstration of the true depth of the Law of God! In the Sermon on the Mount he outlines some of the impossible demands on the sinner's heart; now nobody can ever hope to keep the Law in a way that would satisfy God. It's beyond us – even the little bit that we know about.

But one of the purposes for Jesus coming is so that he could be our hope in this respect also. "God sent his Son, born of a woman, born under Law, to redeem those under Law, that we might receive the full rights of sons." (Galatians 4:4-5) He faced every law in the canon of Jewish Law and fulfilled it to perfection, not missing a single detail, so that at the end of his life the Law was forced to declare him a truly righteous man. He took care of both *overt* and *covert* obedience – that is, he did the things that he must do to be righteous and he refrained from all things that he must not do be righteous. When we realize the smallest part of the staggering demands that God makes on humanity, we have to stand amazed at Jesus' accomplishment. Surely nobody else in history has done such an impossible thing. And because he is perfectly righteous (according to God's ancient promise), "the man who obeys them will *live* by them." (Leviticus 18:5)

But he didn't do it just for his own sake! He came to save us – and part of that means that we too must be righteous in God's eyes. So, now that he has bought that righteousness with his own life, he signs our names on the contract of life with his. Can one man carry many with him to Heaven? He can if he's the Son of God who bought that righteousness! "For if, by the trespass of the one man, death reigned through that one man, how much more will those who receive God's abundant provision of grace and of the gift of righteousness reign in life through the one man, Jesus Christ." (Romans 5:17) We are literally getting into Heaven on Jesus' coattails! Or more properly said, according to historical doctrine, by the merits of Christ and not our own.

• *He makes us children of God.* This is perhaps the most amazing part of our salvation. To think that man, once a rebel and a God-hater, would be allowed to come into God's presence – to think that such an incorrigible creature would be summoned for special honor – to think that man would sit on God's right hand to judge the angels! (1 Corinthians 6:3) – and to think that this once enemy of God would become an adopted child of God, rightful heir to all that God possesses, staggers the imagination. Nobody in all history could have imagined that God would do such an incredible thing.

If Jesus had stopped at restoring us to the righteous state that we had in Adam he would have done us a service to earn our everlasting gratitude. If he had given us eternal life and no more, what blessing could we want beyond that? But the Lord "in love predestined us to be adopted as his sons through Christ Jesus, in accordance with his pleasure and will." (Ephesians 1:5) We have yet to understand this, let alone appreciate it. Because of our adoption we have all the rights that Jesus himself has. Did Christ consider it beneath him to give us his own inheritance? "So Jesus is not ashamed to call us brothers." (Hebrews 2:11) Our standing with God is far above what any other creature in Heaven and on earth can claim.

Not that we deserve any of this honor. That's the whole point. Christ did an unspeakably extraordinary thing when he brought us to the

Father and signed our adoption papers. We had no rights with God! All we deserved was condemnation, and rightly so considering our history. Now, however, we can ask anything we want from our "Father" and fully expect to get it! "Until now you have not asked for anything in my Name. Ask and you will receive, and your joy will be complete." (John 16:24) Perhaps this is the biggest thing that we struggle to believe about God – our right to him and his promises based on our adoption.

• *He serves us.* This is a little-understood aspect of Jesus' ministry and yet perhaps it's the most fundamental one. Jesus, you will recall, didn't come to be crowned king of the Jews in pomp and ceremony. He came as a humble carpenter's son, "despised and rejected," misunderstood by friend and enemy. His very humility confuses us all. In fact, his own followers are careful to call him Lord – and so he is – but forget that this Lord took on the role of a servant for our sakes.

A servant does demeaning work, the work that nobody else wants to do. Didn't Jesus do just this in coming to help sinners? "I have not come to call the righteous, but sinners to repentance." (Luke 5:32) "A friend of tax collectors and sinners." (Matthew 11:19) The Pharisees, too pure to touch the wicked, despised Jesus for his attention to sinners. But Jesus was interested in saving – and that means he'd have to go down where sinners were and rescue them from the mud and the filth of the world. He's interested in healing the broken, touching the lepers, raising the dead, giving hope to the hopeless. He wants to clean the disciples' feet. (John 13:1-17) He wants to teach them the simple things of God's kingdom. He wants to personally oversee the nitty-gritty of building God's house; he will allow nobody else to do the difficult and thankless task.

This is all the more remarkable when we realize how little we appreciate his hard work!

> You see, at just the right time, when we were still powerless, Christ died for the ungodly. Very rarely will anyone die for a righteous man, though for a good man someone might possibly dare to die. But God demonstrates his own love for us in this: While we were still sinners, Christ died for us. (Romans 5:6-8)

Paul understood that humility of Christ and deeply appreciated what the Lord did for him. "For I am the least of the apostles and do not even deserve to be called an apostle, because I persecuted the Church of God. But by the grace of God I am what I am, and his grace to me was not without effect." (1 Corinthians 15:9-10) Surely it was an amazing grace that condescended to lift the persecutor Saul into such a place of importance in the eternal Church! And he personally trained Paul for the tremendous job ahead of him. And we, just like Paul, stand amazed at this humble love as it loves the unlovely.

The Lord

There's been a move in the Church in the past few years to restore some meaning to this title. It was once fashionable to consider just the initial step of salvation – repentance and the first act of faith – as the core of our Christianity; it didn't matter much what followed that as long as you took that first step. But lately Christians have been realizing that this is only step one; step two is living in the *kingdom*. People have often called this "making Jesus Lord of my life," but actually that's an incorrect way of looking at it: he was Lord long before you and I were born! We don't *make* him Lord, we just wake up to the fact that he *is* Lord, as others before us have found.

At any rate, there's a whole new dimension behind the Lordship of Christ that we need to look at. Jesus was just as careful to develop this part of his work as he was any other part.

- *Building a kingdom.* Jesus is building a new world. Men try to rebuild this physical world so that its problems will go away and everyone can be happy, but such a thing will never happen. This world is built on a foundation that can never last into eternity (in spite of what the scientists claim!) and God intends to sweep it all away into oblivion at the end of time. (Hebrews 1:10-12) But Jesus' new world will be just what's necessary: it will have all the characteristics of God himself (eternity, perfection, uprightness, of a spiritual nature, utter fulfillment) and it will be the vehicle for the next phase of God's plan, the eternal life of his redeemed saints.

  This new world requires enormous resources and infinite skill in its construction. Jesus is a master builder, however, and he lays the stones in a way that the result will be a perfect house for the God of glory to live in. He started making plans for it right after the fall of man; he continued the preparations through the experiences of the Israelites; he came in person to lay the all-important cornerstone – his incarnation, life, death, resurrection, and ascension; he laid the foundation in the work and writings of the apostles; he continues to build the house now by laying stone on stone in the work of the Church; and someday he will finish his work and present it as a "New Jerusalem" to his Father, laying "everything under his feet." (Revelation 21; 1 Corinthians 15:24-28)

This is the work he referred to when he told his disciples:

> In my Father's house are many rooms; if it were not so, I would have told you. I am going there to prepare a place for you. And if I go and prepare a place for you, I will come back and take you to be with me that you also may be where I am. (John 14:2-3)

As with any house-builder, he builds it to suit himself. It has all the features that he likes (we will like them too, by the way, because his love always guides his work for us to do us good) and it's perfectly situated – in the Heavenly realms. We can trust this builder to give us a place to live that we would *want* to live in forever! It will be so perfect that we could never get tired of it or want anything else. Does this tell you anything about his skill and his care for us?

The new world will be, for once, a world that God is pleased with. The last time God said he was pleased with our world was *before* Adam sinned; ever since then he's been aching to get rid of it! He's been a long time in anticipation for "a new heavens and a new earth." (Isaiah 65:17) This will be a place that will obey him, that will honor him as Creator and Redeemer, that will glorify him as the source of all good things. There they will say of him, from the bottom of their grateful hearts, that "for from him and through him and to him are all things. To him be the glory forever! Amen." (Romans 11:36) There will be no trace of man's sin, no enemies present, no death; only the goodness of God. This is the world that Jesus is busy right now putting together.

• *Makes us his subjects.* This is no small job. We are used to living by our own opinions and will, and it has always come hard for us to bend the knee to someone else's will. Sometimes we will grudgingly agree with another person but only if we are forced into it or it serves our own purposes, not because we really want to lay aside our own wishes in favor of his. But this is exactly what Jesus has set out to do with us – *make* us conform to his will and *like* it.

He has many ways of doing this. We react to the word "force" with fear and dislike; but he "makes" his people walk in his ways by using gentle but persuasive means. Remember, "a bruised reed he will not break, and a smoldering wick he will not snuff out, till he leads justice to victory." (Matthew 12:20) He *will* lead justice to victory – but he will do it in such a way as to get us there undamaged in spite of our weakness.

Jesus intends that someday all people will bow their knees to him in submission (Philippians 2:10-11), and people ought to be more concerned than they are about how he's going to do that. But now he's interested in getting us to follow his leading, and he uses gentle ways to do it. For example, as he works in us through his Spirit he gradually changes our willfulness into a desire to "keep in step with the Spirit." (Galatians 5:25) The Spirit leads us by teaching us the Truth about Christ. (John 14:26) He helps us cry "Abba, Father" when we want to say something to God and don't know what to say. (Romans 8:14-15) It's by the Spirit that we put to death the misdeeds of the body. (Romans 8:13) So the more we live by the Spirit, the more we will conform to his will – and we do find ourselves conforming to his will, in spite of ourselves, because it's that very self-will (which fights against his will) that the Spirit is crucifying in us. In fact, we become willing slaves as he overcomes our resistance to him! (Romans 6:18)

- ***Defeats the enemy.*** Every good king protects his subjects, and Jesus is the outstanding example of this principle. Nobody can protect us like Jesus can! An earthly king can do his best against physical dangers, but only Jesus can hold the spiritual forces at bay around us and lead us to the safe haven of Heaven. Only Jesus knows how to "overcome the world" and defeat Satan.

We just don't know the dangers that the enemy surrounds us with. We are too often unaware of the physical dangers around us! The child's prayer applies to us all, because we are all helpless much of our lives to things that could go wrong:

Now I lay me down to sleep,
I pray the Lord my soul to keep.
If I should die before I wake,
I pray the Lord my soul to take.

We could all probably relate how many disasters we've narrowly escaped from. But when we get to Heaven we are going to find out a whole new list of spiritual disasters that Jesus saved us from, entirely unknown to us, as he faithfully led us through this "valley of the shadow of death." "Your enemy the devil prowls around like a roaring lion, looking for someone to devour." (1 Peter 5:8) How can we possibly protect ourselves against a spirit that we can't see? A spirit who has been alive far longer than anyone on earth? Who has vast experience at bringing people – even saints of God – to their knees in despair?

Don't underestimate the devastating power of the devil; he led you for years under his yoke of tyranny, doing his will not God's, and making a disaster of your life – which you may yet be struggling to clear up. Jesus has to launch an all-out attack against him to break his strangle-hold on us; then he has to constantly be our forward scout and our rearguard to protect us from further trouble. Paul trusted in Jesus implicitly for his protection: "I know whom I have believed, and am convinced that he is able to guard what I have entrusted to him for that day." (2 Timothy 1:12)

Jesus will prove the victor in the end, over all enemies, no matter what the odds. "If God is for us, who can be against us?" (Romans 8:31) He threw back the devil during his own temptation, and he knows how to keep us safe during ours. "I have prayed for you, Simon." (Luke 22:32) He plans to lead us, his captives, in a victory parade back to Heaven, with the devil and his crew behind us in chains. "For he must reign until he has put all his enemies under his feet." (1 Corinthians 15:25) We might not think, as we look around us in our world, that he's doing that; but appearances are deceiving. Notice for one thing that not one of his enemies has successfully avoided the first curse that God laid on man – death! This in itself is his overruling hand making sure that the enemies of God will eventually be brought down to the dust; nobody will get the last word with him!

• ***Head of the Church.*** Jesus is the Lord of the Church too. Unfortunately you wouldn't know it, the way people try to run things in the Church to suit themselves! We know that unbelievers try to throw off his Kingship (Psalm 2:1-6) and we understand why; but Christians have supposedly already bowed their knees to Jesus – their fellowship should be the place where he rules supreme and does his will perfectly. Isn't it so? No, it isn't – or at least it doesn't appear to be. Men determine what will go on in the Church: *they* decide what will be taught there, what the worship will be like, what "obedience to God's commands" means, what service to God will look like, what holiness really is, and so on. Almost every local church has a list of rules of men – Jesus called them 'traditions of men" – that everyone is bound to follow or they will find themselves outside the church walls.

Fortunately Jesus is bigger than we are; he *is* going to run his Church the way he sees fit even if we try to get in his way. But to see it you have to step off the beaten track and look behind the bushes and trees along the way. He is training people to use their spiritual gifts – but not usually in seminaries and Bible schools; he uses the everyday circumstances of life to train them, and impresses his truths on their hearts by the lamplight late at night while they study the Bible and pray. These humble servants don't get the applause and renown that some others get in the Church, but they are doing more in Christ's kingdom than many an educated preacher.

He is answering prayers of humble saints whom the Church is usually unaware of. Grand prayers are offered in services that he often ignores, because they glorify man and his works too much. But the nobodies of the Church, the old saints that nobody takes notice of, the social outcasts, the rejected of the world, the little ones whom we may be teaching – those are the really useful servants in the Church. The people that the world passes by because they have no beauty or majesty of their own to attract us to them (notice how they resemble our Lord?) are literally holding up the pillars of the Heavenly Temple with their prayers and intercessions. He *is* answering *them!* If the Church is doing anything right in our day, it's due to *their* spiritual insight and their service; the Lord is directing the affairs of the Church through them, the real strength of the Church, and bringing it together into the House of God.

When we see these things happening then we know that Jesus is indeed the Lord of the Church and directing everything according to his will. The affairs and will of men look as if they are doing everything possible to tear apart Christ's Church; but since it's still holding together, still growing, still bringing new saints into glory and teaching them the Truth about God, we have to assume that Jesus is directing its affairs in his own way and through his own people; he will *not* be put off by man's sin but *will* accomplish what he came here to do.

As you read these descriptions of Christ, could you imagine yourself telling them to your children? If you do, you are painting a graphic picture in their minds of someone real who can do anything, who will do what he wants in this world, and who offers us the same kind of exciting life that he lives. This is news of a living Christ, not just a story of a dead man in an old history book!

The fullness of Christ

The above outline of the nature of Christ and his work follows the well-known pattern of **PROPHET - PRIEST - KING** – he serves the three functions that we, as sinners and yet children of God, need the most. But there's so much more of Christ to learn and to take advantage of! We could study him for the rest of our lives and never find an end. There's so much about him that's usable – he exactly fits the needs that we have, and the interests that we have; and there's so much more about him that's mystery and great that we simply stand in awe of.

For example, you could do a study on the Names of Christ and learn worlds of things about him. Philip Henry, a preacher of the seventeenth century and father to the famous Bible commentator Matthew Henry, preached a series of sermons once on the names of Christ. It's a rich feast to read the sermon notes. He laid out 54 names of the Lord in his sermons; here they are:

> Foundation, Food, Root, Clothing, Head, Hope, Refuge, Righteousness, Light, Life, Peace, Passover, Portion, Propitiation, Freedom, Fountain, Wisdom, Way, Banner, Example, Door, Dew, Sun, Shield, Strength, Song, Horn, Honor, Sanctification, Supply, Resurrection, Redemption, Lesson, Ladder, Truth, Treasure, Temple, Ark, Altar, Our All, Husband, Father, Brother, Friend, Master, Teacher, King, Captain, Physician, Advocate, Shepherd, Elder, Inhabitant, Keeper.

Do you see anything in this list that you need for your life? I should hope so! God thinks that you need these things; that's why he sent Jesus to be these things for you. Consider them a spiritual smorgasbord: as you read the Bible, you can see the rich foods on God's table all labeled by name; your hunger will drive you to this food and that food to satisfy you, and the Father stands ready like a chef to serve you whatever you want.

Or, you could do a study on the things in the Old Testament that got the people of God ready for the ministry of Christ in the New Testament. For example, these subjects tie in directly with the ministry of Christ:

- *the types of Christ*
- *the history of Israel*
- *prophets and prophecy*

- *the Law and all its meanings*
- *the Tabernacle, the Temple, and all its furnishings*
- *the prophecies about the Gentiles*
- *the covenant with Abraham, and the other covenants*

As we read the Bible we see things about Christ that convince us that he's bigger and wiser and more capable than we dreamed. For example, Isaiah prophesied that Christ would be called a *Wonderful Counselor* (Isaiah 9:6). So we ought to be able to see this come true in the Gospel accounts. And in fact we do: we find him counseling people all the time about what to think and what to do – with the unerring skill of a knowledgeable and interested counselor. This could make a complete study in itself.

Jesus was the *miracle worker*. You could do a study on just the miracles he performed. It would turn into more than a simple list of his miracles, because you would learn *for whom* he did miracles, *when* and *where* he did miracles, *why* he did miracles, *what happened* as a result of his miracles – and as the picture slowly comes together, you would learn *what a miracle of God is*. Then you can begin studying what we can expect from Jesus in the same way, or in ways far beyond what the Jews experienced under his earthly ministry. The subject of miracles is a vitally important area to understand in the kingdom of Christ.

Jesus was a *Teacher*, more skilled at teaching us about God than any before or after him. He didn't just spit out some ideas that came into his head! He knew what to say and to whom to say certain things. He knew that some people could learn only so much and the rest had to wait until later. He knew how to say particular truths with the greatest effect. He used different methods of teaching, evidently because certain methods are best for certain subjects. This, you must keep in mind, is how God wants these ideas taught – if you want to be a teacher of the things of God, you must learn from the Master Teacher himself. Even further: whoever teaches in the Church supposedly has the spiritual gift to teach (Ephesians 4:11), which means the Spirit of Christ is directing him or her in their teaching. But remember that Christ said that the Spirit would remind us of *his* words – in other words, our teaching must be of the same nature as his, and on the same subjects, to be genuinely from his Spirit.

Finally, we must remember that Jesus Christ is *multi-faceted*. There are hundreds or perhaps thousands of aspects of Christ if we want to learn all about him. Many people make the serious mistake of focusing on just one or two or even half a dozen aspects of Christ and then refusing to look at any more. The problem with this is that he's so full, and so big, that if we just look at a small number of things about him we are liable to get an unbalanced picture of him. For example, we've already mentioned that many Christians spent so much time exalting him as Savior that they forgot he's also the Lord. Jesus is the Wisdom of God, and yet he learned obedience as a Son. (Hebrews 5:8) He's the Husband of the Church and does things that a husband will do for his bride; he's the Shepherd of the sheep; he's the Captain of the army; he's the fulfillment of the Tabernacle's many sacrifices and elements and laws. So when we try to study him in his actions, we have to be able to see him in all sorts of roles – he wears many hats, and many at the same time! – in order to understand him without getting confused. He's never so simple to understand as we often make him out to be.

The Gospels

These four books are our primary sources for our knowledge of Jesus' earthly ministry. For that reason they have become the center of the New Testament Church. In fact, they are the only existing records of the life of Christ – there were no other records made of him in history.

The entire story of Christ is just too big to tell about. John told us that "Jesus did many other things as well. If every one of them were written down, I suppose that even the whole world would not have room for the books that would be written." (John 21:25) That sounds as if he's stretching the truth, but if you consider the possibilities then it may really be impressive what Jesus did! For example, the average person can speak about 230 words per minute. That means he can say the equivalent of what has been written in the book of John in about 1 1/2 hours. If we consider that Jesus could very well have spent 8 hours every day talking to people and teaching them, he would have said enough to fill up these chapters 5 times over – a complete book a day! If he ministered for three years, and if someone would have recorded every word he said, we would have had over 1,100 books authored by him! And that's only what he *said* – a collection of every story of each miracle that he did would have taken many more hundreds or thousands of books to write.

Obviously we can't carry a Bible around made up of thousands of volumes. Nor do we need to. The design behind the four Gospels is that we have been given no more and no less than what we need to know about Jesus. The Spirit teaches us *what* we need to learn about Christ, in the *way* we need to learn it. As much as we would like to know more about him than what's written, the Lord feels that we don't need to know more than what he's given us in the Word.

This means that, as teachers, we need to slow down when we read the Gospels and pay attention to what's going on there. There's definitely a purpose and a method in these books that we need to learn about if we want to teach them:

• ***They testify of his glory.*** Jesus is on center stage in these books. But he's not only the principle character, he's revealed to us in a way that proves that he's the Son of God. Many an unbeliever has started out reading the Gospels with the intent to discredit them, and ended up believing in the Christ that they glorify.

The Gospels show us that Christ is the only solution for the problems of life. That itself is an accomplishment since we usually spend most of our lives looking all over the world for answers. When someone is convinced that Jesus heals the wound, that Jesus feeds the soul, that Jesus counsels with wisdom, that Jesus is the Friend to have, that Jesus is the judge of the heart, then the Gospel writers have accomplished their goal. What they were aiming at, after all, is that "you may believe that Jesus is the Christ, the Son of God, and that by believing you may have life in his Name." (John 20:31)

The word "glory" means *credit* – in other words, who gets the credit for something? To whom should everyone turn for this thing? Who was responsible for this? We can see very clearly in the Gospels that Jesus alone was responsible for salvation and healings and all the miracles that he did. No man or woman, no matter how much they wanted to do what was needed, could help themselves; only when Jesus passed their way did they get God's blessing. In fact, his miracles were designed to teach us this very thing: if you can possibly imagine how Jesus could have pulled those wonders off, then you must be on the same level of power and wisdom and stature as he is! Nobody could (and nobody can now) figure out how in the world he did them. There is only one person who could do such things – the Son of God himself.

When Jesus gets the glory then people turn to him the next time they need such a thing for themselves. Notice that the crowds followed him everywhere with their sick and demon possessed, once they found out he could heal them. When he fed the 5000 on the hillside, they followed him when he moved on from there, hoping that he would feed them again. When we read what he did for people then we also want to get the same thing for ourselves. In other words, people will travel with the man who produces, not just promises; and the Gospels aren't bashful about demonstrating how well Jesus produces the promises of God for whoever will come to take them.

• *Faith looking at the Son of Man.* The Pharisees had a real problem when they looked at Jesus: all they saw was a poor carpenter's son, a nobody, an uneducated troublemaker from the country. If it weren't for the Spirit of God, we would all have the same problem; Jesus wouldn't have gotten the spot in history that he did, and there would be no such thing as the Church today. Jesus even told Peter, a devoted follower, that the only reason why he saw that Jesus was the Christ was that "this was not revealed to you by man, but by my Father in Heaven." (Matthew 16:17)

We of later centuries are at a disadvantage. The disciples were there; they walked and talked with him, and could see him and touch him. Though they needed the Spirit also to see his real nature, they at least had him there in flesh and blood and could watch him work and listen to him teach. We don't have that privilege. What we do have, however, is their written record of his ministry – and they were careful to present him in the way that he needs to be presented for the eye of faith.

The story gives almost nothing about his personal life; this was on purpose, you know, so that we don't focus on what he was as a man but as the Son of God. What little it does give us ties in directly with the purpose at hand. For instance, we are told that as a boy he "grew in wisdom and stature, and in favor with God and men." (Luke 2:52) That's not enough to write a novel about! But it explains the process by which he became ready for his short ministry as an adult. More information than that isn't necessary for our faith in him.

A more impartial observer would have given entirely different accounts of his ministry; but fortunately the disciples weren't impartial toward the Lord. For example, a modern newsman would have reported back to us that a certain woman caused a sensation one day when she supposedly touched his cloak, and Jesus told her that she was healed. That's all that he would have been able to confirm, and that's all he'd be interested in reporting. But Luke tells us that no doctor had been able to help her over twelve years; her bleeding *did* stop when she touched his cloak; Jesus felt the power go out from him; it was her faith that made the miracle happen; Jesus sent her away *in peace*. With these extra details (that any other writer wouldn't have been able to provide) we get a bigger picture of who Jesus really is and what he's able to accomplish.

• ***Disciples giving out the bread of life.*** The story in Matthew 14 provides the idea here. When Jesus was out in the countryside with thousands of people listening to him teach, it came time for people to go home – it was getting late and they hadn't eaten all day. When the disciples asked him what could be done, he answered: "They do not need to go away. You give them something to eat." (Matthew 14:16) As the story unfolds we see that he meant what he said to them; even though he broke the bread and multiplied it, it was the disciples who gave it to the people.

That was an important lesson for them to learn, because they would be required to do the same thing over and over again in their future ministries. *Jesus gave himself to his disciples, and they give him to us.* When the time came to expand the kingdom beyond the local assembly of Christians in Jerusalem, some of the apostles sat down and committed the story of Jesus to writing for the sake of the rest of the Church – including us. The Gospels are nothing less than the disciples feeding Jesus' sheep with the bread from Heaven.

> ... God's household, built on the foundation
> of the apostles and prophets, with Christ

Jesus himself as the chief cornerstone. (Ephesians 2:19-20)

Modern critics ought to take notice of this. These aren't fabricated tales that the apostles made up to start a new religious movement. They are *faithful* accounts of the Lord's words and works; if they had made any of it up, it would be no good for our faith. This must be exactly what Jesus said and did or they would have been lying about him! We can't believe in a fable; the Church can't rest on, or work from, a myth. So the disciples were obligated to take the Truth *as it is* in Jesus: "Surely you heard of him and were taught in him in accordance with the truth that is in Jesus." (Ephesians 4:21) We need the God that these Gospels describe. Thank God that Jesus really is what the apostles say he is, or none of us has any hope of salvation.

• *Multifaceted view.* We mentioned before that the Lord has many sides to his character; he wore many hats, and often we have to unpack a single story into all sorts of pictures and explanations of what he was doing. This is probably where we get into the most trouble trying to interpret the Gospels. We have to remember that Jesus is a vast and complicated subject; be careful, when you focus on one aspect of him, that you aren't overlooking some other equally important side in the story.

Let's take an example. In Matthew 15 we read the story about the Canaanite woman who came to him pleading for a miracle to heal her daughter. Jesus says some harsh things to her; she responds in humility and faith; and then Jesus gives her what she asks. The point of the story, we usually say, is that Jesus is merciful and responds to true faith – even when Gentiles display that faith.

This is true, but there is more about the story than that. The story takes on enormous dimensions when we pick up on that one statement of Jesus: "I was sent only to the lost sheep of Israel." (Matthew 15:24) If you know your Old Testament, you will remember the covenant that God made with Abraham (Genesis 12,15,17) and all his seed. That covenant was the foundation blessing of the Jewish nation; all other agreements and arrangements came after it and never did supersede it. Jesus was bound by the terms of the covenant (the penalties of which you can read about in Genesis 15:7-21) to do good to Abraham's seed – and to nobody else! Does that exclude everyone except Jews? According to Paul, Abraham's seed are *all those who have the same kind of **faith** as their father Abraham!* "Therefore the promise comes by faith, so that it may be by grace and may be guaranteed to all Abraham's offspring – not only those who are of the Law but also to those who are of the faith of Abraham. *He is the father of us all.*" (Romans 4:16) As a matter of fact, Jesus came into this Gentile country looking for Abraham's children and *he found one* in this Canaanite woman – the sign he needed to see was the Abrahamic faith that she had. Here was a "lost sheep of Israel." The story shows all sorts of things about Jesus, one of which is that he is the covenant fulfiller.

• *Ties to the Old Testament.* You probably noticed that the Gospel writers quote the Old Testament over and over. That isn't to impress us with their Bible knowledge! And it isn't just to "proof text" what they are talking about, like modern preachers often do. Their aim was to show us that Jesus and the Old Testament are tied tightly together – you can't understand one without the other.

First, they are telling us that *this is the God of the Old Testament – up close.* Some of the Jews recognized their God when they watched Jesus working and heard his teaching. "The people were amazed when they saw the dumb speaking, the crippled made well, the lame walking and the blind seeing. And they praised the *God of Israel.*" (Matthew 15:31) They knew whom they were seeing because they knew their Scriptures. We, however, not knowing the Old Testament as well as they, might miss the point – Jesus was the Israelites' God come close, close enough to do his work on a person-by-person basis. I don't know what you get from reading about God in the Old Testament, but if you watch Jesus you will see the same God. "Anyone who has seen me has seen the Father." (John 14:9)

Second, they are telling us that *Jesus is the fulfillment of all the prophecies.* We know this side of Jesus' ministry much better; we know that the prophets all spoke about the coming Messiah and what he would do for God's people. The apostles referred to the old prophecies many times regarding what Jesus was doing. Be aware, however, that we may miss the importance – even the meaning itself – of the prophecy, just as the Jews did. Didn't they already know where Jesus would be born – and were any of them there to welcome him? (Matthew 2:3-6) Here was the King come to set up his new Kingdom!

Third, they are telling us that *Jesus is the real sacrificial and Temple system that the Old Testament system foreshadowed.* This we know almost nothing about. We watch him die on the cross, and we know that somehow that relates to the death of the victim that the Law required on the altar of the Temple. But we don't see the vast and complicated ceremonial system that Jesus went through, step by step, in the Heavenly Tabernacle. We don't see much of the Lord in his work as the Great High Priest, interceding in the Temple for his people. We don't see how his nature corresponds exactly with the elements of the Tabernacle and the Temple. This is all true, however, and extremely important to our salvation. The Gospel writers are careful to display before us the Temple of God in the flesh; (John 2:19) we mustn't miss the significance.

Fourth, they are telling us that *Jesus is the fulfillment of the Law of God.* They show us a sinless man, careful to do all that the Law required. He knew and practiced the depth of the meaning of the Law – the spiritual side of the Law, not just its superficial meaning. Now if he did such a thing, how can we look to our own feeble efforts to satisfy God when Jesus offers us his righteousness instead? Here is a man who did what thousands of years of well-intentioned Jews couldn't do! Men have always gone back to the

Gospel stories for the *example* of Jesus' holy life, saying that we must be like him – entirely missing the point! None of us can live a life like this! The purpose of the stories is to drive you to him for help.

There are many other things that the Gospel writers want to tell us about Jesus and the Old Testament. I hope you take the hint and study the story of Jesus in that light; let the apostles guide you expertly through the labyrinth of the Old Testament (which today's Jews would do well to learn!) and show you how the Lord of Glory shines on its pages.

• *Foundation work.* We do well in starting with the Gospels when we first become believers. Here is the stuff that our developing faith will need as problems get bigger and we get weaker. Dying saints have often gone back to the simple Gospel stories to hold up their faith. The Church's work depends on these truths, these pictures of Jesus; without them we have no salvation.

The book of Hebrews calls these things "elementary truths" – "repentance from acts that lead to death, and of faith in God, instruction about baptisms, the laying on of hands, the resurrection of the dead, and eternal judgment." (Hebrews 6:1-2) We all have to start here. There are basic things that every Christian has to get down or he will always be messed up in his thinking or, what is worse, he won't have the necessary knowledge to keep himself out of moral trouble.

Collect together the broad topics of the Gospels and you will find out what's a foundation for our faith. They are always developing the theme of the Son of God – Immanuel, God with us, God in the flesh, the One who made all things, coming close to save us. Another truth they hammer on is that Jesus is the miracle worker – only he can do what we need; no other man can help us. They show him as the great Teacher – so get used to sitting at Jesus' feet and listening to his wisdom and counsel. They teach us what Jesus came to do – save us from sin – and we see him dealing with the problem of sin in people's lives from all sorts of angles. When you get these broad lessons under your belt you will be in a better position to go on to the "solid food" that Hebrews 5 refers to, ready to grow up and become mature in your thinking and life. But if you haven't gotten the Gospel lessons down yet then you need to go back to them, not go on to difficult things!

You will notice that the writers of the various New Testament Epistles assume that you have already done your homework in the Gospels; they often don't go over the same material again for slow learners. This means, of course, that if someone doesn't understand the basics of Jesus then he's very likely going to twist or misunderstand or be entirely ignorant of what the Epistles teach – which often happens. (2 Peter 3:16)

• *A teaching method.* Finally, the Gospels use a teaching method that does the job of instructing us about Jesus remarkably well. Keep in mind that these writers wrote their books under the inspiration of the Holy Spirit – so this is *God's* preferred method of teaching about his Son.

Later we will get more into how the Gospels teach about Jesus. For now we can notice a few points: **first**, they use little stories – what the scholars call "pericopes" (pronounced, pair-IK-oh-pees) – to break down the lessons about Jesus. Instead of using a more Greek approach of a long doctrinal essay (which is a valid method, by the way, since Paul himself uses that method) they stress only a small point at a time. This gives them a lot of room to make the point well, and it gives us a better chance of getting and remembering the point. **Second**, they use a lot of stories. Human beings love activity and movement and examples, and they learn more by their eyes and what they see happening than by any other sense. Besides, we are more convinced by what we see working than a whole book of promises and theory. **Third**, one of the strongest characteristics of the Gospels is that they tell the story several times and from several perspectives. One of the cardinal rules of good teaching, if you want your point to stick in the pupil's mind, is to say it several times over. Three, by the way, seems to be a good number of times, the experts of education tell us.

What Do Children Need From Us?

Children depend on us for everything. And we have been more than willing to take care of all their needs since the day they were born. Feeding, changing diapers, clothing, loving, protecting, entertaining – it's a 18-20 year relationship that takes up most of our time and resources, but we do it willingly because we love them. There's something in the heart of a parent that wants to fulfill the child's every need.

But they are dependent on us for more than physical needs. The Lord gave them to us for a reason; he has a lot to do in their lives, and the time they will stay with us is the first stage on their spiritual journey. Paul said that God arranged even the details of childhood surroundings for his purposes:

> From one man he made every nation of men, that they should inhabit the whole earth; and he determined the times set for them and the exact places where they should live. God did this so that men would seek him and perhaps reach out for him and find him, though he is not far from each one of us. (Acts 17:26-27)

It's a sobering thought to realize that what we adults do will affect their future, either to the good or the bad; the successes and failures of a man or woman are often the result of their parents and what their home-life was like. This has a spiritual side as well: it's up to *you* to teach them about Christ;

if you don't, how will they even know about him? In God's providence you may be their one and only chance of hearing the Gospel! Even if they do hear it later, as an adult, they may have missed years of knowing him and living in his blessings simply because of what you may have failed to do. This is easily avoided.

Paul told us this: "Fathers, do not exasperate your children; instead, bring them up in the training and instruction of the Lord." (Ephesians 6:4) There are all sorts of ways to exasperate children! One way is to treat them as if they don't deserve our full attention, as if they were second-class citizens. They know when they aren't wanted! They can also tell if you are throwing yourself into their training and sparing nothing to teach what they need to know. Jesus warned us also: "See that you do not look down on one of these little ones." (Matthew 18:10) It's too easy for adults to do this to children; but if we aren't careful we are going to leave scars on their souls that will be there years from now.

In our own ways, we can be careless with children and not teach them in the right way. These kinds of things can happen:

- *We impose our limitations on them.* We wouldn't think that, being teachers, *we* have limitations and children don't – we usually think that it's the other way around! But there are simple spiritual lessons that they can get much easier than we can. We have problems now, as an adult, that we didn't used to have when we were younger; we are going to look at some of them in a minute. So when we teach children, we tend to struggle with *our* problems and *our* limitations while they get the point way ahead of us. It's much like gifted children in a class of normal students – they have to cool their heels waiting for the rest of the class to catch up. We adults often hold up spiritual progress in the children because we can't keep up with them.

• *We don't let God do his work – we do it for him.* We are so used to telling children what to do that we are too prone to step into God's role and do his work, things that he alone is entitled to do. In other words, we tell the children *what* they have to do and we expect them to perform for *us*, when really it's God whom they must please; and they have to do it in *his* timetable, not ours, and in the way that pleases him, not us. When it comes to the work of the Spirit we are not the experts – and we are not the child's ultimate authority. We have to remember that children are just as much creatures of God as we are, and they are just as responsible to him as we are. We tend to forget, though, that our biggest job is to stay out of the way while God deals with them. You may not realize how often and in how many ways we get in the way of God and the child when they try to relate to each other.

• *We may work on the wrong things.* We can get confused and spend time on issues that either don't help the child spiritually or can actually hurt him. We have to find out what he needs, not what we think he ought to have to become just like us. The Scripture teaches that one must start at the beginning, with the basic principles; and after those come the things next in line; and so on. It really is a shame when we go to extremes and involve children in social or political issues that don't really concern them – even if the issues *are* important to us – when they aren't well equipped to handle things like that.

Any of these problems will hurt, not help, the child we teach; and we don't want to do that. We need to do all that we can to avoid hurting him spiritually. If an adult isn't careful to help a child along the truth, done in God's way, then he's in danger of the judgment that Jesus spoke about:

> But if anyone causes one of these little ones who believe in me to sin, it would be better for him to have a large millstone hung around his neck and to be drowned in the depths of the sea. (Matthew 18:6)

So instead of being careless when we teach children we need to be extra careful. Ask yourself the question, **WHAT DO THEY NEED FROM ME?**

Unless you become like little children ...

> *I tell you the truth, unless you change and become like little children, you will never enter the kingdom of Heaven. Therefore, whoever humbles himself like this child is the greatest in the kingdom of Heaven.* (Matthew 18:3-4)

This passage teaches us three things that children need from us:

- *You must change first.* This is the point of this entire book, as far as I am concerned; you must get this idea if you don't get anything else. Before you can teach children about Jesus, you *must* change. Or at least we can say this about it: to be a Christian, you must change; and only then will you be spiritually qualified to teach children. Of course we know from John 3:3 that one must be "born again" to see the kingdom of God; but here in this Matthew passage the Lord is telling us about another fundamental change in our hearts besides the new birth. *We must become like children.*

At first glance this doesn't seem to make any sense. If he wants us to become like children, then how could we also be adult enough and wise enough to teach children? But it's not childish ignorance that he's after; it's the child's point of view, the child's natural feelings, the child's heart that he wants to see in us. If he doesn't see that in us – and who can mistake a child's ways! – then he isn't satisfied with us at all.

What's in a child's heart that Jesus likes so much? **First**, they are always in learning mode. They are always asking questions; they want to know how things work; their play is nothing less than training for the real world. They depend on adults all day, every day, to teach them the truth they need in their lives. School is an inevitable (though not always liked!) part of every child's life because it's during their childhood that they must learn and prepare for the coming responsibilities of being an adult. This constant learning is more important for a child than we realize: it's said that a child has his basic world view (in other words, a bare-bones but sufficient picture to understand the world he finds himself a part of) by the time he is six! We don't have much time to get the essentials into his world-view, do we?

Adults, on the other hand, have for the most part quit learning. School is over, and we don't see the need to keep learning things. We are already doing well in our jobs and we don't need to learn more for them; we've already learned social skills and how to fit into our little corner in the world. The really unfortunate thing about this is that we have the same attitude about the world of God and about his Word – we simply will not learn any more than the little bit that squeezed into our heads at conversion! That is so typical of adults. The Lord has no respect for that kind of thing: "My people are destroyed from lack of knowledge." (Hosea 4:6) Then when we display our lack of knowledge in front of the children – not knowing the lesson, not having done sufficient study of the subject, not wanting to use the Bible for a textbook because we are so afraid of it, relying completely on someone else's notes and literature (as good as they may be!) because we don't know anything about it ourselves – they pick up on that. We lose a lot of credibility with them because *we* don't know what we are requiring *them* to learn.

Second, they believe what they hear. A child will accept at face value whatever you tell them. That's a vulnerable spot in children, because they will believe something even if it's wrong; they will believe the fantastic unless you tell them otherwise. Their world includes the possibility of all sorts of things wonderful and strange; their minds enjoy creativity, which you can see as they read make-believe stories. Even their play time includes imaginary characters and situations and things that couldn't possibly happen in real life, but which are nevertheless real to them – or they would like it to be real if they could get it!

But we are grown up now, aren't we? We know that the world is reasonable and logical, and one can't have whatever one wants, and we must work hard for whatever we need. We don't believe in miracles and the impossible. At least we don't believe that such things are for our time! And we don't pay any attention to God's counsel or his point of view on things; it would be nice if the world were a perfect place to live, but the grim realities of life make the Bible's counsel just too simplistic – a child's view, in fact, and not very useful for adults.

This means, however, that we aren't going to believe *most* of the Bible! So, because we don't believe it ourselves, we are only going to half-heartedly teach these stories to children; and since children aren't stupid, they are going to see through our duplicity. The Lord isn't pleased with this either, because what the Bible says – word for word, just as it stands – is *true*.

Before you can be qualified to teach children you must believe every word the Bible says. Maybe you don't understand a lot of it, and your scientific mind rebels at the thought, and the common sense you got by growing up contradicts it. But you've got to put all that aside and believe the impossible. The way God tells you to see things – that's the way you have to start seeing it.

Third, they do what they are told. They get used to taking orders from us because it's necessary: they are still learning what are the right things to do. The amazing thing about this is that they do it without question, without a single thought of whether it's right or not, with not a shred of pride that may get hurt. They know, somehow, that Daddy and Mommy give the orders and they must obey. Their problem isn't whether the parents have the right to command, or whether they are obligated to obey, but obeying and staying out of trouble!

If you tried to tell an adult what to do, however, you may have a fight on your hands! We don't like to be ordered around. We get reconciled to it a little on the job because if we don't do as the boss says then we might get fired. But even there, employees have found ways to protect themselves against the authority of their superiors: labor unions, employee rights, and so on. We feel that nobody else has the right to tell us how to live our lives; we've felt that way about things since our teen years when we discovered we have a mind of our own and we learned how to make our own way in life.

The problem with that is that God requires total, complete, unquestioning obedience from us, without any suggestions from us about what might be more fair or more efficient. He just doesn't want to hear it! The Scripture calls him a *despot* – 2 Peter 2:1. (The English translation is "Sovereign Lord" but the Greek word is δεσποτης – which is where we get the word "despot" from.) *He* rules, we don't, and he expects immediate obedience to whatever he says, whenever he says it. That just doesn't go well with us; but then our independence doesn't go well with him.

Fourth, they are devoted followers. You've heard stories of children who will fight each other for the honor of their daddies. Their love isn't something they can explain to you, either; they just trust their parents and they want to be just like them. They will dress, act, and talk like their parents because they look up to them as their heroes.

By the time we grow up, however, we've become disillusioned about heroes. We've seen enough of the problems and faults in others to know that there's nobody worthy of our trust anymore. So we refuse to become someone's camp follower, or at least we will follow at a distance without committing too much of our time and energy to their cause. We want to have a quick and handy escape in case things get too bad.

We take the same approach with Jesus, unfortunately. Although we might admit that he is worth our time and trouble to follow, we still can't bring ourselves to do as Matthew did:

> As Jesus went on from there, he saw a man named Matthew sitting at the tax collector's booth. "Follow me," he told him, and Matthew got up and followed him. (Matthew 9:9)

We tend to call this "being fanatical about one's religion." But that's exactly what Jesus wants you to do! Things move too fast in his world, the demands are tough, the jobs to get done are too critical, for him to have sluggards and half-hearted followers behind him. He needs a devotion that we have never given anybody else if he is going to use us to help build the kingdom.

• *You must humble yourself.* Besides a complete character change, another way to become like a little child is to learn humility. It's not easy, this business of humility. It means admitting that you *aren't* number one in the universe and that others are at least as important as you are. It means that someone else needs to be telling you how to live, instead of you trusting in yourself. It means admitting that you aren't what you ought to be – and being willing to uncover those sins so that the Lord can take care of them. This comes hard for an adult; this is why Christ aims directly at your pride before he mentioned anything else about how to get to Heaven, because it's the first problem that must be solved before he will trust you to teach his little ones.

One way to humble yourself when you teach children about Jesus is to believe the accounts about him yourself! These are fantastic stories about him – the world laughs at the idea of accepting any of it as true. Turning water into wine? Everyone in modern times knows that can't be true! All the other miracles are just as hard to swallow for a modern, sophisticated American. In fact, even most Bible scholars don't believe in the supernatural world of miracles; they have all sorts of ways of explaining it away with science and psychology. So you're going to look like a fool in everyone's eyes when you solemnly sit in front of your children and tell them that *it's all very true.*

Another way to humble yourself in front of them is to put yourself down, lift Christ up, and respect the children as equals spiritually. You are not the center of attention here; Christ is. Focus on him – show them that he's what they need. He's the life they need, the bread, the wisdom, the Friend of sinners, the strong one. You stand in need of these things just as much as the children do! You aren't anybody special in Christ's eyes, as if you were indispensable in his plans and these children are fortunate that you agreed to spend your precious time throwing them a few crumbs from your table! Rather you are the least of the saints of the Church; you are only Christ's servant, trying in his strength to honor him but liable to sins and ignorance yourself. We are all in this together. And when you reach out to them and help them find in Christ what you yourself depend on him for, the children get the idea that you really do love them – that you want to see them grow to where you are and even beyond. "I have more insight than all my teachers, for I meditate on your statutes." (Psalm 119:99) Can you live with the possibility that one of your students will know more than you do about the Bible? If you really cared about them then you would be working for *all* of them to know more than you do!

A third way to humble yourself is to give your all to the Lord – and to the children as a result. Children aren't a nuisance; but they will feel that they are when you go to class unprepared, half-hearted, and don't much believe these things yourself. They can see through you pretty well. Even if you manage to fool them for a while, their own lives will suffer eventually when you don't care enough to dig in and give them your best. Aren't they worth it? Weren't *you* worth it to someone once? Will you ever see these children again – will they have another chance to hear the Gospel after your classes with them? Their eternity just may hang in the balance! Your time is valuable but their souls are of infinite worth; it's worth it to set aside prime time for their benefit. The service that the Lord calls you to, far from being an inferior station in the Church, is a vital one that he thinks is more productive of spiritual fruit than any other branch of the Church's work. Work on this level is so important that the Lord considers it the first and necessary step to further responsibilities. (Matthew 25:23)

• *You must welcome them in Christ's Name.* In this passage Jesus also tells us about an important duty that all teachers have, and it's going to feel humbling if we take it seriously. When you teach children, you have a duty to do what the Lord called you to do – no more than what he told you and no less. He gave you food for the lambs – very specific food that's specially designed to produce spiritual strength and vision. He gave you instructions for their obedience and growth. He entrusted you with spiritual treasures and powers just so you could bring a blessing into their lives. In other words, we have Jesus in our hands and we must be busy distributing *him* to the children just as the disciples distributed the bread to the crowds. You must set aside whatever your own interests are and *do what he tells you to do*.

Consider yourself an ambassador of Christ. You've been sent with news to tell them, and you must relay the news in exactly the way you yourself heard it from him. A faithful messenger will take great pains to represent his King faithfully in all matters:

A wicked messenger falls into trouble, but a trustworthy envoy brings healing. (Proverbs 13:17)

Like the coolness of snow at harvest time is a trustworthy messenger to those who sent him; he refreshes the spirit of his masters. (Proverbs 25:13)

When a king's ambassador delivers the news faithfully, he not only brings joy to the hearers but he sets his king's heart at rest, who knows that the message got through OK in the form he wanted it to be. This is so much more true about the Gospel of Christ! He evidently is very concerned about the children getting his special blessing, and he doesn't want you to mess it up! We often have our own agenda to follow; we think that certain things are important (whether or not we got that from the Bible!) and that's what we intend to teach to the children. But that may not be what the Lord wants you to teach them! These are his lambs, and he alone knows what they need to survive spiritually. Remember that he's the Good Shepherd who knows where to lead his flock for the food and water that they need. He does *not* need our opinions on the matter!

Consider yourself a doorkeeper in Christ's kingdom. Jesus is calling them, and you stand at the door to let them in so that they can come to him. They are going to ask directions to find him – or at least you should be responsible enough to give them those directions even if they don't ask. The children don't need *you* so much; they need the Lord who calls them into the flock. You aren't there to draw attention to yourself but to guide them to him. As they come in (which is your job – to get them in through the stories and the truth about Christ in the Scriptures) they will head off in his direction through faith and obedience, and your job will be done. No glory in it, is there? But Christ will have a new batch of lambs for himself! The Lord will hold you accountable for making sure they find their way through the door, learn their way through the hallways of God's house, and reach him. You are their temporary guide.

Bring the children to me ...

Let the little children come to me, and do not hinder them, for the kingdom of Heaven belongs to such as these. (Matthew 19:14)

The second thing that we must learn is that we must bring children *to Jesus*. This is the key that many adults miss when they say that all children have the blessing of God – actually the children get no such blessings unless Christ "prays for them." Notice carefully what the text says: the kingdom of Heaven belongs to whom? To "such as these" – in other words, to children like these who were brought *to Jesus*.

A child isn't necessarily blessed by God simply because he's a child. His parents may have baptized him as an infant, and then never taught him a thing about Christ during his childhood or taken him to a church where they teach the truth about Jesus. His childhood, in other words, may (and usually is, if you go by what happens too often in nominally Christian homes) have been *without* the blessing of Jesus.

This passage teaches that Jesus *does* bless children; he even prays for them! But certain conditions must be met first:

- ***You are their door to Christ.*** Jesus has things for them that they need spiritually, and whether they get those things rests literally in your hands. The disciples in this story "rebuked those who brought them." You are Jesus' disciple now, and I hope you don't keep the children away from Christ for whatever reason people do that. Hopefully you realize the importance of your job and dutifully lead them to the Master so he can bless them.

  There are ways to open the door to Christ so that children can come to him; we will see many of them shortly. For now we can look at a couple of ways: **first**, make them very familiar with particular stories in the Gospels that teach a certain thing about Christ. When you show them what the Lord is doing, and why he is doing it, and what happens to people that he does it to – and hammer the point of the passage in so well that the children know it by heart and can refer to it immediately – then you've made a strong link to the Scripture for them that they will never forget. They can use that link in the future when the same set of needs comes up in their own lives, and they will be drawn back to the story (and thus to Christ himself) for his promised help.

Second, show them that what Jesus said and did wasn't limited to Bible times. The reason for these stories isn't just to give them history lessons to memorize! This is the Lord of the entire Church; these are the things he does for *all* his people, everywhere and at all times, not just to the Jewish believers in ancient Palestine. The children have every right to believe that they can go to Jesus for his blessing just as the children in the story did. Your job will be to show them that Jesus is still alive, still waiting for them to come, and still able to do all the things that the Gospels tell us about him.

When you teach like this, the stories of Christ are going to take on special meaning for the children. They just accept what you tell them, being the way they are, which is all the better because such wild ideas are too much for mature adults to accept. So, the children will be blessed when adults won't even come! But you have to open this door for them or they can't come – how can they come to someone they don't know and can't hear? You are their eyes and ears, and you must believe these things yourself before you will convince the children of their reality. The point and result of all your Bible lessons must be that there *really is* someone like this and it's really a wonderful experience to meet him.

• *Bring them to Jesus.* Jesus wants people everywhere, not just children, to come to him. Come to *him*. The reason we spent so much time in the previous chapter on who Jesus is, is so that we will know the right God to bring the children to! We have to know Jesus ourselves so that we won't send confusing signals to the children. John the Baptist knew the Lord – in fact, it was his job to know the Lord ahead of time so that he could point him out to the crowd:

> Look, the Lamb of God, who takes away the sin of the world! This is the one I meant when I said, 'A man who comes after me has surpassed me because he was before me.' I myself did not know him, but the reason why I came baptizing with water was that he might be revealed to Israel ... I saw the Spirit come down from Heaven as a dove and remain on him. I would not have known him, except that the one who sent me to baptize with water told me, 'The man on whom you see the Spirit come down and remain is he who will baptize with the Holy Spirit.' I have seen and I testify that this is the Son of God. (John 1:29-34)

The only way we will know the meaning of any of the stories in the Gospels is if we are familiar with Jesus' face. If we know his ways well then we can point them out as we teach; if we know his thoughts well then we can show the children what Jesus was trying to do. On the other hand, if we have trouble ourselves figuring out what Jesus is up to then we mustn't expect the children to get a good idea of who Jesus is, and they certainly won't be able to trust him in any way.

Every lesson should be a lesson on something about Jesus. It's a shame that teachers waste all their time teaching just our duties and responsibilities before God, and even our blessings. Heaven won't be centered around us but around the Lord – he's the star of the show! Even our obedience doesn't mean a thing unless we start with *his* nature, *his* commands, *his* kingdom, and then move on to the "therefores" in our lives.

• *He will bless them.* We may have a problem believing that Jesus still blesses people because it's been such a long time since he blessed us; but that's because of *our* unbelief, not *his* unwillingness! There are plenty of stories that teach that he's ready and willing to help any who come to him in faith. The children will believe that even if we don't; and he will prove through them if not through us that he's a God who keeps his word.

How does Jesus bless children? Without anticipating our discussion of this below, we can focus on what this particular passage says about it. He "placed his hands on them." "Laying on of hands" is one of the elementary truths that the book of Hebrews refers to (Hebrews 6:2); unfortunately it isn't something that we moderns know much about. Using certain Old Testament Scriptures we can, I think, learn something about this old teaching: **first**, we find Jacob placing his hands on the heads of Joseph's sons to bless them, and the act was *authoritative*. His right hand went on Ephraim's head (he was even the younger of the two boys) to bless him with the greater inheritance, and his left hand went on Manasseh's head for the lesser inheritance. (Genesis 48:12-20) In other words, through his authority as the ruling patriarch he gave out the boys' inheritance rights. Isn't Jesus the Lord who gives the inheritance of Heaven to those who come to him – including children?

Second, we find the priests putting their hands on the heads of the sacrifices in the Temple. (Leviticus 4:15; 8:14; 16:21, and other places) Of course the victim was about to be killed – that's not exactly what Jesus was going to do to these children! But the solemn Temple ceremony symbolized the *sanctification* of the animal, which is no more than an old Hebrew word for "setting aside for God's use." We see the same thing in the New Testament when the Christians at Antioch sent Paul and Barnabas out to the mission field: "So after they had fasted and prayed, they placed their hands on them and sent them off." (Acts 13:3) This is also what Jesus is doing to the children: laying hands on *his* children and claiming them for God.

Don't look down on them

See that you do not look down on one of these little ones. For I tell you that their angels in Heaven always see the face of my Father in Heaven. (Matthew 18:10-11)

Here is another solemn warning from the Lord; he counsels us that we had better step very carefully around the children that we are teaching. It seems that he *is* concerned about their spiritual health, and he thinks that we are just too prone to ruin things for them. Let's analyze this passage:

> • *Why do we look down on children?* You can almost see him, putting the child behind him away from the adults – what concerns him about their welfare? He says that we "look down on" the children; why and how do we do that? He evidently thinks that we often do that, that we do it even without thinking about it – as if it's normal for us to do that. But he just won't stand by and let us do that to the children! His reference to their protecting angels wasn't just pretty language; it was a threat! Why do we look down on children?

> Probably one reason why we consider children to be lower than us is because they are still undeveloped – physically and mentally and socially – and so we think that they aren't going to understand this adult level material anyway. It's as if we can safely postpone their real education until later when they will be able to appreciate it more. The problem with that is that they can understand it very well; they will be able, in fact, to fit it all into their world view much easier than we adults can, since we have to find the rare faith to fit God's truth into our already existing world view, and they simply have to build it into their developing view of life as they grow. We have no good reason for putting their spiritual education off, and every good reason for giving it to them *now* while their lives are under construction and in great need of the truth.

> A second reason we look down on children is that there seems to be a particular stigma about

teaching children's classes. Adults like to be around their peers just like other age groups; if someone has to separate from the group and spend some time with children, it doesn't sit very well. They will often do as little as possible for the children simply because they aren't worth the extra time and effort; one has to keep one's ties with the other adults, right? Children get in the way of that! You will find, however, that the children will sense that immediately and will never accept you; if that's the way you feel, you may as well let someone else teach them because you aren't going to get anywhere with them anymore. Besides, being with other adults isn't always the greatest thing to be doing; adults often don't do things that are any more important than what the children do – they just play grown-up games instead of children's games.

Another reason we look down on children is perhaps the worst reason of all, and the one we will be most condemned for: they won't praise us like adults will when we teach them. Teachers look for glory, although none of them want to admit that, and adults often have rewarding ways of showing their appreciation for your hard efforts. Children, however, show no appreciation for you; they just listen and then leave. There's no personal glory in teaching children! So, many of us refuse to teach them. Of course we find other "good" reasons for refusing instead of the glory issue because it would look so bad. But that's why many won't do it; they need some sort of positive feedback to make them feel important and wanted, and children just can't do that. That, however, is one of the good reasons (there are others) why it's actually better to teach children than adults: you have a better chance of doing something useful with children, and getting real spiritual work done, than you have with adults who have learned the art of letting things go in one ear and out the other – then praising you for your performance at putting them to sleep!

• *Angels for them?* People have used this passage to support all sorts of teachings of the relationship between angels and children. I just don't know whether God assigns an angel for every child on earth; the Bible doesn't say that, though we would like to think that. What I do know, however, is a passage in Hebrews explaining the duty of angels:

> Are not all angels ministering spirits sent to serve those who will inherit salvation? (Hebrews 1:14)

Angels have a unique assignment, one that we don't know much about but the Scripture hints at here and there. Evidently their work is important or the Lord wouldn't bother doing it! In any case, this passage in Hebrews makes it plain that angels help (again, in what way we are not sure) God's people. It doesn't mention anything about helping those who don't belong to God, but then we're not sure about all the possibilities in Heaven.

Next, let's come back to this passage in Matthew 18. Jesus refers to "these little ones" – who are they? The ones who were coming to him! Let's not overlook the fact that he's pointing at the children surrounding him, the ones he's laying his hands on and praying for. Is there a relationship between the two details? **There are angels ministering for the children whom Jesus touches and prays for.** There is more of a dynamic going on here than we may have realized.

Third, notice what Jesus says those angels are doing right now: they are before the throne of God, "seeing the face" of the Father. We will see below the meaning of this phrase; but think about what Jesus did for these children when they came to him. He prayed for them. This means that he asked the Father to do something for them. We can safely assume, then, that the Father turned right around (in answer to Jesus' prayers) and instructed his angels concerning the children – in other words, he told them to do what Jesus asked for them. Are *your* prayers answered so immediately and with such certainty? We don't know what he asked the Father for them, but we can surely wish for such care and looking-after for ourselves! They are in an enviable position spiritually!

• *Seeing the face of the Father.* In those days the people better appreciated Jesus' picture than we do. They were ruled by kings, and when someone had a need that he couldn't take care of himself and the lower officials couldn't help him with, he went to the king. That is, if he could get an "audience" with the king; that wasn't something he could depend on! Often somebody would stop him at the front desk and refer him to some official who probably wouldn't be very helpful. But if the person could get to the king himself he would present his case, and he hoped the king would see the reason for the request and grant it. If the king said "yes" then it was done, no matter who else in the kingdom disagreed!

God is no less a king; in fact he is the "King of kings." Things work the same way in his court. We may not realize that (which is why we live such dry spiritual lives!) and we may not like it that way, but nevertheless he entertains people in need before his throne and passes judgment on their cases. Jesus tells us here that these children's angels have the right of access to the Father, the right to come up to him ("seeing his face") and present themselves as his servants. That's the most powerful position in the entire universe (except for the place at his right hand, reserved for his Son). This kind of access to God means that he is personally interested in the children's case and has ready angels to dispatch for their needs.

Age of accountability

People have argued for centuries about whether children can be held accountable for matters concerning God. There are so many issues involved in the debate: for example, whether or not to baptize infants, what kind of benefits (if any!) the child will have if baptized, whether or not to include children in the communion ceremony, what happens to young children who die, whether or not children are morally responsible for any sin they commit, whether children can actually know the seriousness of sin and whether they can feel true guilt over it, whether a child's repentance is genuine and the same thing as an adult's, whether children should pray, what the differences are between a child's spiritual situation and an adult's, whether there is an age when children do become responsible and therefore able to handle the things of God, and so on. As you can see, this is not an easy matter to resolve.

What makes it harder to solve is that it's something that's close to our hearts. I'm sure that most if not all of us adults are guilty of arguing on the basis of our love for our children – and not much on the basis of *truth*. We can easily analyze a stranger's faith to see if it's up to snuff; we take pains to make sure that we don't associate ourselves with people who don't believe as we believe and live as we live – we are experts at judging the spiritual performance of others. But when it comes to our children, our tendency is to go to the opposite extreme: we will often argue *against* what the Bible may say, simply because we are already prejudiced in their favor. Is this bad? Perhaps not as bad as the judgmental spirit we hold against others outside our families! Perhaps we need more of this attitude of parental love when it comes to brothers and sisters who aren't of our peculiar persuasion but who nonetheless claim the Name of Christ.

An additional problem about this issue is that, in spite of what many people claim, the Bible simply doesn't have much plain, clear, black-and-white guidelines for Christians to go by on the subject of how to handle children in the Church. Most of what it says about children of Christian parents is by inference – you have to read between the lines, so to speak, and use Scriptures for "proofs" that are rather doubtful authorities for the circumstances of the New Testament Christian Church. All sides have to do this; I'm not accusing any particular group of playing games with the Bible. You can see this best in the fact that solid Christian thinkers through the centuries have been divided on this issue even when they agreed on other issues, and they all believed very firmly that they had a Biblical basis for what they said.

Without getting into any matters that divide Christians, I think we can talk about spiritual accountability of children, and the Biblical principles behind that – no matter what your personal persuasion is. In fact, it's very important that we settle some of these issues so that we will know how and what to teach them about Christ.

First let me state the "Age of Accountability" doctrine. It has three points:

- Every person is born under the curse of death, being children of Adam and Eve, because we inherited from them *original sin* – that is, the inclination to sin. We are all doomed to die a physical death because of this original sin in our natures.

- A child has this original sin in his heart, but he isn't old enough to knowingly follow its leading. In other words, sin may happen in his life but he's not responsible for it – he's not *willfully* sinning against God. If he dies at this point, he can't be held guilty of willful sin – and Christ's death covered original sin completely – so he passes directly into the presence of God and salvation. All this is assuming that the child has Christian parents.

- A child reaches a certain age at which time he gets the ability to discern good from evil – and with that ability becomes a sinner by choice instead of simply by birth. Then is when guilt for personal sin becomes a reality and repentance a moral necessity. If he dies at this point without consciously coming to Christ for salvation, he will not receive life but death and Hell.

As you can see, the Age of Accountability would be an extremely important point in one's life – a watershed, as a matter of fact. One passes from complete safety to utter danger. In one sense it would be better to die as a child! At least you would be *sure* that they would make it to Heaven, without any doubts on the matter.

But even those who believe this doctrine have to admit that, while point one is very plainly taught in the Bible (see Romans 5:12-19), the other two points aren't at all plain. They have to make their case by inference. However, our interest here is not so much in *when they are saved*, but *what they need*; so let's attack this problem from a different angle and see if some of the confusion will clear up.

> • ***What can children understand?*** The Bible very plainly teaches that nobody – not even adults – can understand anything about God and Christ unless the Spirit of God opens their eyes to spiritual realities. We can't see who Christ really is – the Savior – and take advantage of that knowledge in any way unless God gives us that ability. "Blessed are you, Simon son of Jonah, for this was not revealed to you by man, [*not even a teacher!*] but by my Father in Heaven." (Matthew 16:17) Our flesh, the world, and our sin all get in the way of the vision of Heaven.
>
>> We have not received the spirit of the world but the Spirit who is from God, that we may understand what God has freely given us. (1 Corinthians 2:12)
>
> Once we do see it, we still don't rely on our own native abilities – either by education or

experience or even age – to understand it and talk about it and live by it.

> This is what we speak, not in words taught us by human wisdom but in words taught by the Spirit, expressing spiritual truths in spiritual words. (1 Corinthians 2:13)

In other words, it's not something *in us* that makes us able to understand Christ but what God *gives* us. Furthermore, Paul goes on to say that it's not age or experience that divides those who know from those who don't; the key is whether someone has the Spirit or not:

> The man without the Spirit does not accept the things that come from the Spirit of God, for they are foolishness to him, and he cannot understand them, because they are spiritually discerned. (1 Corinthians 2:14)

All this is to say that children can know Christ in a saving way, in the same way adults do, if the Spirit of God opens their eyes to the truth. It has nothing to do with age. In fact it has nothing to do with their childlike world view either, because this passage tells us that the Spirit will give them the right way to see things, the right words and thoughts for expressing their faith, to make up for their otherwise limited experience. Being an adult adds nothing to the transaction between the Savior and the one being saved! So whatever people say happens *after* the Age of Accountability can just as easily happen *before* it; and if that's true, how useful then is the concept?

Furthermore, children can learn the facts just as easily as adults. I mentioned above that salvation isn't hindered by a child's limited world view; I didn't mean to say, however, that the Spirit works with someone who is totally ignorant. A very vital piece of the puzzle of the salvation process is our knowledge of God. For example, even an adult can't be saved unless he at least knows who Jesus is and what he can do: "If you do not believe that I am the one I claim to be, you will indeed die in your sins." (John 8:24) Someone must preach and bring the truth, and then the hearer can respond to the truth: "And how can they believe in the one of whom they have not heard? And how can they hear without someone preaching to them?" (Romans 10:14) It's always been that way and it always will be that way.

Well, the children are in the same boat. Whatever insights they might get, whatever working of the Spirit may occur in their heart, whatever God might do in their lives, is never going to be apart from *some* kind of knowledge of the truth. Spiritual fruit always comes from God working with the knowledge that we have:

> ... asking God to fill you with the knowledge of his will through all spiritual wisdom and understanding ... in order that you may live a life worthy of the Lord and may please him in every way: bearing fruit in every good work... (Colossians 1:9-10)

You won't find any Scripture that teaches anything contrary to this.

There's no question that children know far less than adults about almost everything. They are constantly in a learning mode, from the day they are born until they leave the nest to go out on their own. But this is the very beauty of their situation: teach them about Jesus, and then they will have the knowledge necessary to receive the grace of God! When they receive that *grace* is between them and the Spirit of God; but when they receive the *knowledge* is up to you – and remember they can start learning at an early age.

Last, the Scripture teaches us that we are responsible for what we know, not for what we don't know:

> That servant who knows his master's will and does not get ready for does not do what his master wants will be beaten with many blows. But the one who does not know and does things deserving punishment will be beaten with few blows. From everyone who has been given much, much will be demanded; and from the one who has been entrusted with much, much more will be asked. (Luke 12:47-48)

In other words, a child's salvation is literally in *your* hands. If you tell him about Jesus – the same things that an adult needs to hear in order to be saved, not just cute stories about him – then that child has now heard the truth and is capable of acting on it. *When* he does isn't your problem; but he simply can't unless you give him something to work with first! If you back off and don't tell him the plain truth of the matter, it's certain that he will be another sad case that I've seen many examples of: later in life he will say "Nobody ever told me that before!" and he will have lived years in sin and death without the blessings of a long life full of Christ.

What is really scary about this is that the children are responsible to the Law in some way, even if they know nothing about Christ. Paul tells us that God has put the Law in our hearts so that we are all responsible to our Creator and Lord:

> Indeed, when Gentiles, who do not have the Law, do by nature things required by the Law, they are a law for themselves, even though they do not have the Law, since they show that the requirements of the Law are written on their hearts, their consciences also bearing witness, and their thoughts now accusing, now even defending them. (Romans 2:14-15)

That child is responsible for the Law written in his heart! Aren't you going to give him something more promising than what the Law intends to do to him? Won't you lay out the Gospel of Christ before him so that he has a salvation to reach out for instead of a life of guilt and a hopeless death?

• *When are they responsible?* The Age of Accountability doctrine says that children aren't responsible for their sin until a certain age – normally when they reach adolescence. The reason for that is this: they don't understand that they are sinning against God – not until they are able to discern good from evil on their own, without Mommy or Daddy having to tell them that such and such thing was wrong.

Let's back up a minute. **First**, the Tree of the Knowledge of Good and Evil – the fruit of which Adam and Eve ate in the Garden of Eden – was our downfall, not our salvation! It was sin for them to have this knowledge; it was certainly none of God's doing! He *didn't want* them to have it. When they got it, they died – something that God knew would happen. They deliberately turned away from God when they possessed this knowledge. The knowledge of good and evil is not a good thing for us to have but a bad thing. So why in the world are we appealing to this shame of ours, this downfall in us, and saying that it will help us decide for Christ and salvation? It can never do that! (See the *Appendix* on the Tree.)

We saw above that the Law is in our hearts telling us what's wrong; it's there from birth, by God's finger. It's wrong to think that it slumbers until a certain age when it suddenly wakes up and pricks the conscience. There are two kinds of sorrow (according to Paul – 2 Corinthians 7:10) and a child can easily experience the first type – sorrow that he's in trouble. That kind of sorrow comes from the pricking of the Law on our hearts. Nobody can experience the second sorrow, however, unless the Spirit of God moves the sinner's heart to it; and again a child *can* experience that, since it's the work of the Holy Spirit and not dependent on our abilities.

It's true that adolescence brings with it the ability and the desire to make one's own decisions, and this seems to match the Knowledge of Good and Evil of the Genesis story. (See the Appendix for more information about this story.) But we should draw the right conclusions from all that: children actually have a *better* chance of coming to Jesus than we adults do, because of our knowledge! The switch in their minds that makes them want to think for themselves isn't on yet; they tend to accept what authority tells them without getting bent out of shape about it. Adults tend to rebel against what they hear about God, and children tend to accept what they hear about him. So what we gain at adolescence isn't a *spiritual* knowledge – it's not that we finally understand what we have done against God – rather it's the willfulness to do things our way and a hardening of the heart against the things of God.

This relates to the point we made earlier, that any spiritual understanding that we have (at least any correct understanding!) comes not through age or experience or education but by the working of the Spirit in our hearts. This is just as available to a child as it is to an adult. So a child can know very well that he has sinned against God if the Spirit shows him that truth.

Second, we are responsible for our feelings about God. The Age of Accountability doctrine has the first point absolutely right: we were born in sin and are under the curse of death. But it doesn't help things at all to say that we aren't accountable for any sins that we do until a certain age. We are accountable for something far more important long before that age.

Part of the salvation process is our response to God – he saves, but we must love him and trust him. We have to *want* to be with God forever. *This response of ours is not God's responsibility.* There are mysteries about salvation that man will probably never understand; but the Bible does plainly teach that there will be nobody in Heaven who does not love God. After all, Hell is where there are people who don't love him – either they hated him in life or they were indifferent to him. Either way, God claims no responsibility for their reaction to him; he isn't so unjust as to punish someone who doesn't fully deserve it.

Whether or not you believe that God could take a child to Heaven without faith in Christ, you certainly must see that, while in this world, it's the *duty* of every human being to "love the Lord your God with all your heart and with all your soul and with all your mind." (Matthew 22:37) Their judgment hangs on whether or not they do this; someone can't live with God, child or otherwise, unless they do. After all, it's this hatred, this turning away from God, that leads to sin. So teach them that they are responsible to love God first and foremost.

• *Who is innocent?* People always call children "innocent," probably because they are so helpless and naïve. Someone can take advantage of them so easily.

But there's a double meaning to the word "innocent." For one thing, it can mean *guiltless in the eyes of the Law* – in other words, that we are not sinners and that we don't deserve the penalty of death. None of us, not even children, not even babes in the womb, are innocent in this sense. Not only are we all children of guilty parents (all the way back through the family line to Adam and Eve!) but our inborn tendency is to sin – it's not a maybe, but a certainty. We are morally corrupted from birth, unable to please God or keep his Law.

The second meaning of the word "innocent" is *without guile*. *Guile* is an old word, but maybe some of these synonyms will help you get an idea of its meaning: deception, deceit, duplicity, dishonesty, trickery, artfulness, fraud. Jesus said of Nathanael that "here is a true Israelite, in whom there is nothing false" (John 1:47; the KJV has *no guile*). Children are masters at being innocent in this sense. They have no hidden agenda, they take the world as it comes, and they believe what they are told.

Adults have learned the art of being two-faced – being one way inside, and another way to everyone else. They have done this to protect themselves, for good or bad reasons; but once learned it's almost impossible to put aside. Adults wear masks; you can never tell if they're being honest, and they almost never believe anything without a good deal of proofs and incentives.

Children, on the other hand, are an ideal opportunity for teachers, and a fertile ground for anything you want to tell them. They haven't yet learned that there are people out there who want to hurt them. They haven't learned the skills of protecting themselves from dangers; their defenses are down – non-existent, in fact – and it's easy to get to their minds and hearts. Of course this puts a heavy responsibility on you, the teacher, because you have to tell them the *truth* and not what will hurt them in any way. All the more reason to give them words that lead to life!

Children simply believe what they are told and trust completely in the reality of it. They easily follow; they obey and respect the authority. (I'm describing child-like behavior, not what every child always does!) When challenged, they don't hold back; when punished, they don't plot revenge. They are genuinely energetic and enthusiastic. Adults lose all these sterling qualities at the "Age of Accountability" – so what benefit is there, spiritually speaking, in getting older? We only get hardened to the things of God and become good at being sinners, as we lose our child-like characteristics. We all lost our innocence before the Law when we were born; we all lose our innocence of childhood when we grow up.

So we can't say that a child is innocent of sin any more than an adult is. We can only say that he is innocent in the way he approaches God – it's the *way* he receives the things of God, not his moral standing before the Law. This is what appealed to Jesus when he dealt with children.

Whatever you believe about the standing that children have before God – infant baptism and its benefits, what happens when children die, church privileges, etc. – the fact remains that it will benefit children tremendously if you teach them about Christ, in a way that they need to be saved and grow in grace in Christ.

A child's response

> But when the chief priests and the teachers of the
> law saw the wonderful things he did and the
> children shouting in the temple area, "Hosanna to
> the Son of David," they were indignant. "Do you
> hear what these children are saying?" they asked
> him. "Yes," replied Jesus, "have you never read,
> 'From the lips of children and infants you have
> ordained praise'?" (Matthew 21:15-16)

Can a child respond to the Gospel in a meaningful way?
Is it really true that they can only learn some things about God
but they have to wait until they grow up before they will
understand the root of the issue of salvation? I believe that this
passage teaches the opposite! Notice several things about these
remarkable children:

- *A miracle of grace!* When we read this story
we don't usually stop and think about what is
going on here; we think, "how appropriate that the
children would join in with the celebration." But
is this natural? Wouldn't the children that you
know have been *playing* instead of praising? Is it
natural that these children would have been caught
up with what the adults were doing and
participated in it heart and soul? I don't see
anything natural about this! These children
obviously were doing something deeply spiritual,
something even that the Pharisees couldn't do!

We can see the significance of Jesus at the
Temple much easier than the people in his day
(especially the Pharisees) because we are reading

the Bible's account after the event, and we already know by its prompting what Jesus was up to. But for his followers – and especially the children! – to see him in his rightful place as King coming to claim his city was nothing less than the work of God in their hearts. Furthermore, we can understand that the adults would see this, but here is proof that children also can see the simple yet profound meaning in one of Christ's most spectacular moves in the process of salvation. Someone will say, "But they are only parroting their elders; they don't really understand the significance of what they are saying." That's not Jesus' opinion; he says they were *praising* him (verse 16), which means that they knew to some degree what they were saying. Parroted words are *not* praise. He disagreed with the Pharisees on that very point – the motivation of the children's behavior …

• *The Pharisees' problem:* The Pharisees objected to the whole situation. They challenged Jesus, as if to say "This is turning into a circus! Jesus, you are responsible for this mess! Look at the children – they are shouting words of blasphemy, not realizing that they are wrong. Tell them to stop immediately!"

They couldn't see what was *really* going on, however. This wasn't just a party that Jesus stirred up in the Temple; he was coming into Jerusalem as King, and to the Temple because this was his Father's house. The whole procession was highly significant and full of meaning. Not only was he laying claim to all the city, he was marching to his final victory over sin and death, forever completing what the Old Testament had prepared the Jews for. He was the Son of David come back to the City of David to make all wrongs right and bring the remnant back to the house of God.

The Pharisees weren't spiritually astute enough to read all that into the events, however; they stumbled at the physical appearances, his humility, the youth of his followers, and the simple child-like praises of his worshipers.

• *Jesus' pointed answer:* His answer to them was fascinating; he often answered them like this. He used a double-edged sword to pierce their hearts with the truth. First he quotes an Old Testament passage to defend what the children were doing: they were, in fact, saying the *right things* about him – it was the Pharisees who were wrong. Second, he leaves unsaid (what is not said is often the loudest said!) the very next line in that Old Testament prophecy:

> From the lips of children and infants you have ordained praise *because of your enemies, to silence the foe and the avenger.* (Psalm 8:2)

The Pharisees would have known that verse; if they didn't, they would have gone home, looked it up, and boiled in anger at Jesus' hidden meaning. He certainly wasn't trying to make friends out of them, not with an answer like that!

He made his point, however. God uses the simplicity of children, the single-mindedness, the honesty, the lack of pride, to bring out the truth in *the way it must be said.* A child's natural reaction is to say what he sees! He isn't going to be two-faced about it or try to twist it to suit his own ends; he has no ulterior motives, no reason to say differently from what he sees and knows. Jesus was telling the Pharisees, in effect, that if they wanted to know the truth themselves then they would do well to sit at the children's feet and learn the right way to think!

Old Testament examples

To wind up this section we will look at some examples from the Old Testament of children participating in what the adults also experienced. Some of these examples are very significant, because it shows them enjoying the *same* blessings that the adults had and suffering the *same* punishments that the adults suffered through. There was no difference in kind; what the parents' lot in life was, the same held for their children. I'm not trying to make a case of whether children automatically share in their parents' standing before God; denominations argue over this one and can't seem to come to an agreement. But we *can* see that it's possible and does happen that children experience the same kinds of things that adults do, spiritually speaking. If that's true, then it makes a world of difference about what we give them in our teaching sessions.

- **Samuel** – In the book of Samuel we start reading about a little boy left by his parents in the Temple to grow up there. His mother vowed that she would turn Samuel over to the Lord early so that he could serve God. His first experience with the Lord was new to him, however:

Now Samuel did not yet know the LORD:
The word of the LORD had not yet been
revealed to him. (1 Samuel 3:7)

Notice the key words: *had not yet been
revealed to him.* Until the Lord reveals his word
to a child (or an adult, for that matter!) he will not
understand it; but when he does, he *will*
understand it. That's the key for *when* someone
understands the things of God.

What happens next in the story is a little
embarrassing for adults: God speaks to little
Samuel and he doesn't speak to Eli, the priest!
Eli, the man with the authority in God's house,
had to ask the boy Samuel what the Lord had to
say about the situation in Israel.

- **Circumcision** – The ceremony of
circumcision started with the patriarch Abraham,
and continued through all the generations of his
children the Jews. It was extremely important: it
was a sign of the covenant (agreement) between
the Lord and Abraham – and therefore with all
those who shared the sign of Abraham, or
circumcision. In other words, it showed the legal
right to the promises of God. If a man wasn't
circumcised then they were to throw him out of the
camp! (Genesis 17:14)

It was possible for a man to be circumcised, but
it was a lot easier to do it right after birth. Aside
from the practical issue, however, the Lord wanted
it to be done to each male child because he too was
included in the covenant agreement with God – by
virtue of his birth in the family of Abraham.

Growing up isn't what made him come under the covenant! He had those rights by birth, by the circumcision done to him after birth.

How does that apply to us? Without getting into divisive issues, we can notice what Paul specifically says about circumcision in the Christian's heart:

> A man is a Jew if he is one inwardly; and circumcision is circumcision of the heart, by the Spirit, not by the written code. (Romans 2:29)

This too is open to a child, as well as an adult, if God moves in his heart with his Spirit. There is no age limit to this.

• **Korah's family** – The story of Korah is a sobering one. Korah and some of his friends decided that they wanted some of the glory that Moses was getting as leader in Israel. They challenged his authority and refused to obey his orders any longer. At first the Lord was going to destroy the whole camp of Israelites; but Moses persuaded him to narrow it down only to the original troublemakers.

Their punishment was an awesome display of God's power. God opened up the earth underneath them and they fell into the chasm, along with everything they owned. What was so startling, though, was something else that this passage says:

So they moved away from the tents of Korah, Dathan and Abiram. Dathan and Abiram had come out and were standing *with their wives, children and little ones* at the entrances to their tents ... As soon as he finished saying all this, the ground under them split apart and the earth opened its mouth and swallowed them, *with their households* and all Korah's men and all their possessions. (Numbers 16:27, 31-32)

Whatever you may think about God's method of punishment, the point of this story is that children can and do suffer under the punishing hand of God for sin – in this case, for their fathers' sins. God didn't gingerly step around the children! Doesn't that prompt us to get serious about the children that we teach, knowing that God will hold them accountable too for knowing the truth and living in a way to please him?

• **All learned the Law** – The Jews were instructed not only to learn the Law themselves so well that they knew it by heart; they were also told to teach the Law to their children at every chance they got:

These commandments that I give you today are to be upon your hearts. Impress them on your children. Talk about them when you sit at home and when you walk along the road, when you lie down and when you get up. Tie them as symbols on your hands and bind them on your foreheads. Write them on the doorframes of your houses and on your gates. (Deuteronomy 6:6-9)

This Law was literally the life of every Jew, the only rule of faith and practice that he had. He was to teach the Law, *everything* in it, to his children – why? So that they would know the *truth*! So that they would grow up with a correct understanding of God and his requirements, of man and his shortcomings, of the Temple and the hope there that it held out to all the Israelites. His education was to be balanced and complete, in other words, *before* he became an adult. And if a child can learn the Law, he can certainly learn the Gospel which holds out the only One who can fulfill that Law for us.

Jesus And Children's Needs

If you have had anything to do with children at all, you will know that they have another quality about them (besides their simple faith) that adults don't share, except this one isn't so good: they can't take care of themselves. If left to themselves they would eat themselves silly with junk food, live in squalor, and get sick with no idea of how to get well. Their lives would quickly turn to chaos and worse if it weren't for us taking care of them.

That perhaps is our biggest job when it comes to children – taking care of them. We know what to eat to stay healthy; we know that a clean house is a safeguard for physical and mental health; we know what to do in case of emergencies. We've been through all this before, and now we know how to get *them* to adulthood safe and well-trained for life.

When it comes to spiritual matters they are just as helpless. The Bible is a big book to a child, and he certainly doesn't know where to start or how to understand what he reads. He's going to need a lot of help finding the truth that he needs out of it; someone with some wisdom and experience is going to have to carefully lay the foundation for him, lead him through the basic principles, and prepare him for meeting the real world in his adult years armed with the truth. It's a much more serious training program than anything else we do with him; his whole future hangs in the balance.

What we have to do is think through this thing, just as carefully as we would the diets that they need, and decide what they need spiritually to be well-rounded in their knowledge of God and the Scriptures. They need a "firm foundation" of essential knowledge, one that will not be full of holes and that will serve them when the crises of adulthood hit them. How many times have you heard an adult thank God that he remembers the song he learned as a child, or the Bible passage, which now comes back to comfort and help him?

Many Sunday School materials have attacked this problem by working out a multi-year schedule: if a student works through the entire five year course, for instance, he will have read most of the stories in the Bible and hit many of the essentials of the Christian faith. We can't do that here, however; we could spend a lot of time going over all the material that the teacher can use from the Old Testament in teaching children, or the material from the New Testament Epistles, but that's too much for one book! The sharp teacher will know when and how to bring material in from all over the Bible: "Therefore every teacher of the Law who has been instructed about the kingdom of Heaven is like the owner of a house who brings out of his storeroom new treasures as well as old." (Matthew 13:52) Instead, what we want to do now is focus specifically on Christ and the essentials about him that every student should learn.

We can't do more than suggest some areas to study; there is simply an enormous amount of information about Jesus that we can learn and teach. But at least we can touch many important areas. This is how we will go about it: since the children's needs are clear to see, we will look at each area that they need help in and suggest the things about Jesus that you need to teach them to meet that need.

A world view

What I mean by "world view" is this: the way we look at things in life, the things that we consider important, the goals that we've decided are worth working for, the rules for day-to-day living, the way the world works. Getting this all figured out isn't a small job! Different cultures have different world views. For example, a Hindu in India thinks that all life is sacred and one mustn't kill any creature, no matter how small; that has a tremendous impact on their culture! They won't kill the rats, for instance, that eat their grain fields – which accounts for much of the poverty of Indian villages. Here in America there are all sorts of world views, ranging from Ivy League high-brows to the fast-paced business world to "red neck" country boys to the farms of Appalachia, with many more in between. The business of each family in each little sub-culture is to train their children in their own distinctive view on what the world is all about.

The Church also has its wide range of world views, though some of them are very unfortunate. The Eastern Orthodox Church, for example, believes that icons are important for the life of the church, whereas the Southern Baptists are very plain in their outward forms of worship – they don't think that icons do anything for people spiritually. Many of the world views in Christian circles are perfectly legitimate; we shouldn't think that if someone has a different way of looking at things than we do then *they* must be wrong and we are right! Christianity has a wonderful way of fitting into one's peculiar culture. Though it's bigger than any single culture (which means that it can spread over the whole world!), it can fit comfortably into a culture and help people understand how to live in their particular part of the world.

But we don't want to get into issues that make us different here; we want to look at what makes a Christian world view different from a non-Christian's world view. These are truths that all Christians should believe, no matter what part of the world they live in.

Children, the experts tell us, form their world view by the time they are six years old. That's a sobering thought! We haven't got much time to make sure they get it right. With all the competing authorities around, we aren't always sure that they will have our world view! TV and radio are powerful culture-shapers, and since children soak up information like sponges they may be beyond our reach already after sitting at the feet of America's entertainers (who, by the way, have a very deliberate philosophy that they are forcing on us).

Our job is to make sure that Jesus is a major part of their world view. Whether or not they believe that he exists, and is still living, and is still working in the world, will have a profound impact on the rest of their lives. It's not at all easy to see all this! Most people in the world today don't believe that he exists, and they certainly don't believe that they need to bother about him; and it doesn't help matters that they can't see him! This makes it all the more important that we convince them while they are children before they get the critical judgment of adulthood and start judging things by their reason and senses.

> • ***Who is in charge?*** The Gospels start out with Jesus saying "Follow me." (Matthew 4:18-22) He means that. He didn't ask them to follow, he told them to – he expects them to. He doesn't want them to disobey him and go on living like there is no Christ. He's making a new Kingdom (Matthew 4:17; Mark 1:14), and he wants it to run a certain way. He wants to gather a band of followers out of this world and make them ready for his new kingdom. So one of the first things he does is to set them down and explain how he wants things

done – in other words, he makes sure they understand that he's the Boss and things are going to be done as he wants them.

The Sermon on the Mount is his first lesson on this. Don't just read it to children and tell them that they have to live like this; make them understand that Jesus has great expectations of anybody who wants to be part of his kingdom. They have to do it as he says because he's in charge. That's what "Lord" means! It's true that these new kingdom rules are very strict – impossible, as a matter of fact – but then he has the right to run things as he wants. He's the King! And kings make laws that we must obey or we will be in trouble.

The leaders of this world think that they are in charge of things, but they are very mistaken. Jesus is a king not only in name but in fact: his power is much stronger than any earthly power, and that is what gives him the right to rule over all men. When the soldiers came to arrest him, all he said was "I am he" and they "drew back and fell to the ground." (John 18:6) When Pilate said he had Jesus' life in his hands, Jesus answered that "You would have no power over me if it were not given to you from above." (John 19:11) People should understand that Jesus is in charge, and we must do as he says and fear making him angry. "Kiss the Son, lest he be angry and you be destroyed in your way, for his wrath can flare up in a moment." (Psalm 2:12)

Jesus' followers also must learn to get their orders from him. Although we might think we know what we should be doing in life, we really don't know until the Lord tells us first. He sent the disciples out with strict orders about what to do (Matthew 10), and he wanted them to follow his orders or things wouldn't have worked the way he wanted. The disciples thought once that ordering out a demon from a boy would work, but he told them what they had to do first before it would work. (Mark 9:29) Once the disciples were chasing parents away who were bringing their children to Jesus; he ordered them to let the children come to him. (Matthew 19:13-15) Once he told his disciples to "be on your guard against the yeast of the Pharisees and Sadducees." (Mark 7:14-21) In other words, they were to stop listening to those false teachers and start listening to him instead. You can see, in almost every story, that Jesus is the boss, and he expects everyone to do what he says – not what they think is right or what others might say.

So what you must teach the children is that Jesus is in charge of everyone and everything. We must all start going to him to find out what he wants from us.

- *__Who made everything?__* The Bible says that Jesus was there at Creation with God the Father. (John 1:1) "Through him all things were made; without him nothing was made that has been made." (John 1:3) When we say that God created everything, we are really saying that he has power over things – he can make them do what he wants; and he has authority over things – he tells them to be a certain way; and he has wisdom over things – he makes them and arranges them in a perfect way.

All these things are true of Jesus as well as the Father.

He made the seas and everything in them; that's how he had the power and authority to command the storm to quit: "He got up, rebuked the wind and said to the waves, 'Quiet! Be still!' Then the wind died down and it was completely calm." (Mark 4:39) He knew how to do that because he made the water and wind; he had the power to command them because he first commanded them to exist and told them how far they could go:

> Who shut up the sea behind doors when it burst forth from the womb, when I made the clouds its garment and wrapped it in thick darkness, when I fixed limits for it and set its doors and bars in place, when I said, "This far you may come and no farther; here is where your proud waves halt?" (Job 38:8-11)

He knows how to make a blind eye see, because he invented eyes and he knows how they work. (Matthew 12:22) He can raise people from the dead because he is the Life, and that Life is the life of men. (John 1:4) He knows how to turn water into wine – something that modern chemists will never figure out – because he's the Creator of both. (John 2:1-11)

Jesus made us, too, which means he knows what we are and what we can do. (John 2:24-25) He knows if there is sin in our hearts, and he knows the jobs that he intends to give us in life.

He knows when we will sin against him. (Luke 22:31-34) He knows how much suffering we can take and when to send us help. (1 Corinthians 10:13)

If children learn early that Jesus made all things, then they won't turn to science and psychology and philosophy in later years to solve their problems – they will turn to the One who they know made everything.

• ***What are the rules in life?*** This is related to the fact that Jesus is in charge of the world: he also lays down the rules that we have to follow if we want to please him. They aren't easy rules! He expects perfection from all of us, mainly because he refuses to allow sin in Heaven. "For I tell you that unless your righteousness surpasses that of the Pharisees and the teachers of the Law, you will certainly not enter the kingdom of Heaven." (Matthew 5:20)

Some of his rules are these: **First**, you must take up your cross and follow him. (Matthew 16:24) That means that he wants you do what he says, in the way he says to do it; you must obey him even if it isn't fun, or if people laugh at you or others reject you because of it. **Second**, you must love God with all your heart and soul and mind and strength. (Luke 10:27) This means that you want to spend time with him, talking to him and listening to him, and you are ready to do everything he tells you. **Third**, you must love others as much as you love yourself. That's quite a bit! Imagine spending as much time on other people's needs as you spend on your own! But he expects this of us all because we are all very special to him and he uses each of us to touch the lives of others.

In a way, his rules are impossible to follow. We don't like the things he talks about because he wants us to stop sinning and put the world and all its pleasures behind us and do things his way. "With man this is impossible, but with God all things are possible." (Matthew 19:26) He can tell us his rules, but we aren't going to find it easy to please him. He expects us to be perfect! "Be perfect, therefore, as your heavenly Father is perfect." (Matthew 5:48)

But from another point of view, his rules *are* easy – "For my yoke is easy and my burden is light." (Matthew 11:30) He will give us two things to help us: 1) the understanding we need to know what he is talking about, and 2) the power to obey him. He will not leave us alone to do it ourselves! "I will not leave you as orphans; I will come to you." (John 14:18) When he commanded the man to stretch out his hand, do you think the man obeyed Jesus without some divine help? (Matthew 12:13) His rules are tough because they have to be; an eternal Heaven will rest on them and they have to be firm and dependable. But he commits himself to making sure that we can measure up to his expectations.

• ***What are the problems facing me?*** A child needs to know what he's up against in this world. Jesus immediately takes him under his wing and counsels him about the dangers and pitfalls and problems that he's going to find in life. If he listens to the Lord, he will be better prepared than most people are; if he trusts in Jesus then he will know where to go for help when he meets these problems.

Jesus told us once that "In this world you will have trouble. But take heart! I have overcome the world." (John 16:33) What kind of trouble will we meet along the way? Jesus has walked that way before us, and he can tell us:

First, there are always going to be bad people around. God doesn't get rid of them (although they deserve it!) and they are going to make things harder for us when we try to obey God. Don't worry, though – he knows what he's doing; he doesn't want to get rid of them right now. But he intends to keep an eye on them and make sure they never choke out his people. The Lord is instead going to wait for the last day until he gets rid of them; all the more reason to never give up loving and obeying him so that you will be in that rich harvest of good grain! (Matthew 13:24-30)

Second, we saw before that he warns us about false teachers. (Matthew 16:5-12) There are many people who don't teach the truth – they may say that they teach the Bible, but they don't believe much of what it says and they don't want to talk about some things in it with you. They actually teach *not* to believe certain things in the Bible! You need to stay away from those kinds of people; Jesus tells us that we are under no obligation to listen to them: "Leave them; they are blind guides. If a blind man leads a blind man, both will fall into a pit." (Matthew 15:14) It's not safe to play with fire, no matter how skilled you think you are; and it's not safe to spend time sitting at the feet of people who don't believe the story about Jesus.

Third, you are going to have some problems about your own heart. Just when we thought we were pretty good after all, out comes some unclean thought or mean act! Jesus isn't at all surprised when this happens, however; he warned us that ...

> The good man brings good things out of the good stored up in his heart, and the evil man brings evil things out of the evil stored up in his heart. For out of the overflow of his heart his mouth speaks. (Luke 6:45)

If he knows this about us, he must also know how to cure the problem! He must know how to reach into our hearts and clean the dirt out; in fact, he intends on doing just that – he cannot tolerate sin in his followers: "Unless I wash you, you have no part with me." (John 13:8)

There are many other problems that he knows about, and he wants to warn us about them all. Of course we can't take it in all at once; but if we stay close to him then we will gradually become aware of the dangers around us, and by then we will also be good at asking him to help us past those problems, since we are convinced that he knows how to handle them.

• *__What are my goals?__* Parents teach their children from early age that money, fame, and a good job are the most important things in life. But Jesus taught otherwise: he despised the values that people usually have and steered his disciples in another direction.

He said of the man who wanted to build bigger barns for his increasing wealth, "You fool! This very night your life will be demanded from you. Then who will get what you have prepared for yourself?" (Luke 12:20) What he was saying was that there are more important things to live for in this life. He told the man who wanted to go bury his father before following him, "Let the dead bury their own dead, but you go and proclaim the kingdom of God." (Luke 9:59-60) What he was saying was that working to extend God's kingdom is much more important than keeping close to those who aren't in the kingdom. He told Martha that "you are worried and upset about many things, but only one thing is needed. Mary has chosen what is better, and it will not be taken away from her." (Luke 10:41) What he was saying that even though this world's responsibilities look very important, they can and should be set aside when it comes time to do God's work.

Not only did Jesus give us counsel about what are the important things to live for, he showed us that he is worth following, for many reasons. For example, Peter said to him that "Lord, to whom shall we go? You have the words of eternal life." (John 6:68) Matthew, the tax collector, saw that Jesus was worth more than the money he was making, and he left it all to follow the Lord. (Matthew 9:9) Did he think that Jesus could provide for him? Did he think that Jesus would work out the problems about family responsibilities, taxes owed, and all the other things that we must take care of in life? Evidently he did, and evidently he believed that Jesus would train him to do more important things than collect taxes.

A child must know, as much as an adult must know, that only Jesus gives us things worth living for. This world's wealth and honor aren't worthy of our time; it's like so much pigsty fodder. (Matthew 15:11-16) To be called his disciple is the highest honor; to follow him means living on the exciting edge of Heaven's realities. Peter wanted to walk on the water just as Jesus did. (Matthew 14:28) There's no higher calling in life, no more important work, no more precious inheritance to have, no more honor than to be with Jesus. The sons of Zebedee knew this, although they didn't know the cross they would have to carry to get the honor! (Mark 10:35-45)

• *__Who am I? Where do I fit in?__* This is one of the most important questions that a human being must answer during his life. People jump off bridges when they can't find a reason for living; they simply have to see why they are here and whether anybody cares about them. So you must address this issue when you teach children, and be sure to tell them about what Jesus thinks of them.

Jesus is "the friend of sinners." He was accused of spending his time with "tax collectors and sinners" (Luke 7:34) but he didn't seem to be bothered by that. "It is not the healthy who need a doctor, but the sick. I have not come to call the righteous, but sinners." (Mark 2:17)

First you must show children (yes, those sweet innocent babies who don't seem to know anything about sin! In a few years they will be giving enough proof to the world that they have sin in their hearts) that they are sinners, and unless they get straight with God they better stay away from bridges as long as they can – a suicide's future in eternity will be nothing to look forward to! **Second**, show them that Jesus wants to talk to them about their souls. Show them from powerful Scriptures that he looks for and finds sinners – even the worst ones! – and fairly but firmly deals with their sinful lives. **Third**, show them that Jesus has healing in mind; he *can* take away their sin and he intends to, if they will come to him.

I know that people don't like to think of themselves as "lost," but until they do they are just fooling themselves – they aren't nearly as important as they think they are, and they are going to die without accomplishing anything that God thinks is worth keeping. Their lives will be meaningless; they may as well have not lived at all.

What the children have to see, above all else, is that they are *wanted*. Jesus' entire mission is to seek and save those who are lost. God wants them to get their hearts straight (through Jesus, who is the only one who can make them acceptable) and start living the way God says to live. If they do this then their lives will become immensely important; they will be "fellow workers" with God. He wants them on his terms, of course, but nevertheless God doesn't want "anyone to perish, but everyone to come to repentance." (2 Peter 3:9)

• ***What is the purpose of the world?*** Finally, a child needs to know what this world is for. He may be fooled by the glitter of gold and wealth, thinking that money makes one happy. He may think that friends are to be used for one's own ends. He may think that the work he does and the physical things he values are important enough to be part of God's eternal plan. But there are so many Scriptures that prove that such thinking is foolish; read Ecclesiastes for a blistering condemnation on the emptiness of things in this world and the foolish man who thinks he can find something here worth living for.

What we have to teach them instead is Jesus' opinion of this world:

Do not store up for yourselves treasures on earth, where moth and rust destroy, and where thieves break in and steal. (Matthew 6:19)

Life is more important than food, and the body is more important than clothes, and the Father knows that you need certain things in this world to live. (Matthew 6:25-34) But neither is so important that you need to spend all your time getting as much as you can! There are more important things to live for than money and food and cars and clothes and toys.

Jesus told the rich young man that his vast wealth should be for helping the poor, not filling his bank account. (Luke 18:18-30) He told one man that he didn't have time nor the interest to help him get his family inheritance. (Luke 12:13-15) He himself didn't have enough money to pay the taxes he owed at the Temple! (Matthew 17:24-27) He seemed to have a completely different attitude about money and possessions than we have.

Money wasn't the only thing he had opinions about. To him, life in general was the one and only opportunity a person has to get right with God. Jobs and friends and work and play and everything else that we can spend our time and energy on in this world will only distract us from the point. "As long as it is day, we must do the work of him who sent me." (John 9:4) We can get distracted by everyday circumstances, thinking that these are what life is all about. But we are deceived; they are only a context in which God tests the heart. He uses people and circumstances, good times and bad times, family and culture to develop us and mold us and test us. Then when life is done he judges the results to see what we are made of: "The one who received the seed that fell among the thorns is the man who hears the Word, but he worries of this life and the deceitfulness of wealth choke it, making it unfruitful." (Matthew 13:22; read the entire chapter 19 for a good idea of how the Lord uses our lives for his purpose of judging our hearts.)

Now if a child can get this kind of information about the world he lives in, he will be a long way toward living a successful Christian life and avoiding the usual pitfalls that people get themselves into. Getting at children while they are young is a wise move toward building the next generation; everyone knows this and tries to teach children their own philosophies and world views in ways that are extremely effective. The Church needs to become expert at this so that she can head off the pagans and their formulas for sin and cultural disaster.

Don't worry that the child doesn't know how to apply some of these things in profound spiritual ways. It's enough to build them into the child's world, to make sure that he knows who the King is and whose rules he must follow; he will have enough when he knows the sham of this world's "treasures" and what God holds out for the faithful, which is worth living for and waiting for. *How* the child applies this knowledge is between him and God, and *when* he applies it is also not up to you. But he doesn't have a chance of applying the truth if you don't first get it into his head and heart! So stack the truth in his mind like cordwood, and someday the Spirit will have fuel for lighting a heavenly fire.

Protection

Children are so helpless in the face of danger, not only because they can't protect themselves (and don't know how) but also because they don't understand the danger itself. They crawl underneath cars, they reach out to a strange dog, they climb to the tops of trees – all sorts of things that give adults ulcers trying to follow behind them and keep them safe. When they haven't learned yet that the stove is hot then they want to touch it; it's only after they've been burned that they know to stay away. Life is full of dangers, and it's a shame that they have to learn the hard way in so many circumstances. But that's what parents are for: to teach them ahead of time what the dangers are, and to keep them out of trouble.

If we could see the spiritual dangers looming over the horizon, however, we might get really discouraged. The devil is used to getting his hands on children early – by the time we become teenagers we have already spent years in his training:

> As for you, you were dead in your transgressions and sins, in which you used to live when you followed the ways of this world and of the ruler of the kingdom of the air, the spirit who is now at work in those who are disobedient. All of us also lived among them at one time, gratifying the cravings of our sinful nature and following its desires and thoughts. Like the rest, we were by nature objects of wrath. (Ephesians 2:1-3)

> Why is my language not clear to you? Because you are unable to hear what I say. You belong to your father, the devil, and you want to carry out your father's desire. (John 8:43-44)

It's in our childhood that our enemy begins laying the plans for our downfall; we are getting set up for disaster later in life. He's very patient and he knows how to do this; he doesn't love children, and he won't stop short of twisting their little minds to think his thoughts and do his will. We have to get there ahead of him with the only thing that will stop him.

Jesus and the devil have been battling for centuries, ever since the time in the wilderness when Jesus used the Word of God to send Satan running. (Matthew 4:1-11; Luke 4:1-13) Our only hope for defeating the plans of the enemy is, again, the Word – and in the same way – Jesus speaking them into the heart to stop him cold. A child needs a chance to learn the truth about God and about himself; he needs the Lord's protection around him to hold off the enemy's attacks while he gets his thinking straight.

How can Jesus protect us?

• *From the unknown.* There are two kinds of unknown: strange situations, and hidden dangers. Jesus protects us from both of these things. He realizes that he's calling us to live a strange kind of life, and we aren't going to be familiar with any of it. Many times we are going to put our foot out on water without knowing what will happen next! Just as Peter who stepped out of the boat when Jesus called him, we have never before done these things that Jesus is going to lead us into, and we wonder if our next step will be fatal. (Matthew 14:22-33)

The kinds of things that Jesus wants us to do don't make any sense to an unbeliever. He told one person to "sell your possessions and give to the poor, and you will have treasure in Heaven. Then come, follow me." (Matthew 19:21) That was just too risky for the young ruler, however, because he had no idea where he might end up following Jesus and without money. But if he would have had a better understanding of Jesus, as the disciples did, he wouldn't have hesitated to leave his wealth behind – Jesus more than makes up for anything we give up for him! (Matthew 19:27-29)

Sometimes we are called to leave our families behind too. This happens when we want to follow Jesus and they don't; of course we may not leave home about it, but nevertheless it isn't very pleasant living with family members who hate the One you love. What will happen? Jesus assures us that he will see to it that we have lots of mothers and brothers and sisters to make up for our loss:

> I tell you the truth, no one who has left home or brothers or sisters or mother or father or children or fields for me and the gospel will fail to receive a hundred times as much in this present age (homes, brothers, sisters, mothers, children and fields – and with them, persecutions) and in the age to come, eternal life. (Mark 10:29-30)

Another time there was a large crowd who followed him into the mountains to get healing and hear his teaching. You have to think a minute to appreciate the situation: they left their homes and jobs for a few days, and probably some family members, to go out where Jesus was. Who would take care of them? How would they know that things would be OK back home while they were gone? How could they eat and get along out on the mountain where they were miles from the nearest food? But they trusted him to provide – and he did just that in a big way! He took a few loaves of bread and a few fish and fed the thousands of people who were there with him. (Matthew 14:15-21; 15:29-39) We needn't fear the future if we are with Jesus.

Another person who suddenly faced the possibility of being killed was the woman who was caught in adultery. Though adultery is a serious sin, and the Bible says that adulterers must be put to death, Jesus proved to be a refuge for her against her enemies. I'm sure that for a few minutes things were pretty tense because she didn't know what would happen next; how was she to know what Jesus would say about her in judgment? She was never in any danger, however, because Jesus had control of the situation as soon as they brought her to him. He wanted to save her, and when they brought her to him it was exactly what he needed to save her. (John 8:1-11)

• *From the unjust.* Jesus also protects his people from injustice. It's unfortunate but true that there are mean people who do mean things to others. They might think that they are doing something right – Jesus said they would think this: "A time is coming when anyone who kills you will think he is offering a service to God." (John 16:2) – but they will still come under judgment for it.

When someone despises us for being weak or helpless or ignorant, Jesus is especially interested in what's going on: "See that you do not look down on one of these little ones. For I tell you that their angels in Heaven always see the face of my Father in Heaven." (Matthew 18:10) He won't let them get away with persecuting his people. I would hate to be that person who bullies God's people, knowing how powerful and holy Jesus is!

On one occasion even the disciples were being unfair to the children – they wouldn't let parents bring the children to Jesus for his blessing and prayers. Children have as much right to come to Jesus and get his grace as adults do, but the going to do what he can to make sure we get the truth from good teachers, and learn how to stay away from unfaithful, unbelieving teachers.

- ***From things that hurt.*** There are many things in this world that can hurt us. Parents warn their children to stay away from things that will hurt them; Bible teachers, however, have to warn their children to stay away from things that will hurt them spiritually. To get a broken arm is bad enough; but to spend one's whole life in pointless sin is misery, especially when we find out that it could have been avoided, and all we've accomplished is to put our eternal future in jeopardy.

Jesus knows about spiritual dangers in a way that none of us can see. He sees the kingdom of the devil, and he sees the great serpent raging through the earth hurting and destroying as many people as he can. Jesus sees the sin in our hearts and how it has been hurting us all our lives. He knows what Hell is like, and he weeps when he sees someone who is obviously content to end up there. But though he sees all this danger, he isn't helpless to do something about it. He warns us about it and he will step in the way of danger to protect us when necessary.

God's people are like sheep – helpless. They can't protect themselves from danger; they just stand there and bleat while the wolf makes a feast of one of them. But Jesus won't let that happen! "I am the good shepherd. The good shepherd lays down his life for the sheep." (John 10:11) He will send someone to help us just in just in time, or guide us to a Bible passage that sheds light and helps us to understand. He has many ways of reaching a sheep in spiritual danger before the sheep gets hurt.

Jesus knew how to handle dangerous demons too. He never failed to throw them out of children and adults when he ran across them. And he did it with just a word! The legions of the devil were no match for the Son of God; in fact they were terrified of him. They often pleaded with him to go easy on them in his wrath. (Matthew 8:31)

Jesus saved his disciples in a raging storm with nobody getting hurt. (Mark 4:35-41) He protected his disciples from the Roman soldiers when they came out to arrest him. (John 18:8) Jesus prayed for Peter because he could see Satan tempting Peter to do something awful; it was because of that prayer that Peter eventually repented of his terrible sin and came back to Jesus. (Luke 22:31-32) He fed people in the wilderness to keep them from starving. (Matthew 14:13-21; 15:29-39) He healed people from diseases that were killing them. He stood between sinners and the Law and rescued them from certain death. (John 8:1-11) He kept people from sinning, and even warned evil men that if they caused one of his people to sin then there would be a fierce judgment in store for them. (Matthew 18:6; Mark 9:42; Luke 17:2)

So we needn't fear the unknown danger as long as we are close to Jesus. He can see it all, and he can protect us from it all.

There are many passages in the Old Testament – especially in the book of Psalms – that talk about how the Lord goes to great measures to protect his people. The stories of Jesus doing this only underlines this characteristic of our God. It's encouraging to see all those old promises come to life as we watch.

Discipline

Discipline isn't the bad word that we often consider it to be. It doesn't just mean punishment; it's something that we all need, and if we don't get it then we are in deep trouble. Here is how we can define discipline:

DISCIPLINE IS TRAINING SOMEONE TO BE A BETTER CHRISTIAN.

There's nothing wrong with that; we all want to be better Christians, don't we? The problem is that the way God disciplines us isn't always much fun! Sometimes it's a training session in which we learn how to use his weapons for spiritual war, or use his tools for building our part of the kingdom. But other times he disciplines us by making us hurt for sin we got ourselves into, or making us do without things we need, or having us put up with bad treatment from other people. However, he isn't trying to make us feel miserable by using ways like this to train us; he loves us, and that's why he uses effective ways to teach us his truth.

> Endure hardship as discipline; God is treating you as sons. For what son is not disciplined by his father? If you are not disciplined (and everyone undergoes discipline), then you are illegitimate children and not true sons. Moreover, we have all had human fathers who disciplined us and we respected them for it. How much more should we

submit to the Father of our spirits and live! Our fathers disciplined us for a little while as they thought best; but God disciplines us for our good, that we may share in his holiness. No discipline seems pleasant at the time, but painful. Later on, however, it produces a harvest of righteousness and peace for those who have been trained by it. (Hebrews 12:7-11)

Jesus is interested in disciplining his people. If he doesn't, he won't be a good Savior. He intends to save them from sin and death, but he expects them to learn of him and learn his ways – so that they won't always be working against him. This is going to take much training, counseling, and hard work on both sides. Sanctification is a long but important process of being a Christian; it will be a great testimony to the rest of the world when it results in our living holy lives.

Now I want to show some examples of when Jesus either encouraged discipline or used it himself on someone.

- **THE BLIND MAN**. *John 9:1-41* There was some discussion about why this man was born blind – some thought that he must have sinned against God and now he was getting what he deserved. But Jesus pointed out that many people, this man being one of them, are suffering some hardship because God plans to use them for a great work. He will either heal them and use that to show the Pharisees that there really is a God who does miracles (as he did here in this story) or he will give them such a faith in him that they don't mind the hardship, again a strong witness to others.

- **THE WANDERER**. *Luke 9:58* A man said to Jesus that he wanted to follow him. Jesus answered that he has no place to call his own, no home to go to at night, no bed to sleep in every night. He had to live this way to do the work that God sent him to do. Anybody who wants to follow Jesus has to be willing to share his lifestyle – it will be hard training (which the disciples found out!) but in the end they will be hardy workers who can forget the comforts of this world and work effectively for the better things of Heaven.

• **HOW TO PRAY**. *Matthew 6:5-15*   Here Jesus trains his disciples how to pray. Prayer is so important that we mustn't do it any way we please. God won't listen to sloppy prayers! We have to learn how to talk to God, and what kinds of things to ask him for. You will find that if you take seriously his teaching on prayer, it will be one of the most difficult things you ever tried! This way of doing prayer is like long distance running to an athlete: it will take a long time to master, and yet it will be very satisfying when you start getting answers to your prayers.

• **CARRY THE CROSS**. *Matthew 16:24-28*   Jesus knows what lies ahead for him – he must eventually end up on a cross, dying like a common criminal, hated and despised by everyone. That's a hard way to end life, let me assure you! But he was willing to carry that cross because of the many benefits it would have for all his people even to our day. Here he says that the cross will do *us* good as well! What a strange thought! But what he's saying is that the hard times, the lonely times, the times of suffering that our Father gives us to live through, will be good for us in the end. So we need to learn how to carry those hardships and failures and pains and disappointments as blessings, not curses, hoping in the day that all of it will be gone and we will get our reward for being faithful soldiers.

• **HOW TO USE WORLDLY WEALTH**. *Luke 16:9* This command isn't very popular with people because they love their riches too much to give them away. But it's great discipline for Christians to exercise their love for each other! It also gets us used to depending less on what we own and start depending more on what God has waiting for us in Heaven. Heavenly treasures are more valuable than all the riches of this earth; we show how much we value them when we willingly give up the cheap riches we have here to help others.

• **STUDY THE SCRIPTURES**. *Luke 24:25-27* He can use people who know the Scriptures to build his kingdom; he isn't very pleased with people who don't know the Bible very well. You can't know what's in the Bible unless you read it, and you can't understand it unless you study it well. Think about what it says, pray over it, ask God to send the Spirit to help you understand it – and someday you will know more about it than your teachers! It's going to be hard work – study always is – but when you learn it well, he will be pleased with you and you will be able to teach others the truth about him.

• **PRAY CONSTANTLY**. *Luke 18:1-8* Prayer is not only difficult to do well, but one needs to pray constantly about things until the answer comes. Jesus tells us here that the Father is much more willing to give justice to his people than this unrighteous judge; however, one needs to keep praying until God sends an answer. The Lord has many reasons for holding an answer back (none of which he may tell us about!) but he's mightily pleased when we value what he has so much that we keep coming back for it, vowing never to give up until he gives it to us. This kind of prayer is not for the faint of heart. His promise to us is that answers go to the persistent prayers.

• **THE NARROW DOOR.** *Luke 13:24* The road to Heaven is not an easy one to follow; in fact it's a very difficult one. Though Jesus stands ready to give us whatever supplies we need, we have to walk and fight and pray and hope and never give in to the enemy. We have to take time out to read the Bible, to pray about what God wants us to pray for, to hear the Word of God taught and preached, to praise and worship God, and to do good to others. Not only do we have these duties that we are responsible for, we must find the true God (amidst all the false gods of this world) and learn about him. We must find out what Jesus does for sinners to save them. Looking for and learning about the truth about God is often a difficult job in itself! It takes a lot of dedication and it especially takes courage for what you might find him to be.

• **WATCHFULNESS.** *Luke 12:35-40* Jesus wanted his people to be ready for his coming. This involves all sorts of ways to be prepared. For one thing, we must deal with the sin in our hearts if we want him to be pleased with us when he arrives. Another thing is that we have to give an accounting to him of the resources he gave us to disciples thought that children are better off if they are "seen and not heard" as the old saying goes. They found out differently! Jesus rebuked them for what they were doing; he ordered them to bring the children to him instead of stopping them. They didn't argue with him! (Matthew 19:13-15)

One other time we find Jesus being careful to protect his disciples – this time about the Pharisees' bad teaching. They had, of course, grown up with this teaching all their lives, and it was natural for everyone in Israel to respect and listen to the Pharisees; these men were the leaders of the nation and the teachers of the Law. It would have been unwise to ignore them. But Jesus saw how hurtful the Pharisees really were, even though nobody else could see it. He saw that the Pharisees were demanding that the people obey unfair laws and give too much of their money for the support of the rulers of the land. He knew that the Pharisees themselves didn't even try to be as good as what they were telling the common people to be. So he warned his disciples:

> Be on your guard against the yeast of the Pharisees and Sadducees … then they understood that he was not telling them to guard against the yeast used in bread, but against the teaching of the Pharisees and Sadducees. (Matthew 16:6,12)

God's people need the truth, not lies. They need to hear about how Jesus saves, how he helps the lost and heals the sick. They need to learn what the Bible says, just as it says it, and believe it if they are going to be saved themselves. Jesus is use to build his kingdom. Remember the parable of the talents! We mustn't get sleepy and give up our duties, nor must we get sloppy about our work.

• **GOOD SEED**. *Matthew 13:1-23* Jesus has many reasons for telling this parable, but one of the most important reasons is to warn us about hearing the Word of God and acting on it. Notice why the other types of soil didn't produce a good fruit! They lacked self-control and couldn't resist the temptations of the world; they weren't careful to pay attention to the Word as someone taught it, so they didn't even remember what it said. Only those who were careful to listen and careful to use it were able to produce a crop that God was happy with.

Please understand something about discipline, though. We can work hard at any of these things and still not get anywhere! Just because we pray every day, with all the care in the world, doesn't mean that we will please God with what we say in our prayers. Our discipline is only half the story; Jesus stands ready to *make it work* when we do our part. Discipline is simply getting our cups ready to better receive the free grace of God.

Food

We all need food to live, but children need food to grow. They use up food at a much faster rate than adults because it builds a growing body with growing needs. They seem to be a bundle of energy – their body processes are running at top speed to keep up with the demands of changing from a child to an adult.

Their spiritual needs are also more intense than ours are. We've already seen that it's now when their world view is coming together, so it's very important that they get all the necessary information to do that. What they need is a steady diet of the truth – truth from the Word of God – and they need it served to them in just the right portions and in the right balance.

Food comes in all forms, some better for you than others. It's not good to live on just sweets and fats, though we like a taste of that now and then. It's much better to get a healthy mix of all kinds of foods. The same holds true with the Bible, believe it or not. People think that you can jump in anywhere and get spiritual benefit from it. Apart from the fact that adults are fooling themselves if they think this way, it's definitely not good for the children to get the Bible like this. Someone has to portion out the Scriptural truths to them just like giving them portions at the dinner table. If you let a child get whatever he wants at a restaurant he will come back with something that will make him sick! If you don't carefully instruct him in what he needs from the Bible, he will get all sorts of crazy ideas in his head that will definitely make him spiritually sick!

Above all, feed them Jesus. Make sure that they know all about him – who he is, what he does for people, what he expects from us, the kinds of miracles he can do, his commands and promises, all sorts of things about him. Since he will be their only hope for a fulfilling life *for the rest of their lives*, it's necessary to get them as familiar with him as possible at this early age.

Next, be careful to balance the diet that you give them. Don't just harp on his commands all the time! In every story try to tell them something about what he is like, even if it's just a little detail. Show them how glorious he is – how amazing he is, how much power he has, how interested he is in us. If you need to, use the same story across several lessons, bringing out a different angle each time – once on the need of the person he helped, another on his miracle and how nobody else could have done that, another on the wisdom he used in dealing with people who didn't like him. If you need to, make a list of the things you want the children to learn about Christ and then work through particular lessons that will teach them those things – checking off each item as you accomplish it.

Finally, make sure that they know where to go get more of this kind of food. Jesus said that "I am the bread of life." (John 6:35) You need to feed Christ to them, but they need to know where to get more. Hopefully you have done your job so well that they wouldn't go anywhere else for truth and happiness. "Lord, to whom shall we go? You have the words of eternal life." (John 6:68) Hopefully your children will be so satisfied with Jesus and what he has to offer them that they will get used to eating his spiritual food for the rest of their lives.

Conclusion

The biggest needs that children have are care and encouragement, training and the necessities of growth. As long as they get these needs met, they will grow up healthy and able to handle life in the world as responsible adults. We adults *want* to help them – we certainly devote most of our time getting children to adulthood – but we can't forget the important spiritual growth that they need. Unfortunately we often do, because the physical needs are so pressing, they are so much in the foreground in the normal day-to-day operations. For some reason we think that spiritual growth and all the things necessary for that to happen aren't as important, so we put less emphasis on them or even put them on the back shelf for later years. That's a very serious mistake: they need these things now, in their spiritually formative years, so that they won't become spiritual cripples. Their future is in your hands; God has given you the responsibility to tend to these very real needs of theirs.

Section Three:

Teaching from
the Gospels

The Gospels are a unique kind of literature for the Church, different even from the Old Testament and the New Testament Epistles. We need to study *how* they present the story of Jesus so that we can get the point across most effectively in our teaching.

The Gospels

The Gospels are unique books. They focus on just one person – Jesus Christ – and they slow way down to tell the story of this man's life in detail. Most of the 28 chapters of Matthew deal with only three years of Christ's life! Nobody else in the Bible gets such close attention, but then nobody else is so interesting and crucial for our faith as he is.

Since the story of Jesus is told by four different writers, it's inevitable that there are going to be problems understanding the Gospels as a whole. We want to look at some of those kinds of problems. But we will also have problems with the *way* they present the story of Christ. Since we are twenty centuries after the fact and our way of doing things is much different from theirs, we often don't understand the point of the stories, and we can't see the overall sweep of what they were trying to do. Hopefully we can look at some of those problems too.

Problems and solutions

The Gospels appear to have some problems, at first glance. There have been many arguments over the centuries about whether they are genuine and how carefully the writers recorded the events they wrote about. Since they are the story of the life of Christ, we would like to be able to clear up some of these problems because our faith and the trustworthiness of the writers hang in the balance! So these aren't just academic questions that we are raising. Besides, the children that you teach are going to be sharp enough to pick up on these things, and you will have to have a reasonable answer for them.

Let's look at four problem areas and try to find solutions:

• ***Why four gospels?*** It seems as if the writers could have collaborated a little better and produced just one book on Christ! Especially since so many of the stories are the same from book to book. The first three Gospels – known as the "synoptic" Gospels (from *syn*, meaning "together, the same"; and *optic*, meaning "vision, that which is seen") – are almost identical. They share most of the same stories, and the details in each story are almost the same. John at least has much new material in it that the Synoptics don't have, though even he re-tells some of the stories from the earlier three.

Why is this so? I think that if you go back and read the Gospels again and this time keep in mind *who wrote them* then you may find significant differences between them. **Matthew** was a Palestinian Jew, a Hebrew, who understood the Law, the Old Testament and the prophecies of the Messiah King. **Mark** was a young man who heard the stories of Jesus from his mentor Peter. **Luke** was a Gentile medical doctor; not only was he interested in the healings that Jesus did and how he did them, he had a cosmopolitan outlook on the world – he was careful to dig out the history, and he sees the story of Jesus set against the backdrop of the rest of the Roman world. **John** is more of a philosopher; he thinks through the deeper spiritual significance of what Jesus said and did, yet uses simple words to describe these profound truths. Now go back to each book and find traces of the author's peculiar traits in the stories – things that make one say "Yes, this *is* the way Matthew would want to say it."

Another reason we have four Gospels is that no one man can see the entire truth of Jesus. Jesus is bigger than we are; he transcends our common categories and shows how little and feeble-minded we are when we try to understand the Almighty God. The issues that he introduced into our lives would take worlds of books to work out! But since the Lord's intent behind the writing of the Gospels wasn't to tell everything Jesus said and did (John 21:25) he limited the material to what the entire Church would benefit from. That means, though, that each writer is going to see Jesus from a small window, due to his own perspective and background, and tell what he saw in his own context. To get the bigger picture of who Jesus is, we must look through each writer's window and catch a glimpse of someone who is just too big to be seen through any one of them.

A third reason we have four Gospels is because "A matter must be established by the testimony of two or three witnesses." (Deuteronomy 19:15) Though the case in Deuteronomy concerned convicting someone of a crime, it seems to me that today's society would be in a fix if we only had one Gospel. Suppose the writer got it wrong? we would ask. How do we know that Jesus did such fantastic things? So instead of giving our modern unbelievers the opportunity of accusing the early Church of making this up, the Lord wisely provided four witnesses to the Lord's bodily presence in Israel, doing the things that the Gospels all record. Remember that these writers have much different backgrounds, they wrote their books at different times (ranging from possibly right after Christ's death and resurrection to 50 years later), and they had different reasons and audiences for writing their books. All this is much good evidence that such a man did live and say these things.

• ***Not all the details.*** You will notice as you read that the writer almost never gives all the details of a story. If someone from the New York Times would have been there, he would have taken pictures, interviewed everyone on the scene, and filled columns of newsprint with irrelevant details. Fortunately there was nobody there like that! The Gospel writers only wrote what God wanted us to hear – no more, no less.

Details about Jesus' personal life have nothing to do with our salvation. They only tempt man to make an image in the form of a creature and then bow down to it and worship it. It's not just the man Jesus that we worship, however; he's the Son of God, which is what the writers were much more concerned about showing us. The style in which he wore his hair, the color of his clothes, the kind of food he liked to eat – all this only fogs the picture of what we really need from Jesus.

Even all the details from the miracle stories aren't given to us. You would think that these would be more important, since they helped to make the miracle what it was. But actually that's not true: the writer told us just the details that are useful for anyone who meditates on this miracle, in ancient Palestine as well as in our own day. They don't even write about much of that day's culture – because it isn't the same as our culture, and they didn't want you to think that the works of God can only happen in ancient Israel! So every detail that they *do* give us has much significance simply because it's something that will figure into your situation too when Jesus works for you.

• **_Broken story line._** Sometimes we catch a glimpse of a succession of events, a clue that this event followed that one. But for the most part, that isn't how the writers presented the story of Jesus. They arranged the stories in an order that probably made sense to themselves, but it seems to escape us. Even if we think that we are following one writer's train of thought, another writer has those same events in a different order – and upsets our theory!

Except for some obvious places (for example, the story of his birth and childhood, his baptism and temptation, and his crucifixion and resurrection) the Gospel writers aren't really concerned about putting things in a sequential order. Sometimes they want to group similar ideas together; sometimes they want to set one event over against another. You just have to study the bigger context (in other words, not just the story that you are teaching but several of them above and below it) and see if you can catch the writer's overall point. For example, the entire chapter of Matthew 21 seems to be looking at a common theme but from different angles – even the story about the fig tree fits in.

The stories often stand very well on their own. The writer's purpose isn't to show the flow of Jesus' life, instead it's to focus on *what Jesus is like* – which has nothing to do with a time-line. He simply moves from characteristic to characteristic. He shows the kinds of things Jesus can do, which requires many examples. He lets us listen in on Jesus' teachings that are about the many issues that Christians have to be working on. There are things here for the young and the old, for the worker and the child, for the skilled and the unskilled. It's more like the approach that the book of Proverbs takes: so many different issues to talk about in the space of a book, and each one is worth studying and thinking about for a long time to get to the bottom of it and benefit from it.

• ***Different details.*** One aspect of the Gospels is that, even when two or more writers tell the same story, they don't use exactly the same details. In fact, sometimes they seem to use contradictory details!

One famous example is the story of the two – or one? – demon possessed men in the region of the Gadarenes – or Gerasenes? Matthew says that there were *two* men there in the tombs, and the area was called the region of the Gadarenes. (Matthew 8:28-34) Mark and Luke both say that there was *one* man healed, and it was the region of the Gerasenes. (Mark 5:1-20; Luke 8:26-39) But in looking a little closer at the story, we find out that the Matthew reference has a footnote at the bottom of the page: evidently some other early Greek manuscripts of Matthew *do* say that the area was called the region of the Gerasenes (you have to be careful of those manuscripts; we often see disagreements between them, and we aren't always sure which is the original reading). So the three could be agreeing with each other after all! Second, it isn't hard to think of some reasons why they disagree about how many men were involved: Matthew, you will notice, was called to follow Jesus right *after* this miracle; he would have heard the story immediately after it happened from the other disciples, whereas the other two writers were simply writing about the *kind* of miracle that happened at this place and time.

Another reason that one writer will have details that another one won't is because those details have something important to do with the point he's making about Jesus; the other writer is making a different point and doesn't need those particular details in his story. That's not being dishonest but efficient. For example, Matthew tells us that Peter also walked on the water when Jesus came to them over the sea. (Matthew 14:22-33) Mark doesn't mention anything about Peter's experience; instead he focuses on the fact that *all* of them had "hardened hearts" in spite of the miracle they had just seen him do with the loaves of bread. (Mark 6:45-52) He isn't obligated to tell us everything that happened; he has a point he's trying to make, and he uses just the information that will make that point.

The purpose of the gospels

John tells us very plainly what the purpose of the Gospels is:

> But these are written that you may believe that Jesus is the Christ, the Son of God, and that by believing you may have life in his Name. (John 20:31)

That means that the things that these books tell us about him, in the way that they tell us, will best bring about our faith in him. It couldn't have been told from any other perspective, or using any other information, and still result in faith. A case in point is Josephus, the early Jewish historian and contemporary of the apostles, who did mention Jesus a couple of times in his writings. Those writings weren't exactly calculated to honor him as the Son of God! Jews who read his short notices didn't go out and join the Christian Church based on what he said. But people *do* believe in Christ when they read the Gospels; the only books that do bring people into the Church (and have for twenty centuries) are the Gospel accounts of his life.

The Gospels are the most effective means that God has given us for the following things to happen:

- *__Jesus looks like his Father.__* "Anyone who has seen me has seen the Father. How can you say, 'Show us the Father'? ... Don't you believe that I am in the Father, and that the Father is in me?" (John 14:9-10) Anybody who has read the Gospels comes away with a definite impression that here is someone who is different from any other man who has ever lived. If these stories are true, this is none other than God in the flesh! "No one ever spoke the way this man does." (John 7:46) When he did his miracles the people were simply amazed: "The people were amazed when they saw the dumb speaking, the crippled made well, the lame walking and the blind seeing. And they praised the God of Israel." (Matthew 15:31) We read those same stories with a ho-hum attitude; but the problem is our hardened hearts, not that the stories about Christ's miracles are any less astonishing. "Familiarity breeds contempt," as the saying goes, and we have heard these stories countless times. Unfortunately, until we see them happen we aren't going to believe them.

If you look closely at what Jesus did, you will recognize (if you know your Bible, that is!) the works of the Lord described in the Old Testament. That wasn't accidental! He's the same God of the ancient Israelites, doing the same things for us that he did in their day. He feeds bread to his people (as in the story of the manna – Exodus 16); he has complete control over great waters (as in the story of the parting of the Red Sea – Exodus 14); he lays the Law down for his people (as in the story of the giving of the Law to Israel at Sinai – Exodus 20); he builds a kingdom (as did the Lord through David – 1 and 2 Samuel); he provides a suitable sacrifice (as the Lord arranged in the Temple ceremonies – Leviticus). Of course his healings, and raising people from the dead, and prophesying the Word of God to the people, all call back images of similar happenings in the Old Testament. The people who watched him do these things thought of this, I'm sure!

You will also recognize, in Jesus' works, the same *ways* that the Lord did things in the Old Testament. The Lord not only has certain works that he likes to do, he has characteristic ways of going about those works. For instance, he likes to use little people to build his kingdom. So God used David the shepherd boy and Abraham the alien and the boy Samuel; Jesus used Peter the fisherman and Matthew the tax collector and the Samaritan woman at the well. Another one of his ways is that he doesn't use much of this world's materials to work a miracle: he used only 300 Israelites to rout the entire Midianite army; he only used five loaves of bread to feed thousands of people.

The things that Jesus taught also remind us of the Old Testament God. He came to fulfill the Law of the Old Testament. He dug into people's hearts and exposed their sin – the same thing that God did through Israel's prophets. He even used parables and stories to make his point, which is the way that God spoke to the Israelites – but you have to back up to see this and view the historical events of the Old Testament as symbols and picture lessons of deeper spiritual truths. You will never find Jesus contradicting what God taught in the Old Testament; rather he will deepen and make plainer those things that used to confuse the Jews in the old days.

This is one of the primary values of the role of Jesus: if we didn't know who God was before now, we can see him in Christ, in the Gospel stories, and know what God is really like – right here where we live, doing the things that he wants done among men, in words and deeds that please him. There's no mystery to God anymore, no guessing about what he thinks of us and expects of us. He made it very plain in Jesus.

• *We finally see the truth.* When we read the Gospels we are hearing God's opinion of things, which is the only true opinion. The world is full of contradicting lies and half-truths that have fooled people for ages. Life is too short and the problems are too pressing to allow this to go on for much longer. We *must* have a source for truth, something that will explain what we must do to be saved.

The Gospels don't pull any punches. Jesus said it like it is: whether he was talking to Pharisees or fishermen, he went straight to the point. He tells us that we are sinners, and that unless we give it all up and follow him wherever he leads us we will die in our sin. He tells us that the religious leaders of this world who hide behind their man-made rules and traditions are leading us astray; they are "blind guides" and we must stay away from them. He tells us the real value of worldly wealth – it has none – and he holds out a lasting treasure that is worth living and dying for.

The Gospels also show us Jesus at work. People nowadays don't believe in miracles, and they think the stories of Jesus' miracles are fables or a determined effort of the early Church to get credibility, through "dishonest" stories, for its new religion. But the Gospel writers simply wrote what they knew, and that simplicity is the biggest argument against modern unbelief. He just went about doing good, and the writers are simply telling us what he did! And it's staggering to think that someone could do these things – even more staggering is the fact that he has come among *us* to do them! We have here a determined Savior who brings the firepower of Heaven to bear on our problems; nothing in this world will stand before him. Although the world and the devil have been busy trying to discredit Jesus, the Gospels still hit a new reader as refreshing good news – finally, here is someone who can help me!

When we read the Gospels and watch Jesus at work and listen to him teach us, we know in our hearts that it's *true*. The books have a penetrating ability to convict the heart. They are a *testimony* of Jesus: this isn't a weak and pitiful witness that we ourselves often prove to be, but the power of God's Word – which, remember, created the world and still controls all aspects of it! The Gospels have power to present the Savior to us so that faith happens; no other testimony, no work of man, has that power over our minds and hearts. Call it what you will, one can't argue with the Word; you can avoid it, maybe, but that may not last long either if the Spirit has anything to do with it!

- **_He deals with our problems here._** We consider ourselves to be sophisticated descendants of those early primitive peoples. So much happened in Western civilization in the last 500 years that we usually don't identify ourselves with any of the civilizations before us. Just look at what science has done for us! In a short time we have become masters of the earth like no other generation in history. They would be astonished to see just the simple modern conveniences we now have in our homes.

One thing about us hasn't changed at all, however: our hearts. We have the same problem of sin that the first human beings had. For all our new powers, we haven't been able to solve that problem; unfortunately it's the one thing that's killing our souls. This is why, when we read the Gospels, we can identify so well with what they teach us – they hit us where we live.

Jesus uncovered the human problem so effectively that we shudder to think that God knows us so well! When he called hatred *murder*, and lustfully looking at another woman *adultery*, and showing off your righteousness as fatal *pride*, he touches us where we all live. He *does* know what we are like! The reason many people don't want to read the Gospels is that he knows them so well, and he's going to uncover the ugliness in their hearts. Too often we don't believe in him any more than the people did back then; we're like the Pharisees in our puffed up pride; we steal as Judas did; we judge others instead of loving them; we love money and store up treasures on earth instead of in Heaven. If we will at least read the stories, and think about them in relation to our own situation, they have a deadly aim straight at our hearts.

The good thing about this is that this means he can do the same for us that he did for them. If he could save the adulterous woman, he can save us from the same judgment. If he could raise the dead, he can raise us too. If he knew the sin in

Peter's heart and prayed for his recovery, he will do the same for us. Exposing our sin isn't the end of the story, not by a long shot. As long as he has our hearts opened up, he's going to kill that sin, with the skill that only God has, and we will join the ranks of countless millions before us who have found the Gospel testimony to be perfectly true. In other words, when God reveals our sin during our reading of his Word then that's reason to hope, not fear.

- ***The solutions are overwhelming.*** Jesus didn't do things by halves. When he healed somebody he healed them fully and permanently. He had solutions that nobody before him and nobody since him have been able to duplicate. The woman with a twelve year hemorrhage who came to him for healing had been to many doctors, none of which could help her. We say now, however, that *our* doctors can heal all sorts of diseases – but *can* they heal as Jesus can? And aren't they still stymied by many diseases, helpless to heal many accident victims, and hopeless when death sets in? Jesus isn't! With a word he can do the miraculous and completely restore to health and life, immediately.

The reason that Jesus' solutions take care of human problems so well is because they are directly from God, the Creator of all things. Jesus can see the root of any problem; he isn't mystified by causes that we can't see, and he knows "the end from the beginning" (Isaiah 46:10) – which means he understands all processes and means, and he has plans to change the human condition.

His enemies just couldn't stop him. Even when they all ganged up on him to take him out of town and kill him, he simply walked through the crowd and left the scene. (Luke 4:16-30) The Pharisees and Sadducees were always laying traps for him that he escaped easily. Only when *he* decided to lay down his life could they do anything to him. (John 10:18)

His disciples couldn't predict him. They saw him settle storms with a word, throw out demons that they were helpless before, and feed thousands with a few loaves of bread. Their entire three year experience following this remarkable man convinced them that there wasn't anything he couldn't do!

The people he helped were amazed at what he did for them. They watched him heal incurable diseases and even raise the dead. They followed him by the thousands wherever he went because they knew he could do what they needed, whatever that may be. He was a dream come true for them.

Of course people look to the Gospels for things that they *don't* have, too. You won't find the following things in these books:

- *A human interest story.* The story of Jesus isn't something that you can take or leave at your pleasure. This isn't just interesting history, though there are many people who hope that it's no more than that! This is something that you need for your life; you need to read this and believe it and let it change your life to suit God's expectations of you. If you walk away from reading it without your heart changing then you didn't get the point.

Many people read the Gospels as if they were nothing more than early Oriental literature. They analyze the stories and the overall structure as if the apostles were aspiring novelists, creating literary works that must stand up under the modern critic's expectations. Even Biblical scholars put the Gospel stories through the wringer and, unfortunately, offer suggestions on how the disciples could have improved them!

Modern unbelievers enjoy the story of Jesus only if they don't have to believe that these stories are written for them, with their sins and their salvation in mind. They appreciate his strict moral code, his political views, his love for people, his organizational skills – everything except the fact that he came to save sinners from sin and death. If they can keep him at a distance, if they can avoid the personal dimension of the Gospels, then they are willing to talk to you about it. But if you once mention that they need to meet this Jesus to take care of the sin in *their* hearts, they disappear. They don't want to think about that.

The problem is that it's difficult to get away from that personal side of the Gospels. There's so little there to feed the sensational; it seems that it's always either pointing at our sin or at our unbelief, and it's always showing us a God that we need. The Gospels are all business.

- ***The lies of the world.*** You will find none of the world's "common sense" or scientific outlook in the Bible. Modern theories on man's psychology, social behavior and values, philosophical systems, political structures, or economic systems will be disappointed in the Gospels – it doesn't cater to any of them. It's just the simple truth, naïve as it may sound. And it's not as if the Gospels are dealing in religion and therefore don't have anything to say to those other disciplines; it has a lot to say about them! Modern man will find himself condemned and outdone by the truth of God; *we* must change to suit the Lord's standards, not the other way around.

A lie, it has been said, is a half truth. That's why so many people are fooled into thinking that the world's answers are right; they sound reasonable, they stroke us the right way (making us feel as if we are important and drawing us deeper into "mysteries"), and the people we respect tell us that they have tried it and it really works! In the meantime hardly anybody takes the Bible's answers seriously (not even many Christians!) because it runs contrary to man's wisdom, from beginning to end, and it sounds too simplistic.

For example, people in our day have a million ideas of who God really is; it seems that everyone has their own God in their minds and no two ideas are alike. Some think that God hangs back from getting very involved in man's world, and it's up to us to make our world better. Others think that God needs man as much as man needs him; both are evolving and changing over the centuries to become something better. They try to prove their idea from a verse here and there from the Bible (always taken out of its context, of course).

But a careful reading of, for example, the Gospels will prove those ideas dead wrong. Jesus' very presence among us and the things he did for us show that God is very much involved in our world, down to the little details of giving us food to eat! And man certainly does need God (as we see from the crowds who followed Jesus waiting for his miracles) but God doesn't need man at all. The God we see in Jesus isn't a bit different from the God of the Old Testament (he hadn't changed at all, in other words) and Jesus looked forward to going back to share in the glory he had *before the beginning of the world* – a glory that's the same now as it was then!

• ***Subjects other than Jesus.*** The Gospels are also disappointing to some people because they focus on just one subject, the life and work of Christ. They would like it better if Jesus had spoken on more issues that relate to our modern situation. In fact, Christians often make the mistake of considering the Gospels to be the gate that gets us into the fold of God and then are of little use to us after that. For more exciting issues they turn to the Epistles or the types and symbols of the Old Testament. They've quickly plumbed the depths of the Gospels (so they thought) and are looking for something more useful or more exciting elsewhere in the Bible.

There are other sources of information in our society for understanding current events; let them go there for that kind of help. Libraries have been written on every subject under the sun and people can spend all the time they want sitting at the feet of men learning all that. But for what Jesus is, for the things that Jesus does, there is only one source – the Gospels – and they keep strictly to that subject and rightly so. If they are the only source of information on Christ's life, would it be right for them to waste time on lesser subjects? Thank God they do such a good job of staying to the point! We can't get this information anywhere else; what kind of shape would we be in if they didn't give us as much of Jesus as possible?

Ways they teach us about Christ

When you read the Gospels you should have a careful eye on *how* they teach about Christ. They don't just list some doctrines about him that we can memorize and live by. In fact, they often take a very indirect approach to the whole matter and many people therefore miss the point. It's possible, ironically, to read through much of the Gospels and not know much more about Jesus than when you've started – like reading a math book and not understanding what you read!

It's *not* enough to simply know the stories of Jesus; there's too much going on here that we mustn't miss out on if we want an in-depth understanding of Christ. The careful reader should be aware that the Gospels have several important *ways* of teaching us about Jesus:

- ***Ties to the Old Testament*** – We've seen already that the Gospels like to show us the Old

Testament God in action, in flesh and blood this time instead of sitting in Heaven somewhere working through his prophets by proxy. Jesus does things that his Father does, and says things that his Father says, and by his own hand works miracles and by his own Word rules over men. The point is unmistakable.

What we will often miss, however, is that the stories of Jesus should remind us of many more things from the Old Testament as well. **First**, the Old Testament used a device called a *type* – an earthly thing, person or situation that represented in some way a Heavenly reality. There are many types in the Old Testament, and most of them have to do with teaching the Israelites about the things that Jesus would do when he finally came. For instance, David was a type of Christ – he was Israel's first successful king (a man after God's own heart) who ruled Israel in the way that God wanted his king to rule. The things he did in his kingdom were a lesson to the Jews of what the Messiah would do when he came. If we don't actually read in the Gospels about the ruling that Jesus did, or we miss the point on how he was setting up his Kingdom, we need to go back to the story of David and learn the lesson that the type teaches us. This is true of so many things in the New Testament! It simply won't take the time to re-teach us the lessons that the Old Testament already did so well; we have to go back to the Old and catch up before we can go on with what the New is talking about.

Second, the Old Testament is full of prophecy, and much of that also dealt with the works of the

Messiah. We know many of the prophecies made about him, such as the circumstances of his birth and the details of his death on the cross. What we may miss, however, is the fundamental point of the prophecies: that the King is coming to earth, to sweep away his enemies and set up a new Kingdom in which peace and righteousness would reign instead of sin and death. For instance, we read the stories of how he fed thousands of people with just a few loaves of bread, and we think that this is a nice story – it shows how powerful he is. What we may not realize is that this what the Old Testament said the King would do for his people!

> The eyes of all look to you, and you give them their food at the proper time. You open your hand and satisfy the desires of every living thing. (Psalm 145:15-16)

Another example is Isaiah's prophecy that Christ would be a Wonderful Counselor. "And he will be called Wonderful Counselor." (Isaiah 9:6) We ought to be able to go to the Gospels and watch him counsel people and make good on that prophecy; as a matter of fact he did just that, which you can see if you study the record closely.

So we need to get used to looking for the Old Testament passages that predicted these things that Jesus did in the Gospels; it would make our study so much more meaningful to see that God planned, and is doing, the entire thing for his eternal glory, from beginning to end.

Third, the Gospels quietly show us the most extraordinary transaction in human history signed and sealed in blood. In Genesis 12, 15, and 17 we read the story of Abraham and God making a covenant together: a legal contract in which God would call Abraham and his descendants his people and they would have faith in him. That legal agreement is what held the Jewish nation together for the next two thousand years. When Jesus came, he put the finishing touches to the agreement (which included putting the Law in their hearts and opening up the family tree to include the Gentiles) and put the dimension of eternity in the whole thing.

The story of the Canaanite woman is an exciting example of this covenant-work that Jesus was doing. He told her that "I was sent only to the lost sheep of Israel" (Matthew 15:24) – meaning that he had no interest in going outside the legal agreement that God made with Abraham. She answered him with faith, the *same* faith that Abraham had, demonstrating to him that she was one of Abraham's spiritual descendants (see Romans 4 for a discussion of this) and therefore rightfully an heir to the Abrahamic covenant! So he gave her what she asked based on that legal right of hers.

• *Pericopes* – A pericope is a story-size passage from the Gospels. The story of Jesus walking on the water, and the story about him healing the demoniacs in Gerasene, are pericopes. All of the Gospels consist of pericopes that a teacher can handily deal with in a class session.

They aren't there just for handiness, however. There are good reasons why the Gospels divide up the story of Jesus into these smaller sections. We already saw that the writers weren't very concerned about giving a time-line of Jesus' life, because this isn't a human interest story. What it *is*, however, is a window on the character and ways of the Lord.

An old writer once called the Gospels "the galleries of the King." When you walk into these galleries you are actually there, among the crowd, and you are watching Jesus do real things that affect you too. This isn't just your wild imagination, however; the Spirit really does transport you to this timeless world where Jesus still lives and works among his people. This is why you can get so much benefit from reading God's Word – it's a living thing that brings you into his presence where he can work on your heart and heal your soul.

If the Gospels were a running novel you would miss out on the spiritual good that he wants you to have. Take a story and immerse yourself in it. Watch him; listen to him; think about your surroundings there; look at the people he deals with; think about what he is saying to you. Live the moment just like the other people in the story, who are standing there beside you. Worship the God that you see, the One to whom you have brought your problems. He wants to deal with you on this issue right now; don't run off from story to story as if the important thing was to collect data! You don't need the next story yet, not until this one does its eternal work on you. Don't move on until he blesses you with this truth: "I will not let you go unless you bless me." (Genesis 32:26)

Another reason why the Gospels consist of pericopes is that they are dealing with his character, and the kinds of work that he does. They could have simply listed these items out and made it like a memorization lesson; but instead they teach by example, by picture, by showing you in action the truths of Christ. Would it really be sufficient for the writer to tell us that "Jesus feeds his people"? Would that persuade us to depend on him? Or is the story of feeding the 5000 a tremendously effective way of showing us that he does indeed feed his people? The first way is a doctrine that we may not accept; the second way is an unarguable demonstration of what he's capable of, and what he wants to do for us.

- *__Multifaceted views__* – If you study the stories and think about them (especially in light of the Old Testament) you will begin to piece together the kind of God that you have. No one story tells everything about him. Jesus is like a diamond that has to be seen from many angles to be appreciated. He's so complex – a fact lost on most people because the Gospel stories seem so simple and naïve – that nobody has him completely figured out yet.

What we take as a simple action on his part is really a small piece of a vast and unimaginably complex puzzle that only he can unravel. Take the process of salvation, for example. We think it was just a matter of dying on the cross; to him, however, he had to bring the limitless resources of God to bear on the problem:

- God spent thousands of years getting the Jews ready for the step of final salvation, including the Temple system and the Law and the Abrahamic covenant and the Messiah prophecies and all the types.

- Jesus came into the world as a humble man, an extremely important step in the process that provided a constant foundation for all his ministry.

- He learned obedience as a child and "grew in favor with God and man."

- He launched his ministry across Palestine going from town to town teaching and doing miracles.

- He had to take care to fulfill every single detail of the Law – something that no man before him had ever successfully done – in the short space of a lifetime, so that the Law pronounced him righteous solely on the basis of his perfect life.

- He called a group of men who would be the foundation of the future Church and trained them in his ways.

- He suffered persecution at the hands of both Jews and Romans and was finally put to death.

- His tomb and the events of the resurrection showed that salvation wasn't done at the cross – it was just getting started!

- Then he had to ascend to Heaven or God could give nothing to his fledgling Church!

- Next he sent his Spirit to forge the Church together into the new body that he planned to continue into the future – down into our day. Imagine all the work that he has done for the last 2000 years to get millions of followers into the Kingdom, taught, and sent on their way to eternity!

- The job isn't done until all the world is gradually put under his feet and he hands it all over to his Father.

Salvation, as you can see, was not a simple process! Nobody has ever pulled even *one* of these things off, let alone the whole job. And yet Jesus did it all single-handedly! When we read the Gospels we ought to keep this vast scheme in mind so that we don't forget how complex and many-sided his nature and work are. It took someone who was a King, a judge, a shepherd, a provider, a seer, a prophet, a legal expert, a friend of sinners, a religious expert, and many other hats; his ability to excel in all these areas simply astonish us. He succeeded at everything he had to do because he's the Master of all things.

Because he's doing so much, we should remember that at any one time he may be juggling dozens of issues. We make a mistake when we focus on one single aspect of a story and refuse to consider other issues that may be involved. For example, we already noticed that he was involved with far more than a simple miracle in the case of the Canaanite woman; he was keeping in mind the Abrahamic covenant that he was bound by God's oath to keep; and he was also working on the fulfillment to bring the Gentiles into the covenant, an Old Testament theme that goes all the way back to Genesis.

• *__Same story, different angles__* – You will read the same story in different Gospels and they will give different details; not always do they tell the story identically to each other. We discussed this before. The idea is that each writer had a different point in mind when he told the story; but there's nothing wrong with different details. A single detail will make the whole difference in what the writer wants us to see in Christ.

For example, in Matthew 13:53-58 we read of his cold welcome in his home town. They took offense at him because they didn't like his appearing to be better than they were. So it says that "he did not do many miracles there because of their lack of faith." We learn then the vital importance of faith: **no faith, no miracles**.

In Mark 6:1-6 we read the same story but with a different punch line. "And he was amazed at their lack of faith." Why is this idea tacked on to the end of the story? I believe that Mark is telling us that, far from being understandable, **a lack of faith is incomprehensible to Jesus!** He expects us all to believe that he does the miraculous! He expects us all to see that this humble carpenter's son is the Son of God, in spite of appearances, and he does have what we need in spite of reasons to doubt him. In other words, the world of the impossible is normal to him and he can't understand why we don't share the same world view!

• *The eye of Faith* – Perhaps the most important thing that the Gospels are doing is presenting Jesus from the perspective of faith. In spite of what many people think of it, faith is *not* an easy thing to do – it's a deeply spiritual act that we can't do on our own. If someone has faith, you just can't account for how they came to have it – there's no visible reason why they should have it.

Consider the odds against it. We are asked to believe that this single man is the Savior of the world; is there any visible proof of that? If so, why didn't the religious leaders of his day testify to it? What background did he have to prove his credentials? What eventually happened to him – isn't that a statement *against* the truth of his message? Where is he now? How can the Church justifiably ask the world to believe in someone that nobody can see or hear or touch?

Jesus once told his disciples, "Because you have seen me, you have believed; blessed are those who have not seen and yet have believed." (John 20:29) That's us! We have never seen the Lord as the disciples saw him and yet we know that he lives, that everything the Gospels said about him is true, and that he works in our hearts. We know that only because the *Spirit* shows us how real he is when we read the stories of him.

Faith, you will find as you study the Bible, is the spiritual ability to see, and be convinced of, the world of God. Our world throws up all kinds of smoke screens and veils to blind our eyes to the reality of Heaven; but when God gives us Heavenly X-ray vision, so to speak, to penetrate the smoke and see into the throne room of God, we see things that convince us of its power. We feel it in our hearts. That's why Jesus kept referring to "eyes that see and ears that hear," because it takes that to know that Heaven is real. The Pharisees couldn't see past their sins and the humility that Jesus took upon himself as they looked at him; they thought he was just an upstart from the country. Peter, however, saw somebody else: "You are the Christ, the Son of the living God." (Matthew 16:16) Jesus told him that, if left to himself, he would never have seen such a thing; but "this was not revealed to you by man, but by my Father in Heaven." (Matthew 16:17)

Thank God that the Gospels aren't disinterested and impartial accounts of the Lord! The writers believed in his divinity, in his special nature, and they worked hard to portray him *in this glory* of his. A modern writer wouldn't have been so keen to show Jesus in a spiritual light; he would have backed off and given more limelight to less important details and people, and he wouldn't have "interpreted" the sayings and works of Jesus in a spiritual way. The Gospel writers, however, were quick to point out how Jesus fulfilled this and that Scripture, and they built up each story of healing so that we, in effect, have front row seats to his glory – we can see his greatness and love and desirable qualities that impartial observers would have missed. They *want* us to believe that he is the Son of God!

Yes, they are slanted in their outlook – but you needn't distrust them for that. They are leaning you towards the *truth* about Jesus that any other source can't and won't do for you. This is the way you *must* see him if you want to be saved too.

Sample Stories

It might help to take a story or two from the Gospels and see how to develop the point – how to get the children interested, help them understand what's going on in the story, and most importantly to see the thing about Jesus that they need to know.

The first story was a lesson I gave to a group of 15 children in a school chapel setting. The second was in a mixed Bible study with about 12 children and 8 adults – a much more difficult thing to do! The adults tend to pull the discussion off into tough theological points, and I had to try to juggle the story details so that the children would understand the point of the story while the adults would get *spiritual food*, which is what they, as spiritual children themselves, need anyway.

Notice that the story starts out with some context; it helps if you explain how this story fits with the preceding one, and why Jesus went home with Peter afterwards.

When Jesus came into Peter's house, he saw Peter's mother-in-law lying in bed with a fever. He touched her hand and the fever left her, and she got up and began to wait on him. (Matthew 8:14-15)

Jesus and his disciples were just coming home from synagogue. Back then the Jews

You should do some studying to know the cultural background. You don't need much, but it makes a world of difference when explaining things to children. They really like association: make them feel as if they are there too, as if you are all looking in the window and watching. It's important to get them this familiar and close to Jesus in these stories; whatever they feel a part of, they remain very loyal to.

went to synagogue just as we go to church; and they did many the same things in synagogue that we do in church. And they went to synagogue on Sabbath – on Saturday, that is – so their Saturday was like our Sunday. Then when the service was over they did another thing that we like to do: everyone went home for a big dinner. You probably go home after church to eat a big dinner too!

Well, Jesus didn't have his own home to go to because he was traveling around from town to town teaching and doing miracles. So on this Sabbath his disciple Peter invited Jesus to his house for Sabbath dinner.

Did you know that Peter was married? This story says that he had a mother-in-law! In order to have a mother-in-law you have to be married; if a man has a wife, her mother is his mother-in-law. Your father has a mother-in-law – can you guess who that is? That's your grandmother!

Some more cultural background. Notice I'm showing how important grandmother's role is, in order to set up for the main point later: the *need* for what Jesus can do.

Work at developing a picture for the children. They think in pictures; they respond so much better to what they see. So use some sanctified imagination when you are painting the scene for them; sanctified, that is, in that you can easily back up whatever you say with facts from somewhere else!

One of the strange things in those days was that usually everyone lived in the same house: father and mother, all the children from babies to teenagers, maybe some uncles and aunts, grandmothers and grandfathers, cousins, and maybe a few dogs and cats thrown in too. That's a lot of people! We only have two parents and some children in our homes; but in those days land was very scarce, and everyone was poor, so they saved money by living together. There could be 20-30 people in one house! They also worked together in the fields so that they could make enough for everyone to eat. They didn't seem to mind all the confusion in one home, at least if everyone did their job and tried to get along with each other.

Now everyone had their own job to do. And grandmother's job was very important: she usually cooked the meals, because everyone else was too busy to do that. Mother was too busy watching all the children and Father was out in the fields.

In this and the next paragraph I'm setting up for one of the elements of a miracle. A miracle, you will discover from your own study, consists of four things: *first*, it is something that only God can do. *Second*, it is something that man cannot do. *Third*, we really need it – this is what I'm developing here, and the children as well as adults have to be convinced from real examples how desperately we need the hand of Jesus in our lives. *Fourth*, it works – it does the job.

How would you know these things about miracles to build them into your story? **Study!**

So grandmother stayed in the kitchen and made sure meals were ready on time.

Peter's mother-in-law, though, was sick this Sabbath. In those days having a fever was very dangerous; she could have died from it! Everyone was very worried about her, I'm sure. What made it worse was that as long as grandmother was sick in bed the meals didn't get cooked! Mother was too busy taking care of grandmother and nobody else knew how to cook! The house probably looked like a mess because everyone was worried about her: she couldn't do her job, and so Mother had to take care of her which means she couldn't do *her* job, which means the children were probably running around the house making a terrible mess and a lot of noise – it sure wasn't any fun when grandmother was sick, let me tell you! The whole family fell apart.

I realize that this isn't in the story, that I'm reading between the lines; but I'm doing two things: *first*, this *is* typical of human nature. After all, even the disciples did their best to keep children away from Jesus! *Second*, I need this dimension in the story to show *when* Jesus wants to help us – not at our best times but at our worst; not when we want him to see us but when we don't want him to see us.

In comes Peter, then, with a guest for dinner! I'm sure Peter's wife was surprised and maybe a little upset with him. "*Peter*," she probably said, "how could you bring home someone for dinner with this place looking such a mess! And we don't have a proper dinner to feed him. What were you thinking of, bringing him here now? He'll think that I'm an awful housekeeper!"

Peter, though, wants to introduce his new friend to his wife, and he tells her that Jesus has asked to see grandmother. "Peter, no!" she gasps. "Mother looks terrible now! She's in bed and in her PJ's and her hair is a mess, and you just can't let him in to see her in such a state!" Mothers worry about things like that.

Jesus insisted, though, that he wanted to see grandmother. So he went into her room and there she was – in just as bad a shape as Peter's wife had said. Then Peter's wife found out that this was no ordinary

When you are dealing with a miracle of Jesus, don't pull any punches. Set the scene carefully and then dramatically show the amazing nature of what he did. There is no human explanation for it! Show the result – that it worked immediately and that it was complete. What you are trying to achieve is nothing less than a hero-worship: He is someone who does the *impossible*. You need to fix it in their minds that when they need the impossible done for them, the only place they can look to is to Jesus – and they *will* find it there in him.

This paragraph ties the need of grandmother in with our needs. In other words, grandmother wasn't a special case; Jesus does these things to *anybody* in need, then and now.

guest! He bent over her bed and touched her hand, and immediately the fever left her. Just a touch! I would have loved to have been there to see it. Grandmother sat right up in bed, feeling completely better. In fact, she was so much better that she got out of bed that very minute, got dressed, combed her hair, and headed out to the kitchen to make the Sabbath dinner for her special guest!

You see, Jesus was no ordinary guest. Peter brought the one person that grandmother needed to see! Jesus heals – he can heal fevers as well as do all sorts of other things that nobody else can do. When he touched grandmother, she was glad he had come to see her in her illness. He was glad to be able to help her, too.

In fact, he wants to see us just when we are at our worst – just when we can't help ourselves, and just when we can't do our job around the house for others. He knows when we don't want anybody

Here is the result of Jesus' action: I'm careful to give credit where credit is due! She responded *after* the work of God in her heart, not before; *he* was responsible for her service. This makes us look to him in our weakness.

Finally, I want them to know that Jesus is still looking for people who need help. This isn't poetry, either; when I teach the story of Jesus to them from the Gospels, I really am bring them and Jesus together, through knowledge and faith and the Spirit, and good things can happen.

to see us, but that's just the perfect time for him to show up – *he* can help us. He wants to come just when you need him the most.

Grandmother was so well that she jumped up right away and started doing her chores – she went straight to the kitchen and fixed a big Sabbath meal, and everyone in the family was happy because she was well again. That's what happens when Jesus touches us: we can serve him, the way he likes to be served. We can do what God wants, we can obey him, when Jesus touches us and heals us.

I brought a friend with me today. Maybe you don't feel like meeting anybody right now; maybe you think that you need to get over being sick, like grandmother, before you want anybody to see you. But my friend wants to see you: Jesus knows that you need help and that's why he has come with me, to see you and to help you. Ask him to touch you and make you well again, so that you can be pleasing to God and serve him.

They came to Bethsaida, and some people brought a blind man and begged Jesus to touch him. He took the blind man by the hand and led him outside the village. When he had spit on the man's eyes and put his hands on him, Jesus asked, "Do you see anything?" He looked up and said, "I see people; they look like trees walking around." Once more Jesus put his hands on the man's eyes. Then his eyes were opened, his sight was restored, and he saw everything clearly. Jesus sent him home, saying, "Don't go into the village." (Mark 8:22-26)

This is probably one of the strangest stories in the Gospels, and for two reasons: first, Jesus seems to have a big problem about the village Bethsaida; and second, this is the only miracle where he has to try a second time before it works!

Again, you need to set the context for them. In this instance it would help them to understand some of the issues coming up if you had already shown them the kinds of welcomes Jesus had been getting from different towns around the Sea of Galilee – for instance, Matthew 9:35; 11:20-24; 13:53-58; 15:21; Mark 7:31-32.

Don't assume that you understand the story! Ask tough questions that will force you to look at the surrounding context and through the rest of the Bible for answers.

Jesus just came from across the Sea of Galilee (which he often did – he crisscrossed it as he went from town to town doing his miracles) and now he comes into Bethsaida. Bethsaida is a little village at the northern tip of the Sea of Galilee. It is special for one reason: this is where three disciples grew up! (Peter, Philip, and Andrew – see John 1:44) There was a large crowd following him around, too; not everyone who surrounded him in the village square that day lived in Bethsaida. Some of them came from a long distance away.

Some people brought a blind man to Jesus so that he would heal him. The first thing that Jesus did was to lead the man out of town! Why do you suppose he did this? I think, for one thing, that he didn't want the situation to turn into a circus. He didn't heal people just to amuse the crowd! They often wanted to see miracles because they liked "magic" shows; he wasn't doing this for show, however! He healed people because they needed help. Performing miracles just to get attention to himself wasn't his way of doing things; he preferred to work quietly, off in a corner somewhere, helping people out of their problems because he loved them. He couldn't care less about the crowd; in fact, he never did trust the crowds that followed him around!

I think there's another reason why he left the village to do the miracle, but we will get to that in a minute.

When they were out of town in the country somewhere, Jesus stopped and spit on the man's eyes. What a strange way to heal somebody! We saw something like this in another miracle he did for someone. (Mark 7:31-37) Why did he do it that way? If a doctor from our century would go back in time and ask Jesus how spit can heal blindness, and if Jesus would have explained it to him, I'm sure he wouldn't have understood it even then! This is something that nobody can understand; Jesus is God's

I hope you can see what I'm working on here. It bothers me to hear people say that the miracles of Jesus are understandable, if only we had enough knowledge. They are *not!* That's the point about Christ: he knows what we can't know and he does what we can't do, because he is God. A creature will never see things from God's perspective. This is why we need his miracles – if he doesn't do them for us, we will have to go without!

Son and he understands how to do miracles. Whatever he does is impossible for the rest of us to do.

What makes people consider this miracle a failure at first is because they are reading too much into the man's answer. It could be that this is the answer Jesus was expecting at this point.

At any rate, the next step was very interesting: he asked the man if he could see anything yet. Instead of saying that he was completely healed, the man told Jesus that he could see only fuzzy objects – they must be people, even though they looked like trees, because they were moving around!

Then Jesus put his hands on him again and this time the man's sight was restored. (Notice that it says *restored* – the man must have been able to see before now, and the blindness was an accident or because of an illness.)

Again, don't be afraid of hard questions. At first glance we see a potential problem here; it's too bad that the unbelievers are ready to capitalize on it! But because we already know who Jesus is (at least we are supposed to!) a hard question isn't going to throw us; we must look at the issue fairly and trust that there is some solution somewhere.

Now I want to ask a question: Why did it take two times before the man was healed? Was there something wrong? Usually Jesus just spoke a word or touched someone and they were healed immediately! What was the problem here?

This is where much groundwork on who Jesus is, and what he does, and how he does things will make the tough lessons go smoother.

Let's get one thing straight first: Jesus doesn't fail. Someone might look at this story and think, "Well, he didn't heal the man the first time – he evidently isn't as powerful as people say." But that's not right. He *never* fails at things; the problem is always somewhere else. Once the people from his hometown refused to believe in him, and therefore he couldn't do many miracles there. (Matthew 13:53-58) You see, if something fails it's because of us, not him; he is the Son of God and can never fail.

This is a tough story, I know, but that means we have to do a good job and learn about Jesus from other stories that are easier before we come to this one and study it. We know better than to say that Jesus was having problems here, because we've seen too many other places where Jesus always succeeded and it was others who had the problems.

You see, there *are* possible solutions – but you have to dig around in other Scriptures to find them! And they seem to have a lot to do with the strange details in this story.

One problem may have been that the man himself was having difficulty believing in

Jesus. Do you remember any other Scripture that talks about this particular village?

"Then Jesus began to denounce the cities in which most of his miracles had been performed, because they did not repent. 'Woe to you, Korazin! Woe to you, Bethsaida! If the miracles that were performed in you had been performed in Tyre and Sidon, they would have repented long ago in sackcloth and ashes. But I tell you, it will be more bearable for Tyre and Sidon on the day of judgment than for you.' " (Matthew 11:20-22)

Evidently Jesus and Bethsaida were not getting along very well! This is probably why Jesus didn't want to do the miracle in town: he had "dusted off his feet," (Matthew 10:14) and he wasn't going to give them the blessing of seeing this man healed. Furthermore the man himself might have heard some bad things about Jesus in town, and his lack of faith was getting in Jesus' way. Of course when he got some of his sight back his faith probably shot up immediately!

I think the real reason the miracle happened like this is because this time Jesus wanted to do it in *two* steps; he knew exactly what he was doing. Remember that once he met his disciples trying to heal a boy with epilepsy; they weren't getting very far. He told them that "This kind can come out only by prayer and fasting." (Mark 9:29) That tells us that not every sickness is alike; he will use different ways to heal different people.

Notice that he did the first step and then asked the man, "Do you see anything?" That is the clue to me that he wanted to do step one first, check on the progress, and then finish up with step two. Otherwise he would have assumed that it had worked and not asked the man anything!

Now I focus on Christ himself and his ways of doing things. This is always the high point of the lesson, because it is him that we want to learn about – what he does and how he does things.

Sometimes you have to be very careful about the wording in the text. With so little to go on, little clues like this may provide the key or the verification that we are on the right track with our ideas.

It's always a good idea to test your point against a few other Scriptures; the Bible will always confirm itself, somewhere.

Do you know of any other places where God used several steps to heal someone? How about Naaman dipping into the Jordan *seven* times! It's not as if God *can't* do it in less time, it's just that this is just the way he *wants* to do it.

I know another place where Jesus is doing something in steps like this. He is working now in children's hearts, teaching them the truth about him and making them learn who he is and what kinds of things he does. Of course right now they don't know everything he wants them to know; someday he wants them to "see clearly" and come to him for salvation. For now, all they can see are some fuzzy things about God. One day, however, he will touch them again and they will see him clearly; this is what has happened to us adults, and that is the stage we are in now. We are learning about him so that we can see him clearly, so that we can trust him for all the salvation that we need from day to day.

Now we wind up with application – not much on what to do, but on how Jesus is doing this same thing with us too. This is very important that they see that the story isn't just history but a guidebook to living with Jesus, a manual on the kinds of things he does.

Let's think back on these stories and try to see what we've done:

- *Know the context.* You must study the story first, and look around a little bit before you teach others about it. You can find so many clues that way! Plus, it prevents you from just jumping to some crazy conclusion based on a word or phrase. You may have to go far afield for the material that you need; in fact it isn't a bad idea to find passages from all over the Bible that may relate to what this passage teaches.

- *Create a problem.* What I mean is this: paint a live picture of somebody in *need*. Jesus only helps the needy, those who can't help themselves. What he has to offer is something that man can't do for himself. That's why he's such a treasure! So don't be too hasty to get to the climax of the story. Develop the problem in such a way that it's obvious that Jesus comes at just the right time with just what is needed. This impresses people. And this isn't being dishonest with the text – painting the picture, that is; because we're at a disadvantage being twenty centuries after the fact; we weren't there while the events unfolded. We need aids to our faith!

- *Show Jesus in action.* Set the situation up so that you can show his glory. Don't spend time on side issues in the story; paint the picture and then focus on Jesus – what he is, what he did, how he did something. Make sure that your point is clear: that nobody else is like him in this; he is very unique. In other words, make the point about Jesus so plain and so simple that the student will know what to ask of him when he has the same need.

• ***Bring it into our world.*** There are many ways of applying the point of a lesson, and they don't all have to be "Now you must do as they did, Johnny!" These applications focused on making the children feel that Jesus wants to come to them too. Hopefully the story was real enough to them that they will make the conclusion themselves: Jesus did it for those people, he is here with me now, so he will do the same thing for me too. You want to bring the children and Jesus together into the same spiritual world, not leave them in our world and Jesus way off in the next!

The Wider Scope

Jesus isn't only in the Gospels. You can find him all over the Old Testament, in many ways, as well as the very foundation and main subject of the New Testament Epistles. The Bible is, in a very real sense, his book.

The Gospels are the easiest place to see Jesus at work; that's why, for the most part, we have spent our time there. Children like to see action, and they relate well to stories, especially if you can paint a vivid picture for them. The Gospels, for that reason, are the best place to start to teach them about Christ. But we need the rest of the Bible to fill in some necessary details that the Gospels don't have. The apostles often didn't feel the need to go over the same material that the Old Testament already treated so well; they assumed that you and I would have done our homework on those issues and they just don't bring it up. So if we *haven't* done our homework, we will certainly get a wrong understanding of the Gospels! We're going to have holes in our interpretations, or possibly even heresy, that could have been avoided had we studied the Old Testament better.

There's a lot of depth in what the rest of the Bible has to say about Christ. The types, the Covenant, the sacrificial system that we read in the Old Testament teach us much foundational truth that the Gospel rests on. The Epistles – the books after the Gospels – go further and explore all the implications and "therefores" of the story about Christ. Can we use these things when we teach children about Jesus? Certainly, but with some wisdom. "Therefore every teacher of the law who has been instructed about the kingdom of Heaven is like the owner of a house who brings out of his storeroom new treasures as well as old." (Matthew 13:52)

The Gospel was in the Old Testament but it was veiled – the Jews didn't know that it was all pointing to Jesus. The Old Testament gives us the truth about salvation in Christ by using "shadows," or physical realities that point to the spiritual fulfillment in Jesus. The Jews themselves had a difficult time interpreting it; so a Christian teacher also has to use some wisdom in presenting a "veiled" Gospel to children. And the Gospel in the Epistles is deep water; the teacher must first give out the milk of the Gospel – the story of Jesus – and then move on to meat when the students are ready for it.

What we want to do now is just taste the possibilities of finding Christ in the rest of the Bible. These subjects are more comprehensive and complex (and therefore fruitful!) than we can do justice to here. You can go on, at your leisure, to explore these topics and find ways to incorporate them into your lessons on Christ.

The Old Testament – where is Christ?

Where is Christ in the Old Testament? According to his own testimony, the Old Testament did teach about him! "You diligently study the Scriptures because you think that by them you possess eternal life. These are the Scriptures that testify about me, yet you refuse to come to me to have life." (John 5:39-40) Jesus also said that the Old Testament saints knew about him: "Your father Abraham rejoiced at the thought of seeing my day; he saw it and was glad." (John 8:56)

Not only are there incidental items about Christ in the Old Testament, but the very foundation, the fabric that the stories are made from, deal with Christ – and someone can see this if he truly understands who Christ is. The Jews should have recognized their God when they watched Jesus work; this is because the God of the Old Testament did those very things that Jesus himself would again do when he came among them. It was the same God! Paul and the other writers of the Epistles saw Christ all through the Old Testament in its structure, its themes, its purposes – to them, you would have to be blind not to see the Lord in it from beginning to end.

There are obvious and not so obvious ways that Christ fills the Old Testament:

- ***The Covenant with Abraham.*** In Genesis 12, 15 and 17 God made a covenant with Abraham and all his seed. We have mentioned this before. We mustn't underestimate the importance of this Covenant for the Jews: it was their introduction to the *grace* of God, something that no man or race had ever seen before.

    The terms of the Covenant were these:

    God would give him a son.

    God would give him the land of Canaan.

    God would give him many descendants.

    God would make him a blessing to the nations.

Abraham, for his part, was to be circumcised and make sure that all his male descendents were circumcised. He also believed the Lord's promise (Genesis 15:6) – an important characteristic of God's Covenant people.

Now this Covenant was the glue that held God's people together. They later were delivered out of Egypt, they received the Law, they cleared the Canaanites out of Canaan, they built a temple to worship in, they had kings and ruled the land, they were deported and then returned home. The reason the Jews were unique, however, is that they had legal rights under this Covenant that their forefather Abraham received from God. The Covenant secured benefits for the Israelites that no other people on earth had the right to.

But to a discerning Jew, the physical fulfillment of the Abrahamic Covenant just wasn't very fulfilling in itself. It was nice to have a land of their own to call home, but what is a dusty piece of real estate, anyway, when one must die after threescore years and ten and give it up? Isaac was a miracle baby, it's true, but what benefit was he to the rest of the descendants of Abraham? Was it really a distinction to be known as a Jew? Millions of people could claim the title, but their hearts weren't like their father Abraham's heart; they were always going astray after false gods. And after centuries of disobedience and ignorance, the Jews weren't much of a blessing to the nations!

This is where the spiritual dimension of the Covenant kicks in. The discerning Jew was right: Palestine isn't the point. Isaac, in himself, wasn't much use to Israel. Only a few Jews were really like their father Abraham, and the Jewish nation was pretty much a spiritual failure. There had to be something more, something eternal, something worth staking one's soul upon.

But they could live only on the *physical* plane of this Covenant until the Messiah came. As it says in Hebrews, "They did not receive the things promised; they only saw them and welcomed them from a distance." (Hebrews 11:13) At this stage the grace of God was strictly by faith! Seeing a goat die for you will probably not do much for your conscience, if you know anything about your sin and the holiness of God! But they had the promise that the Covenant would keep them in God's favor until a more acceptable sacrifice would come along.

The reason the Abrahamic Covenant is so important to the Church is that Christ was the Seed that God made the covenant with – see Galatians 3:16. The Lord always did intend to draw the Gentiles into this Covenant, from the very beginning; he promised that Abraham would be a blessing to "all peoples on earth." (Genesis 12:3) So the Covenant with Abraham ties together the ancient Israelites and the modern Gentiles into one body, one family, under the same father Abraham. And they all have legal rights to the terms of the Covenant.

There are glimpses here and there that the Lord always did have a spiritual covenant in mind.

But will God really dwell on earth with men? The heavens, even the highest heavens, cannot contain you. How much less this temple I have built! (2 Chronicles 6:18)

You do not delight in sacrifice, or I would bring it; you do not take pleasure in burnt offerings. The sacrifices of God are a broken spirit; a broken and contrite heart, O God, you will not despise. (Psalm 51:16-17)

I will give you a new heart and put a new spirit in you; I will remove from you your heart of stone and give you a heart of flesh. (Ezekiel 36:26)

In other words, we should be looking for hints that the land is a picture of *Heaven*; that the son of promise is the *Son of God*; that the many descendants are the *Church*; and that the blessing to the nations is *eternal life* in the Kingdom of God.

Even the part that man plays in the covenant has always been the same: **faith**. Faith has always been the key that opens up the treasures of Heaven, both to Abraham and to modern believers. God responds to that same kind of faith no matter who has it, no matter what age they live in; Abraham got righteousness when he believed and so do we.

So the Covenant to Abraham was the first and critical step to building the kingdom of God; it forms the all-important foundation for everything that God intended to do for the Jews first and then the Gentiles. And of course all this is fulfilled in Jesus, the Seed of the Promise.

• **_The Sacrificial System._** From the sacrifice of Isaac to the ceremonies of the Temple, the Old Testament teaches that sin must be dealt with through the sacrifice of an innocent victim. It seems that our religion is too bloody to suit many "sensitive" people of our day. Unfortunately, *somebody* must die for sin – if it will not be the substitute that God provides, then it must be the sinner himself! Nothing has changed as far as that goes, from the days of the Old Testament till now. Judgment Day will be a fearful time for those "sensitive" people. What do they plan to do about *their* sin?

Everything in the Old Testament sacrificial system shows a God of mercy at work, the same God who would one day send the perfect Sacrifice for man's sin. The types of animals that one could offer, the ways that the sacrifices were made, the Tabernacle (and later the Temple) and how they were to build it and what they were to put in it – all this has profound spiritual significance that we can now see in New Testament times. The discerning Jew may have been able to see what God was getting at in demanding such exacting details; the Spirit often opened up someone's eyes to see the spiritual meaning in this ritual.

There's a fascinating passage in Exodus that lets us in on a secret about the staggering importance of the physical ceremonies of the Temple:

> Then the LORD said to Moses, "See, I have chosen Bezalel son of Uri, the son of Hur, of the tribe of Judah, and I have filled him with the Spirit of God, with skill, ability and knowledge in all kinds of crafts." (Exodus 31:1-3)

> So Bezalel, Oholiab and every skilled person to whom the LORD has given skill and ability to know how to carry out all the work of constructing the sanctuary are to do the work just as the LORD has commanded. (Exodus 36:1)

At first glance this looks as if they were simply given wisdom to do a good job. But Hebrews tells us differently:

> They serve at a sanctuary that is a copy and shadow of what is in Heaven. This is why Moses was warned when he was about to build the tabernacle: "See to it that you make everything according to the pattern shown you on the mountain." (Hebrews 8:5)

In other words, the physical Temple of the Old Testament looks like (in a way that a physical object *can* look like a Heavenly one) its original pattern in Heaven – the Heavenly Temple. You might say that the Temple was God's mission church on earth! The work of Christ, that we are so familiar with, was shown to the Temple architects; and they faithfully built it into the earthly copy. This means that the Jews were getting a foretaste of God's eternal plan of redemption, whether they had the eyes to see it or not. Since we know now what the Heavenly Tabernacle looks like, we can go back to the Old Testament and find the corresponding parts.

• ***Grace and Law.*** One thing that many people don't realize about the Old Testament is that God based everything he did for the Jews on grace, not Law. Grace always came first. He had mercy on Abraham and led him to Canaan in order to make a Covenant with him; *then* he laid the law down with him. He rescued the Israelites out of Egypt and made them a nation and his own people; *then* he brought them to Sinai. He gave them a system of sacrifice for forgiveness of their sins; *then* he laid down the rules of the kingdom. He repeatedly pleaded with the Israelites through the prophets to repent and return to him, and promised to forget what they did against him; he could have simply brought down his fist of judgment at the first sign of sin and been entirely justified in doing so!

God showed himself from the very beginning to be a God of mercy. "I will have mercy on whom I will have mercy, and I will have compassion on whom I will have compassion." (Exodus 33:19) "But in your great mercy you did not put an end to them, or abandon them, for you are a gracious and merciful God." (Nehemiah 9:31) And my favorite passage in the Old Testament, the definition of the very Name of Yahweh:

> The LORD, the LORD, the compassionate and gracious God, slow to anger, abounding in love and faithfulness, maintaining love to thousands, and forgiving wickedness, rebellion and sin. (Exodus 34:6-7)

Doesn't this look like the Christ that we know? The Jews could depend on his mercy and grace; they could go to him in repentance and expect his forgiveness. He made it plain to them in many ways that he wanted them to believe this about him! You remember how David put his life in God's hands one time, after committing two sins for which the Law demanded his death, and waited on God for forgiveness. (Psalm 51) Nobody can say that the God of the Old Testament was hard and unforgiving!

The Law, on the other hand, was a real thing that the Lord expected the Israelites to take seriously. It was *not* the basis of their relationship with God, however, contrary to popular belief. The Covenant with Abraham was the basis of the relationship. They were God's people not because of the Law but because of the Promise. The Law was a "schoolmaster" (Galatians 3:23-24) designed to keep the Jews outwardly in line until the Messiah would come and put the Law in their hearts, enabling them to please God from the heart – which the outward Law was never able to do. If nothing else, the purpose of the Law was to show them what Christ's righteousness would look like! And what ours will look like when we live by the Spirit. (See Romans 8 on this.)

• *__The History of the Jews.__* Even the very history of the Jewish nation is a lesson on Christ. They were a small people, a nobody among the nations of the world. (Jesus was a carpenter's son, born in a stable.) God made a Covenant with them alone, a special relationship that was exclusive – only the children of Abraham could claim legal rights under the agreement. (Jesus was God's own Son, sole heir of God's throne and inheritance.) They were taken into Egypt for protection, and then brought out again. (Jesus went to Egypt to escape Herod and then came back to Nazareth.) David set up the model kingdom and launched Israel as a force to be reckoned with among the nations. (Jesus came, as King of the Jews, announcing the arrival of the Kingdom of God.) They were taken into exile. (Jesus was persecuted and put to death.) The remnant was brought back and the Lord restored them to the land. (Jesus was raised from the dead and brought into Heaven.)

• ***Prophets and Prophecy.*** We know of course that Jesus' ministry was prophesied many times in the Old Testament. But what we may not be aware of is the role of prophecy itself. Prophecy is the announcement of the coming Kingdom of God. The prophets confronted men with the message of doom to the kingdoms of the world, and the eventual peace and righteousness that God intends to set up in their place. It was a confrontation between God and man (through a servant) in which God's power was often made plain through signs and wonders, and man's heart was uncovered through the discerning work of the Spirit.

The first prophet was Enoch, which we learn from the book of Jude:

> Enoch, the seventh from Adam, prophesied about these men: "See, the Lord is coming with thousands upon thousands of his holy ones to judge everyone, and to convict all the ungodly of all the ungodly acts they have done in the ungodly way, and of all the harsh words ungodly sinners have spoken against him." (Jude 14-15)

Notice the elements of prophecy: **first**, an announcement of God's opinion of their moral character. He was putting it in their face, so to speak, so that they had no mistake of what he thought of them. He used words calculated to uncover the nature of their acts; we are too prone to call sin by any other name so that we won't look so bad! **Second**, an announcement of what the Lord intended to do about it. This is where the prophets often got into future events. Their kind of "fortune telling," however, differs from astrologists in this way: the future that they predicted is what God intends to do on earth, in person! If they would listen and repent, it will go well with them when the King arrives.

The reason I'm calling prophecy "Christ in the Old Testament" is that the New Testament calls him the *Word of God among us*; when he came, this is exactly what he did with people. He put the truth of God under their noses so that they would not mistake his meaning. They knew they were facing Jehovah because of the powerful stinging in the words, the conscience-wringing effect that it had on them. The Old Testament prophets were operating under the power of the Spirit of Christ, that same Spirit that would one day pierce the hearts of the Jews in a profound way:

> And I will pour out on the house of David and the inhabitants of Jerusalem a spirit of grace and supplication. They will look on me, the one they have pierced, and mourn for him as one mourns for an only child, and grieve for him as one grieves for a firstborn son. (Zechariah 12:10)

The greatest prophet in Israel's history wasn't Isaiah or Jeremiah – it was Moses! In bringing the revelation of Yahweh to Israel, then by frustrating Pharaoh and leading the Israelites out of Egypt under the hand of God Almighty, then by bringing the Law to them in all its entirety, and setting up the new nation Israel with God as their King, then by leading them through the desert to the Promised Land, he certainly put the Word of the Lord before them in powerful ways.

> Since then no prophet has risen in Israel like Moses, whom the Lord knew face to face, who did all those miraculous signs and wonders the Lord sent him to do in Egypt – to Pharaoh and to all his officials and to his whole land. For no one has ever shown the mighty power or performed the awesome deeds that Moses did in the sight of all Israel. (Deuteronomy 34:10-12)

Study carefully, however, this special prophet. The way he did things, the things he said, and the results are all characteristic of a Prophet yet to come:

> The Lord your God will raise up for you a Prophet like me from among your own brothers. You must listen to him. (Deuteronomy 18:15)

So Moses is the model prophet; what he did and said would be a pattern that all the other prophets of Israel would follow. And Jesus is a prophet "like Moses." The whole subject ties together.

- ***The Types.*** A "type," as we've seen already, is a picture in physical form of a spiritual reality in Heaven. Types can be in all forms and kinds, either human or animal or plant or historical event.

The point of a type is to teach the observer something of what Christ is, or something about Christ's kingdom. Take Joseph for an example. To the observant Jew, the story of Joseph has so many details of the way that God wants to rescue his people from disaster that he could have learned a lot about Christ long before the event! Childhood prophecies told of Joseph's eventual success; Joseph was sold into slavery by his brothers; he was held in prison for crimes he didn't commit; he was put second in command over all the land and from that position of power was able to save his family from starvation and death. Was this only for the sake of Jacob and his family? Did all that happen simply to get Israel a good start in the world? Many Jews think so! They don't see the spiritual significance behind it all, that this is the same way God intends to save his people from sin – the real enemy – and the kind of kingdom he intends to establish – Christ ruling at God's right hand.

Now one can get carried away with types; some have unfortunately seen types where there aren't any! There are many stories in the Old Testament that stand well enough on their own without having to find a typical meaning in them. The student must walk carefully when dealing with a potential type: is there a direct correlation between the details of the type and the truth in Jesus? Are there any details that would justly speak against it being a type of Christ? Are there other passages in the Bible that agree that this is the correct interpretation?

Once you have a genuine type in hand, however, you can use it for what it was intended: to learn the truth about Christ, in the *way* God wants you to look at it. The New Testament writers certainly relied on types to understand the mystery of Christ! Otherwise the confusing appearances of this humble carpenter's son in his short and seemingly unsuccessful career would have prevented them from understanding him, just as the Pharisees were confused about him. Types push the envelope, so to speak, out beyond the local events of the Gospels into the wider realm of God's eternal kingdom.

The New Testament – how do they see Christ?

The rest of the New Testament is like a shocked and excited afterthought of the atomic blast that we saw in the Gospels. Jesus' earthly ministry was short but effective; he did everything he came to do and then suddenly left in a hurry! In the excitement of the moment, the disciples wondered if he had left in *too* much of a hurry. It wasn't until after Pentecost that they discovered the rich supply that he left them through the Spirit, and the careful foundation that he laid down for them to build on. From that point on they could carry the Gospel out to the "uttermost ends of the earth" full of confidence that Jesus *had* done his foundation work very well.

The letters of the New Testament are really a careful look at the event of Christ – looking at it from all angles, getting the most profit from what happened, a slow but sure analysis of what God had done for us in that most important event in history. For this reason, it's the second step for anybody who wants to learn about Christ. The Gospels are the first stop for the traveler in God's kingdom to see, and the Epistles are the second stop.

The Epistles do at least four very important things for us:

- ***They draw conclusions.*** These apostolic letters are so full of spiritual applications from the Gospels that it would be impossible to list them all here. The writers were grappling with the impact of Jesus' message and work on the life of the believer; they continually saw new ways that faith and obedience could take advantage of these new spiritual treasures from God's throne.

    You will notice that the applications for life that they drew are usually in the second part of their letters; the first part is a doctrinal discussion of the truth in Jesus. Let's take Ephesians for an example. The first three chapters (roughly half the book) are a spiritual feast of facts about the Lord Jesus! Perhaps you didn't see these things in Christ when you read the Gospels; Paul did, and he is helping you see them here. He discusses our redemption planned from the beginning of the world, being made alive in Christ, Christ uniting Jew and Gentile in himself, and the mystery of Christ that Paul has been able to understand and preach. What would we do without the apostle's insight into these truths of Christ?

Then, in the last three chapters, he starts drawing conclusions from these doctrines – something that I wish modern preachers were better at doing! The application to life comes *after* doctrine; it's *based* on truth, not the other way around! He talks about everyone in the united Church doing their part to build up the body, living as befits children of light, taking one's personal duties toward others seriously, and finally protecting ourselves with the armor of God. *These applications* are what you should be getting from the Gospel of Christ. Because Jesus is what he is and did what he did, that means that you should be living like *this*. Paul, fortunately, draws our conclusions for us so that he makes sure we will get it right. Notice how often he uses the word "therefore!" Certain Christian duties must and will come from certain doctrines of Christ.

• ***They open the Gospel to the Gentiles.*** If we only had the Gospels to go on, we Gentiles might be a little worried about our right to partake of the salvation in Jesus. There isn't much there to base our case upon! In fact, Jesus seemed to be a bit reluctant at times to even have anything to do with the Gentiles. This is why the Epistles are so crucial for the life of the Church: they open the door wide to all nations and all peoples, and on the authority of Christ himself offer the Gospel to any who will come. (John 6:37)

There are several places where the letters of the apostles particularly focus on opening the doors of the Church to the Gentiles. **First**, of course, the book of Acts gives us the precedent and the strongest case, particularly the story of the conversion of Cornelius (and the Lord's command to Peter that he go to the Gentiles with the Gospel) in Acts 10-11; and most important the job given to Paul to be the apostle to the Gentiles. (Romans 11:13)

Second, Paul discusses it at length in several places, including Romans 4 and Ephesians 2. He based the whole thing on the work of Christ – that is, he claims that Jesus himself was responsible for bringing the Gentiles into God's Church (which the Jewish Christians, until then, had always considered their own domain!) and had intended that all along. In other words, it wasn't a modern invention on Paul's part to boost flagging membership rolls! Christ was behind the sudden burst of activity of the Gospel among the non-Jewish nations.

This is more important than you may realize. You may think that it was appropriate for God to be nice to us – he was simply doing what was fair to everyone; as if limiting the Gospel to the Jews wouldn't have been fair to the rest of us. If so, you underestimate the power of the Covenant! That contract with

Abraham was a legal agreement that God *swore* he would keep – the penalty for breaking it was the same treatment that the animals received: cut down the middle with a sword! (Genesis 15:7-21) Of course God can't be cut with a sword; the point is that he fully intended to keep his side of the bargain. That means that *only* the descendants of Abraham had a right to the promises in the Covenant, and God's honor and very glory were at stake. He can't just indiscriminately give out spiritual presents to willy-nilly anybody! They must prove their ancestry back to Abraham or they will get nothing.

Now, with that in mind, go back to the Epistles and see if you can follow their argument on *how* a Gentile can claim the inheritance in the Covenant – the blessings that God put in Christ.

• ***They describe the new Church.*** Jesus did more preparation in his short ministry than we often give him credit for. He laid the foundation for the Church, a spiritual building that the rest of us would be a part of for all of eternity. The apostles take time to study that foundation and lay the living stones (us) into a house that God would be pleased to live in.

A foundation is perhaps the most important part of any building. It has to be strong and well-laid in the ground, because there's going to be a lot of weight resting down on it and it can't let the building sink into the ground and collapse. It has to be made of a strong material and not crumble under the massive weight of the walls and roof. It has to be laid straight in the ground, or the walls will be crooked and weak. I wish we had time to explore how Jesus is all this to his Church!

What the Epistles do is describe the Church that the Lord is building on this firm foundation. This is, we find out, perhaps the most important work that Jesus is doing among us right now. He always did want a *people* that was united in him, and one with him. He wants us to have his characteristics; he wants us to have his mind on things; he wants us to love him and others as he loved us. The apostles simply describe that work that the Lord Jesus is doing among us! Instead of keeping us in the dark and springing the news on us when we get to Heaven, the Lord includes us in the building planning committee, so to speak, and shows us the way he intends to build us up and what it will look like in the end.

- **_They tie it all back to the Old Testament._** When a Christian reads the Old Testament he may get a bit confused about what's going on. After all, the Jews are still confused about its real meaning after reading and studying it for the last 4000 years! Even though we have the Spirit of enlightenment, can we hope to do better than the "People of the Book" themselves?

This is where the Epistles are invaluable. The apostles studied the Old Testament thoroughly; don't forget that the Old Testament was the only Bible they had! Since they knew the truth about Jesus so well, and were trained by the Master himself, and the Spirit helped them understand Jesus in light of the Old Testament, they were eminently qualified to teach us how to tie the New and the Old together.

Some of the more important discussions are these: the definition of a real Jew (Romans 2); the importance of the Covenant with Abraham (Romans 4); what God is doing with the Jews now (Romans 9-11); the relationship of a Christian with the Law (Galatians); the new Covenant compared to the Law covenant (Hebrews); the work of the prophets (2 Peter 1); and the present decadence as prophesied by the Old Testament (Jude).

You must follow their leading. They know how to interpret the Old Testament so that you won't be pitting the Old against the New – the Lord never intended for anybody to use the Gospel to put down the Law, or to lift up Christ and ignore the foundation that Christ's work rests upon in Abraham and Moses and the Prophets. This kind of poor scholarship only shows how little we know about the real meaning of the Old Testament. Sit at the feet of the apostles who were trained by Jesus himself, and learn from them what to use and how to use the truths in the Old Testament.

The Church – how is Christ working?

It's too bad that often adults send mixed signals to children when it comes to the Church. When we talk about the Old Testament or the Epistles it's easy to stay in the world of theory, talking about this angle or that angle without ever putting shoes on what we believe. But in the Church we can't help but live out our beliefs; we do and say there what we *think* our God has called us to do and say. But, as is typical of our real-life applications of spiritual truths, they are usually impure and inconsistent at best. Which means that what the children see when they are at church may not be what they read about the Church in the Bible.

Church ought to be a powerful witness to the presence and wisdom of Christ. This is where the Lord meets with his people, to accomplish his will on earth, to get glory to himself by our worship and obedience. It should be an object lesson of the truths of the Gospel that children can't mistake. Whether it is or not depends, I believe, on whether we adults are being "like little children" as the Lord told us to be. Too often we let our adult sense of "what is reasonable" or "what is workable" get in the way of the Lord's work; or we let petty issues divide us; or we refuse to obey the Lord's command and do things his way. The result is that we teach our children more about how *not* to do church! For proof, witness the poor showing of our children when they grow up and refuse to become involved in church themselves – they evidently get their fill of it in early years!

But if we can get past these stumbling blocks (a miracle in itself!) we have a tremendous opportunity to show them what's possible when God lives on earth among his people; this Christianity business really does work.

Children will see, when we adults take care to follow the Lord's instructions about church ourselves, these things:

- ***Jesus is the Head.*** "And he is the head of the body, the Church; he is the beginning and the firstborn from among the dead, so that in everything he might have the supremacy." (Colossians 1:18) It isn't difficult to see, in a local church, who is running things. The Lord *should* be running things! Every church is his church, his special work, his responsibility; and he will not share the glory or the duties with anybody else. We all have our jobs to do, but we should never do his work – which is the direction and authority of the church overall.

  We can get a glimpse of how he feels about this issue when we consider a wife/husband relationship. The husband, the Scripture says, is the head of the wife. (Ephesians 5:23) He does *not* want someone else telling his wife what to do! Just try it once and you will find out what "angry" means! He reserves complete rights to deal with his wife; he loves her, and they have a special way of communicating with each other that you are not part of. Don't get in the middle of their relationship!

  In the same way, "the husband is the head of the wife as Christ is the head of the Church, his body, of which he is the Savior." (Ephesians 5:23) It is *not* the pastor's duty, or a teacher's duty, or anybody else's to interfere with Christ's bride! He's even more jealous over his special people than a husband over his wife. The one who preaches is to say only what the Lord told him to say *and no more.* The one who oversees the funds is to do exactly what the Lord told him to do with the money and no more – and no less! They do *not* have the right to make their own decisions and do what they think best when the Lord made their duty to him plain. Such a thing is getting in the middle of Christ and his people; beware the husband's wrath!

When people in a Church take the Lord's authority seriously, things work out so well! He knows exactly what he's doing; he tells us to do something at the right moment because he can see "the end from the beginning." Like a general who stands on the highest hill to see the entire battle, he stands over the Church to best command it and bring it to victory. He expects strict and careful obedience to his orders or we are going to be responsible for ruining the outcome of the battle! Church officers and workers end up helping everyone when they get their orders from Jesus alone.

Another mark that Christ is the head of a local church is that nobody is taking the glory for things. Glory, as we've seen already, is *who gets the credit.* When people praise the pastor, the pastor is getting the credit – not the Lord. Somehow that pastor is doing something to direct all eyes to himself. But when people are amazed at what the *Lord* is doing among them (**key:** he does what man *cannot* do – that's a sure sign that he's the one at work) then man doesn't get the credit, the Lord does, which is the way it should be. Children aren't fooled; they can see when someone struts his stuff in front of everyone and acts big. They know other kids who do the same thing! What they need to see is adults shaking their heads in wonder and saying, "This is the hand of God among us! There's no other explanation!" That's an opportunity for the children to learn what it is that Christ does in the Church.

Another way that Christ becomes easy to see in the Church is when people seek his counsel on things. Church is probably the fiercest battle ground of men's opinions in the entire world. It's so ironic that Jesus said that the world would know us for our love for each other; it's often the opposite that's true – all because of our opinionated wars and divisions, and not being able to agree on the truth. The whole thing is easy to solve when we admit to ourselves that we are not the last word on what truth is – Jesus is. When adults start admitting that they don't know everything, that their views are limited, that it takes more than one person to come to the mind of the Lord on any matter, then the logjam will break and love will start flowing again. They will turn to the only one who does know the truth. They will learn to be patient as the Lord gives us *what* we need to know, *when* we need to know it. They will get along with those who know less (or more!) because they are God's people after all. Everyone starts having the same gentle attitude that Paul had: "All of us who are mature should take such a view of things. And if on some point you think differently, that too God will make clear to you." (Philippians 3:15) Children, when they see this, learn that they need to go to Christ for wisdom when they need the truth.

This is related to another sign in the Church of Christ's presence: when *everyone*, not just children, learn from Jesus. This is perhaps an adult's biggest failure in the church. There's simply an enormous amount to learn about Christ and the kingdom of God, and it has so much to do with our lives and pleasing God; and here we are sipping little drops from sermons (*when* we can remember what was said!) and doing no more. What children see is that when someone finally becomes an adult then they don't have to study the Bible any more! Everyone can have an *opinion*, but evidently nobody is under any obligation to find out what the *facts* are!

The Lord wants us to study, however – *all* of us. Study means digging, spending time in his Word, sharing notes with others and gaining from their insights. It means going back to school (a dreaded thought to most of us!) because there's so much to learn from Jesus. The writer of Hebrews rebuked his readers for stalling, for being slow to learn:

> We have much to say about this, but it is hard to explain because you are slow to learn. In fact, though by this time you ought to be teachers, you need someone to teach you the elementary truths of

God's word all over again. You need
milk, not solid food! (Hebrews 5:11-12)

That's our generation. The valuable things
that the writer has to say about Christ and faith
in him, further on in the letter, depend on us
being learned enough to handle it; so,
unfortunately, most people never get the point.
It's a rare saint who is still in the learning mode
(and therefore the *growing* mode). Children
need to follow *his* example, not the ones who
lay back on their conversion experience and do
little more than attend church services.

• ***Jesus gives gifts to his people.*** The Lord
has special work to do in his Church and he
can't afford to let unskilled workmen mess it
up. So he gives them gifts – spiritual gifts –
that enable them to do spiritual work with
spiritual results. He's not an irresponsible
King! He will make sure that the supplies are
in place, that we have the skill we need, and
the opportunities are there to bring about God's
Kingdom. He wants to see results! And those
results have to measure up to the demands of
eternity.

A "spiritual gift" is the supernatural ability
to do work *in the Kingdom of God*. That last
phrase is the difference between a spiritual gift
and a natural talent. A teacher, we say, has
natural talent when he's successful at getting
knowledge to stick in his students' heads. But
that doesn't necessarily do anything for the
Kingdom! Jesus needs eternal results, things
that accomplish what he needs to do among us.

He needs to save us; so someone has the gift of evangelism and people are saved under his preaching. Jesus needs to convince us of Heaven's treasures; so someone has the gift of teaching so that his students get the faith to see that those treasures are real.

The Spirit's two main jobs are these: to **enlighten** (which means to reveal to us what's really there) and to **empower** (which means to give us the ability to do something). When someone exercises a spiritual gift, therefore, the results of his work bring Jesus plainly to the eyes of those he works with; and they are suddenly able to believe and take hold of the things of God. Spiritual results happen, in other words.

We wouldn't want the Church to be any other way, would we? Isn't this the place where God lives? Shouldn't things be happening here that simply don't happen anywhere else? Wouldn't it be nice if, at the end of the year, we would take inventory of the Church's work and find that much spiritual results came about from the ministry of the Church? This would be so much more meaningful for the purpose of the church than a financial report!

Children need to see this too. They won't be satisfied with a materialistic church, or a church that fails spiritually. When they grow up they will remember boring sermons, proud leaders, disinterested members, financial squabbles, political brawls – but no spiritual work. They won't be very interested in going to church themselves if that's all there is to show for it! They *will* remember, however, if a church changed lives and sowed peace and love among enemies and attracted the sick and helpless with its message of healing and salvation. When it comes time for their turn to be healed, they will turn with confidence to God's appointed means for bringing about those kinds of miracles.

• ***Jesus is among them.*** Paul once remarked that unbelievers should be impressed with our church services that something strange and unexplainable is going on:

> But if an unbeliever or someone who does not understand comes in while everybody is prophesying, he will be convinced by all that he is a sinner and will be judged by all, and the secrets of his heart will be laid bare. So he will fall down and worship God, exclaiming, "God is really among you!"
> (1 Corinthians 14:24-25)

Does this happen in our churches? Some people may respond that this isn't a fair question! That was the apostolic church, and Paul was talking about tongues and prophesying and other supernatural events that don't happen nowadays. But I answer that *wherever the Lord is, unexplainable things happen.* If we are really satisfied with a God who can't do any more than we can, and who can't overcome man's problems any better than the government can, then we deserve the dead church that we have.

But a church in which God is present is an exciting, dynamic church that is always getting spiritual results. Jesus once made a serious promise about this:

> For where two or three come together in my name, there am I with them. (Matthew 18:20)

This accounts for why people fear God in a church, why people take time to study his Word, why people put aside things that hurt and divide, and work at loving each other. There's no other explanation than the fact that the Lord himself is there and they know he's watching them.

It's not an imaginary thing when God visits his people. There's something in the air, something that moves the heart, that can't be explained by psychology or philosophy. God gives joy to his people; he brings tears of repentance or happiness; he motivates people to do things that they wouldn't otherwise spend time with. You will find that the children will believe that God is there, even if they themselves don't sense his presence, and they will accept the testimonies of those who feel the hand of God in their lives. As far as they are concerned, such things are very possible!

- *__We are built up in him.__* Paul describes what must inevitably happen in a local church when Christ works there:

> It was he who gave some to be apostles, some to be prophets, some to be evangelists, and some to be pastors and teachers, to prepare God's people for works of service, so that the body of Christ may be built up until we all reach unity in the faith and in the knowledge of the Son of God and become mature, attaining to the whole measure of the fullness of Christ. (Ephesians 4:11)

The church should be growing together, not apart. The family of God takes precedence over blood relationships. There should be hurts being healed, hatred turning to love, personal funds going to the relief of those in need, teaching the young, taking care of the elderly, and many other ways that the Church shows how unified it really is. It should be easy to see that people feel at ease among each other, that they prefer each other's company – in Church or away from it – to anybody else's.

What usually happens, however, is that everyone is fighting one another! We don't trust others, we don't give anything to anybody, we don't want to help each other, we look down on each other – when we have feelings like these, "church" is just a word we stick on an unpleasant social function that we feel we *have* to go to!

Jesus went through a lot to make us one in him. This was always an important aspect of his work, and he won't be satisfied until we are one. "I pray also for those who will believe in me through their message, that all of them may be one, Father, just as you are in me and I am in you." (John 17:20-21) And Paul pleads in a similar way with the Church:

> If you have any encouragement from being united with Christ, if any comfort from his love, if any fellowship with the Spirit, if any tenderness and compassion, then make my joy complete by being like-minded, having the same love, being one in spirit and purpose. Do nothing out of selfish ambition or vain conceit, but in humility consider others better than yourselves. Each of you should look not only to your own interests, but also to the interests of others. (Philippians 2:1-4)

If people would do this, they would find themselves in a unique society that you can't find anywhere else on earth. Good things happen in a church like this. The Spirit pours out all over them, like the oil over Aaron's head. (Psalm 133) Light dawns, life quickens, and what used to be a lot of cranky individuals becomes one fighting force against which the gates of Hell cannot prevail. Do your part to make a church like this, and you will have a precious legacy for your children.

Section Four:

Results

When you teach children you will get further if you are careful of *how* you go about it. And you need to know the signs that show you are getting through: they aren't necessarily the same signs that you see in adults.

Teaching Children: Results

Sometimes we wonder if anything is going on inside those little heads. They listen, they answer questions, they seem eager to participate in the story, but then they run off after the lesson and act as if nothing ever happened. We are used to the predictable praises from adults: "That was a wonderful sermon, pastor" or "You have such a gift of teaching." Children, however, *never* praise you for your efforts. If you are gauging your teaching performance on the response you get back, you will always be in the dark with children. It just never occurs to them to give you any glory.

That's wonderful, isn't it? Perhaps this is part of what Jesus meant when he counseled us adults to become as little children; instead of praising each other, we need to praise God instead who is the giver of all good things. Although we need to encourage each other and show our appreciation for each other, what we need to do first is give credit where credit is due. If we see the truth about God while someone is teaching, it was God who impressed us and touched our heart: "Blessed are you, Simon son of Jonah, for this was not revealed to you by man, but by my Father in Heaven." (Matthew 16:17) We have to respond to God first, in faith and obedience and love; then we can respond to others through our testimony.

We're actually after the *same thing* with children that we are with adults. Our goal is that they might "believe that he [*God*] exists and that he rewards those who earnestly seek him." (Hebrews 11:6) This is the whole point in teaching the Bible to anybody! What children do with that knowledge will be different from what adults do with it, of course; some things haven't turned on their minds yet that adults struggle with, and their important matters of life seem childish to us and unimportant. But I can't think of anything else I want them to be impressed with from my teaching besides the existence and fear of God. If they have that, they have it all. What more they might learn as adults will only enforce and build on that.

If that's our goal, then we need to think about how to reach it. There are ways to get appropriate results with children. And we need to know what those results are, because how they respond will look different from the way adults respond to us.

How to get results

Jesus gave us some wise counsel once:

Suppose one of you wants to build a tower. Will he not first sit down and estimate the cost to see if he has enough money to complete it? (Luke 14:28)

Although teachers will usually make plans about an individual lesson (on the day before!) they rarely set long-range goals. But the purpose of making goals is so that we can see better how to proceed. If you are taking a trip to a particular city, you will start by buying a map. Then you can see what roads will take you there, what resources are along the way, perhaps the sightseeing that you can do, and then decide which is the best route. Teaching is supposed to be the same way! If you have already decided that you want the children to believe that there is a God, and that he rewards those who earnestly seek him, then you have to make some decisions on how to get that result.

There are several ways to reach our objective when we teach children:

- *__Memorization.__* This is a well-known and age-old approach in teaching children. They memorize things so easily anyway! They can and do memorize entire chapters of Scripture, while adults struggle to remember the words in a single verse. Remember, they are in learning mode – their minds are like sponges at this age. What we want to do is take advantage of that and put the right things in front of them to learn, instead of letting the world do it with their garbage.

  The human brain is a remarkable creation; it can store billions of pieces of data away during your life and never forget a thing. We find out how true that is when events come back to us that we experienced years ago, things that we hadn't thought about since the day they happened. Little things can trigger a memory and we relive the event again in our minds.

  This is the kind of thing we want to do with the Bible – store away as much as we can, as well as we can, so that when something in their adult lives triggers the memory they will bring back old truths they learned as children. The words will come back in order, without any effort, as a welcome fresh breeze amidst the trials they may be going through. When we need help we often don't have time to study, and we don't know where to go for help; those old Scriptures that we learned while we were young will become precious to us then.

So what we want to do is get the Bible into their heads now while we have the opportunity. But let's approach it with some wisdom: let's ask some important questions first. *What* will they need in daily trials? What is it that will give them hope and comfort? What do we want to teach them now that will be the best help possible? We don't want to fill their brains with facts that, however interesting, won't save them in their need! We have to narrow our focus to Christ:

> **CHRIST'S WORDS** – As Peter once testified, "You have the words of eternal life." (John 6:68) "No one ever spoke the way this man does." (John 7:46) Whatever Christ said enlightens any subject; he sees what is there and can tell us the truth about anything. His counsel is perfect; follow it and you will never go astray. You have to be careful with the words of any other man; you just don't know whether it's right or not until you check with God's Word first. But you can accept Christ's words immediately as the full revelation of God's truth.

So it's critical that you get the words of Life into children's heads. Have them memorize his teachings, his sayings, his responses to people, his insights, his rebukes, his peculiar phrasings and favorite words, his descriptions of things. Paul said that a Christian has "the mind of Christ" (1 Corinthians 2:16), which means we know what Christ thinks and says about things. Children should be so familiar with Christ's own words that they would know, in any circumstance, what Christ would say if he were there.

His words are the truth; he wasn't just reciting something he had read from someone else. Jesus spoke what he knew, what he saw, and he spoke accurately about it. If you teach those very words to the children they will be wiser than all the philosophers and teachers throughout history, who have never had and still don't have a clue as to the real meaning of life.

CHRIST'S CHARACTER – To give someone hope for forgiveness and eternal life, we need to see the greatness of the salvation that God has given us. Focus on Scriptures that show how righteous Jesus is, how wise he is, how powerful he is, how loving and caring he is, how thoroughly upset he is with sin and pride and hypocrisy. Find the verses that paint a picture of what kind of person Jesus was; that's the Jesus they will need in the future.

Probably the biggest problem that people have with God in general is that they don't know who he is. They think he winks at sin; they think he won't accept sinners and forgive them; they think he has little to do with men's affairs; they think he has the same values that they do. If children can learn the truth about God from the beginning, however, by watching Christ in action (remember that he said that "anyone who has seen me has seen the Father" – John 14:9) they can see for themselves what God is really like; if they don't like that, of course, that is a problem – but at least they have seen the truth!

CHRIST'S WORKS – There are two things they need to know about Christ's works: what he does, and how he does it. It's important to know what Christ does because of the confusion that so many people have about why he even came into this world. You need to show them and drill them on the miracles he performed, the subjects he spoke about, the places he went, the things he did in his "free" time, the kinds of people he surrounded himself with and spent his time with, and all the other things he did. Every event in Christ's life means something to someone; there will be a day when that child (then an adult) will wonder whether Christ can do a particular thing for him – and like the leper who came to him for healing (Matthew 8:1-4), he will *know* he can, because you taught it to him.

WHO NEEDS CHRIST – Work on who Jesus helped and what their problems were. We

like to identify with someone when we read
stories – we are like this person in this way,
and not like that person in that way, and so
on. The Gospels are specially designed to
pull us into the story and show us how
human these people were; they had the
same weaknesses and sins and needs that
we have. Make the different characters and
their needs familiar to the children. Songs
often do this in a helpful way; you can
think of other methods to make the
characters come to life for them.

The important thing is to drill them on
the kinds of needs that people came to
Christ with. But first you have to make it
plain to them the precise need! Not
everyone who followed Christ for bread got
it from him. "I tell you the truth, you are
looking for me, not because you saw
miraculous signs but because you ate the
loaves and had your fill." (John 6:26) And
others who needed something badly
couldn't bring themselves to admit it to
him. After you describe the real needs that
people have, make them familiar with the
stories of how those people came to Jesus
and how the needs were taken care of.
Seeing that happen is a strong testimony,
not only to children but also to adults, that
Jesus does in fact take care of the kinds of
things that we also need.

- ***How to come to him.*** If you want the
children to get the point of your lessons and
take advantage of what God has to offer us in

Christ, then you *must* show them how to come to Jesus. Maybe you don't realize what a difficult thing that is to many people! When the trial of fire comes in someone's life, they often don't know how to pray or what to believe or whether God will even be inclined to help them. What use is a treasure box if you don't know how to get it open? What use is a God if you don't know how to approach him?

The other side of that coin is that God requires someone who wants anything from him to approach him in the *right way*. You can't just do whatever you like! The Lord is big on ceremony; the Old Testament and the New Testament both teach about the proper and improper ways of approaching God. People get results with God when they are aware of and use the right methods with him.

So you must show the children how they have to come to Jesus. Show them how people approached Jesus in his day; analyze the story and find out why their prayers worked. Look at the kinds of words and attitudes that Jesus responded to, and what turned him off about people. He did give us an example, you know, of how to pray if you want answers. (Matthew 6:9-15) The story of the Canaanite woman is a wonderful example of how we can turn an impossible situation into an answered prayer. (Matthew 15:21-28) Look for methods like these, one-two-three steps that will make clear to them the kinds of things they can expect from God when they approach him in the right way.

• ___How to follow him.___ This is very important for a Christian to know, and therefore for a child to be trained in. Not everyone who calls himself a Christian is truly a Christian, simply because one must follow Jesus – in other words, do as he does, go where he goes, and trust in him for everything – if one wants to claim the name. Many people don't get out of the starting gate because they find out there's a price to pay for the privilege of being in God's family. That price is too often more than they want to pay.

The children must learn what Jesus said about following him. He said it would mean carrying a cross (Luke 14:27); he said we would have to put up with no place to lay our heads (Matthew 8:20); he said that the world would hate us (John 15:18-21). Each of those things needs to be spelled out, so that we know what it looks like, and we know what to expect.

The children need to know where Jesus is going if they are to follow him. Drill the words into their heads: "I am going there to prepare a place for you." (John 14:2) "Come, follow me, and I will make you fishers of men." (Matthew 4:19) "I was in prison and you came to visit me." (Matthew 25:36) You, first of all, will have to find those places where Jesus goes, and then teach it to the little ones so that they know exactly where he is. When they get older they will need those resources to know what part of the world to stay away from and what direction to head for in their careers, their families, and their churches.

• ***Examples.*** As you teach them the Scripture, be sure to use concrete examples of people in the Bible doing what you are teaching about. Children, the psychologists tell us, aren't able to think abstractly. You can fill them with theory if you want, but they don't see it. For example, when presented with a choice of a tall thin glass of drink or a short squatty glass, they will always take the tall one — because it *looks* bigger. They can't grasp the concept of volume yet (even though the short one may have more in it than the tall one!)

If you teach them that Jesus –

- is the propitiatory sacrifice for sin
- is the fulfillment of the Law's exacting requirements for righteousness
- is the union of Jew and Gentile in the Messianic kingdom

... they will memorize the words but they won't understand it for another ten or twenty years! But if you show them Jesus on the cross, dying in our place; and Jesus loving God and loving people, which *is* the fulfillment of the Law; and Jesus helping the Roman centurion and the Canaanite woman as well as his fellow Jews, they will get the same ideas in concrete forms. Besides, seeing the truth in action is a lot more convincing than hearing essays about concepts.

What results will you get?

Children will respond very much differently than adults will to Bible lessons. For one thing, they are still in a frame of mind where everything is very physical and concrete; adults, on the other hand, are able to deal with things on a theoretical and conceptual level. Children understand the stories of Jesus much faster, however, because of this – those stories are concrete examples of who Jesus is! They are the doctrines of the Old Testament put into flesh and blood so that we can see what God is like instead of going by what we've heard about him.

For another thing, children don't have the same issues and problems to work through that we adults have. We struggle with taxes and church fights and work problems, and we need the Bible's answers for these issues. On the other hand, the problems that children have may not be as different qualitatively as they are quantitatively; in other words, they have the same *kinds* of problems but not to the extent or complexity as ours. They do worry about allowance and fights with brothers and sisters and having to do their chores!

So when you look for results, keep these two limitations in mind: they will need *concrete applications* for what they learn, and they will apply those things to *their own world* and its peculiar problems. You are wasting your time and theirs to expect them to respond in an adult way to the Gospel.

What will the children do in response? They will have all this knowledge stored away in their heads, for one thing! Having the Word of God so available is a resource that we adults wish we had more of. Children who know the

Bible are in an enviable position for hard times, when they will need what those words are talking about.

For another, children will see their world in terms of what the Bible plainly says. Since they haven't yet learned the world's lies and haven't come up with their own opinions to contradict God's truth, they will simply accept the Bible's account of things. "Who made you?" we will ask; "God did!" they will answer. Though they won't jump to any adult-level conclusions about that, they at least see it the way it is without the fog of men's confusing ignorance. Then when they get older it will be hard, if not impossible, to lose what they know; they won't easily fill their minds with things that aren't true.

Will their lives change as a result of what they have learned in the Bible? Yes and no. If they know a concrete way of putting some application to work, they will do it and with a lot less fuss about it than adults make. They simply fit it into their world view and go on. Since they have yet to wake up to the possibility of doubting God's Word, practicing it will be more a matter of fitting new things into the daily routine (which you can help them discover). We adults, however, have to overcome formidable hurdles to get the truth into our world view, and if something does make it into the heart it's like a rose in the midst of thorns. Our obedience is more like a victory than a growing process.

In the end, however, you are after the same thing in them that you would be with adults. They must believe in God, they must learn how to come to him, they must walk in obedience to his Word, they must believe the story of salvation and who Christ is. If children do this so much easier than we do, we can only envy their simplicity of faith; we can only pray that our walk will be more like theirs. We must not burden them with our limitations and demand that they agonize over our kinds of sins.

You really have to do your homework here. Remember that you have to give the same truth to them that you give to an adult; God's Word isn't split into stuff for the children and the rest for the adults. You will have to teach some things in a *different way* if you want them to understand the lesson, but the truth that the Bible holds out to all sinners is the hope of knowing God and being saved out of sin and death and going to Heaven. This is the same goal for a child as well as an adult. The key to getting the point across to them on their level is for you to get on their level: Jesus said, remember, that *you must become like a little child yourself* if you want to enter Heaven. This is how you will be able to teach the truths of the Scripture to children.

If you are successful you will be accomplishing another task that you probably won't have the privilege of seeing. All this teaching that you do is like laying the foundation of a building; later someone else will raise the walls and put on a roof and the house will be built. Not only will that child come to depend on your faithfulness in his early years, but that pastor or Bible teacher will greatly appreciate finding a plowed heart full of the seed of God's Word when they press God's claims on that young adult. It will be to your credit that this one whom you taught will cross the "great divide" into adulthood still interested in the things of God, and continue to build on the foundation from his early training and grow even more in the knowledge of God. That fruit, somewhere in the future, is also part of the results of *your* teaching.

Conclusion

Let's summarize what we have found in this study:

- There are problems when teaching about Christ – some of those problems are peculiar to children and some of them are ours.

- Our first job is to learn who Christ really is.

- Children have specific spiritual needs – and they aren't what we expected.

- Christ gives children critical things that make their spiritual growth possible.

- You must understand what the Gospels are about and how to teach them.

- Learn from Christ in the Old Testament, the Epistles and the Church – this provides a firm foundation in your teaching.

- There are certain results to aim for, and there are ways to get them.

There are many things about teaching that we haven't discussed: the necessary credentials of teachers, teaching methods, the psychology of children, lesson preparation, and so on. There is quite a lot to consider when one teaches, especially in the Church setting. It's not without reason that James tells us: "Not many of you should presume to be teachers, my brothers, because you know that we who teach will be judged more strictly." (James 3:1) Teachers have a heavy burden of responsibility: the spiritual future of these children is in our hands, and we can either bless them with what we know or curse them with our ignorance.

But for those whom the Lord has called to teach his little lambs, he has promised all the resources of Heaven. We can't claim any of the success when little ones learn of him and come to trust in him themselves; we know who is responsible for such miracles. We will only be able to say (and gratefully, I might add!) this about ourselves –

> So you also, when you have done everything you were told to do, should say, "We are unworthy servants; we have only done our duty." (Luke 17:10)

APPENDICES

The Prophecies Concerning Christ

The Old Testament is filled with prophecies of Christ. We know many of them because the New Testament was careful to point them out to us. There are many prophecies about him, though, that we would miss if we aren't careful. It requires a careful reading of the Old Testament and some digging in the New to pull some of them out and make the connections.

The following Scriptures are the standard prophecies concerning Christ's person and life. In the left column is the Old Testament prophecy, and in the right is either the New Testament passage that is the direct fulfillment of it, or it is an illustration of how the prophecy was fulfilled (you can find several more of your own if you wish).

These prophecies, hopefully, will help you find a deeper value in the story of Christ, which ought to spill over into your teaching about him. Sometimes you may wish to use one of them for a lesson; usually, however, they will provide background knowledge about him that you will keep in mind when you work through the Gospel stories.

GENESIS 3:15 And I will put enmity between you and the woman, and between your offspring and hers; he will crush your head, and you will strike his heel.

GENESIS 17:19 Then God said, "Yes, but your wife Sarah will bear you a son, and you will call him Isaac. I will establish my covenant with him as an everlasting covenant for his descendants after him."

GENESIS 18:18 Abraham will surely become a great and powerful nation, and all nations on earth will be blessed through him.

GENESIS 22:18 Through your offspring all nations on earth will be blessed, because you have obeyed me.

GENESIS 49:10 The scepter will not depart from Judah, nor the ruler's staff from between his feet, until he comes to whom it belongs and the obedience of the nations is his.

NUMBERS 24:17 I see him, but not now; I behold him, but not near. A star will come out of Jacob; a scepter will rise out of Israel. He will crush the foreheads of Moab, the skulls of all the sons of Sheth.

DEUTERONOMY 18:15 The LORD your God will raise up for you a prophet like me from among your own brothers. You must listen to him.

GALATIANS 4:4 But when the time had fully come, God sent his Son, born under Law.

MATTHEW 1:2,16 Abraham was the father of Isaac, Isaac the father of Jacob, and Jacob the father of Judah and all his brothers ... and Jacob the father of Joseph, the husband of Mary of whom was born Jesus, who is called Christ.

ACTS 3:25 And you are heirs of the prophets and of the covenant God made with your fathers. He said to Abraham, "Through your offspring all peoples on earth will be blessed."

EPHESIANS 2:13 But now in Christ Jesus you who once were far away have been brought near through the blood of Christ.

LUKE 3:33 The son of Amminadab, the son of Ram, the son of Hezron, the son of Perez, the son of Judah.

LUKE 3:34 The son of Jacob, the son of Isaac, the son of Abraham, the son of Terah, the son of Nahor.

JOHN 6:14 After the people saw the miraculous sign that Jesus did, they began to say, "Surely this is the Prophet who is to come into the world."

PSALMS 2:6-9 "I have installed my King on Zion, my holy hill." I will proclaim the decree of the LORD: He said to me, "You are my Son; today I have become your Father. Ask of me, and I will make the nations your inheritance, the ends of the earth your possession. You will rule them with an iron scepter; you will dash them to pieces like pottery."

PSALMS 2:12 Kiss the Son, lest he be angry and you be destroyed in your way, for his wrath can flare up in a moment. Blessed are all who take refuge in him.

PSALMS 16:10 Because you will not abandon me to the grave, nor will you let your Holy One see decay.

PSALMS 22:6-8 But I am a worm and not a man, scorned by men and despised by the people. All who see me mock me; they hurl insults, shaking their heads: "He trusts in the LORD; let the LORD rescue him. Let him deliver him, since he delights in him."

PSALMS 22:16 Dogs have surrounded me; a band of evil men has encircled me, they have pierced my hands and my feet.

PSALMS 22:18 They divide my garments among them and cast lots for my clothing.

EPHESIANS 1:20-22 Which he exerted in Christ when he rasied him from the dead and seated him at his right hand in the Heavenly realms, far above all rule and authority, power and dominion, and every title that can be given, not only in the present age but also in the one to come. And God placed all things under his feet, and appointed him to be head of the Church.

PHILIPPIANS 2:10 At the Name of Jesus every knee should bow, in Heaven and on earth and under the earth.

LUKE 24:6 He is not here; he has risen!

MATTHEW 27:43 He trusts in God. Let God rescue him now if he wants him, for he said, "I am the Son of God."

JOHN 19:18 Here they crucified him, and with him two others -- one on each side and Jesus in the middle.

MARK 15:24 And they crucified him. Dividing up his clothes, they cast lots to see what each would get.

PSALMS 27:12 Do not turn me over to the desire of my foes, for false witnesses rise up against me, breathing out violence.

MATTHEW 26:60-61 But they did not find any, though many false witnesses came forward. Finally two came forward and declared, "This fellow said, 'I am able to destroy the temple of God and rebuild it in three days.'"

PSALMS 34:20 He protects all his bones, not one of them will be broken.

JOHN 19:33 But when they came to Jesus and found that he was already dead, they did not break his legs.

PSALMS 41:9 Even my close friend, whom I trusted, he who shared my bread, has lifted up his heel against me.

MARK 14:10 Then Judas Iscariot, one of the Twelve, went to the chief priests to betray Jesus to them.

PSALMS 45:2 You are the most excellent of men and your lips have been anointed with grace, since God has blessed you forever.

JOHN 1:14 We have seen his glory, the glory of the one and only Son, who came from the Father, full of grace and truth.

PSALMS 68:18 When you ascended on high, you led captives in your train; you received gifts from men, even from the rebellious -- that you, O LORD God, might dwell there.

LUKE 24:50-51 When he had led them out to the vicinity of Bethany, he lifted up his hands and blessed them. While he was blessing them, he left them and was taken up into Heaven.

PSALMS 69:4 Those who hate me without reason outnumber the hairs of my head; many are my enemies without cause, those who seek to destroy me. I am forced to restore what I did not steal.

JOHN 15:23-25 He who hates me hates my Father as well. If I had not done among them what no one else did, they would not be guilty of sin. But now they have seen these miracles, and yet they have hated both me and my Father. But this is to fulfill what is written in their Law, "They hated me without reason."

PSALMS 69:21 They put gall in my food and gave me vinegar for my thirst.

JOHN 19:29 A jar of wine vinegar was there, so they soaked a sponge in it, put the sponge on a stalk of the hyssop plant, and lifted it to Jesus' lips.

PSALMS 109:4 In return for my friendship they accuse me, but I am a man of prayer.

PSALMS 109:7-8 When he is tried, let him be found guilty, and may his prayers condemn him. May his days be few; may another take his place of leadership.

PSALMS 110:1 The LORD says to my Lord: "Sit at my right hand until I make your enemies a footstool for your feet."

PSALMS 110:4 The LORD has sworn and will not change his mind: "You are a priest forever, in the order of Melchizedek."

PSALMS 118:22 The stone the builders rejected has become the capstone.

PSALMS 132:11 The LORD swore an oath to David, a sure oath that he will not revoke: "One of your own descendants I will place on your throne."

ISAIAH 2:4 He will judge between the nations and will settle disputes for many peoples. They will beat their swords into plowshares and their spears into pruning hooks. Nation will not take up sword against nation, nor will they train for war anymore.

LUKE 23:34 Jesus said, "Father, forgive them, for they do not know what they are doing."

ACTS 1:21 Therefore it is necessary to choose one of the men who have been with us the whole time the Lord Jesus went in and out among us.

1 CORINTHIANS 15:25 For he must reign until he has put all his enemies under his feet.

HEBREWS 6:20 Where Jesus, who went before us, has entered on our behalf. He has become a high priest forever, in the order of Melchizedek.

1 PETER 2:4 As you come to him, the living Stone -- rejected by men but chosen by God and precious to him ...

EPHESIANS 1:20 Which he exerted in Christ when he raised him from the dead and seated him at his right hand in the Heavenly realms.

EPHESIANS 2:15 His purpose was to create in himself one new man out of the two, thus making peace, and in this one body to reconcile both of them to God through the cross, by which he put to death their hostility.

ISAIAH 7:14 Therefore the Lord himself will give you a sign: The virgin will be with child and will give birth to a son, and will call him Immanuel.

ISAIAH 9:1-2 Nevertheless, there will be no more gloom for those who were in distress. In the past he humbled the land of Zebulun and the land of Naphtali, but in the future he will honor Galilee of the Gentiles, by the way of the sea, along the Jordan -- The people walking in darkness have seen a great light; on those living in the land of the shadow of death a light has dawned.

ISAIAH 9:6-7 For to us a child is born, to us a son is given, and the government will be on his shoulders. And he will be called Wonderful Counselor, Mighty God, Everlasting Father, Prince of Peace. Of the increase of his government and peace there will be no end. He will reign on David's throne and over his kingdom, establishing and upholding it with justice and righteousness from that time on and forever. The zeal of the LORD Almighty will accomplish this.

ISAIAH 11:1-2 A shoot will come up from the stump of Jesse; from his roots a Branch will bear fruit. The Spirit of the LORD will rest on him-- the Spirit of wisdom and of understanding, the Spirit of counsel and of power, the Spirit of knowledge and of the fear of the LORD .

MATTHEW 1:18 This is how the birth of Jesus Christ came about. His mother Mary was pledged to be married to Joseph, but before they came together, she was found to be with child through the Holy Spirit.

MATTHEW 4:12 When Jesus heard that John had been put in prison, he returned to Galilee. Leaving Nazareth, he went and lived in Capernaum, which was by the lake in the area of Zebulun and Naphtali -- to fulfill what was said through the prophet Isaiah.

JOHN 18:37 You are right in saying I am a king. In fact, for this reason I was born, and for this I came into the world, to testify to the truth.

.

JOHN 1:32 I saw the Spirit come down from Heaven as a dove and remain on him.

ISAIAH 28:16   So this is what the Sovereign LORD says: "See, I lay a stone in Zion, a tested stone, a precious cornerstone for a sure foundation; the one who trusts will never be dismayed."

ISAIAH 42:1   Here is my servant, whom I uphold, my chosen one in whom I delight; I will put my Spirit on him and he will bring justice to the nations.

ISAIAH 50:6   I offered my back to those who beat me, my cheeks to those who pulled out my beard; I did not hide my face from mocking and spitting.

ISAIAH 53:3-5   He was despised and rejected by men, a man of sorrows, and familiar with suffering. Like one from whom men hide their faces he was despised, and we esteemed him not.   Surely he took up our infirmities and carried our sorrows, yet we considered him stricken by God, smitten by him, and afflicted. But he was pierced for our transgressions, he was crushed for our iniquities; the punishment that brought us peace was upon him, and by his wounds we are healed.

ISAIAH 53:7   He was oppressed and afflicted, yet he did not open his mouth; he was led like a lamb to the slaughter, and as a sheep before her shearers is silent, so he did not open his mouth.

EPHESIANS 2:20   Built on the foundation of the apostles and prophets, with Christ Jesus himself as the chief cornerstone.

MATTHEW 3:16   As soon as Jesus was baptized, he went up out of the water. At that moment Heaven was opened, and he saw the Spirit of God descending like a dove and lighting on him.

MARK 14:65   Then some began to spit at him;   they blindfolded him, struck him with their fists, and said, "Prophesy!"   And the guards took him and beat him.

MATTHEW 8:16-17   When evening came, many who were demon-possessed were brought to him, and he drove out the spirits with a word and healed all the sick. This was to fulfill what was spoken through the prophet Isaiah: "He took up our infirmities and carried our diseases."

MATTHEW 26:62-63   Then the high priest stood up and said to Jesus, "Are you not going to answer? What is this testimony that these men are bringing against you?"   But Jesus remained silent.

ISAIAH 53:9 He was assigned a grave with the wicked, and with the rich in his death, though he had done no violence, nor was any deceit in his mouth.

MATTHEW 27:57-60 As evening approached, there came a rich man from Arimathea, named Joseph, who had himself become a disciple of Jesus. Going to Pilate, he asked for Jesus' body, and Pilate ordered that it be given to him. Joseph took the body, wrapped it in a clean linen cloth, and placed it in his own new tomb that he had cut out of the rock. He rolled a big stone in front of the entrance to the tomb and went away.

ISAIAH 53:12 Therefore I will give him a portion among the great, and he will divide the spoils with the strong, because he poured out his life unto death, and was numbered with the transgressors. For he bore the sin of many, and made intercession for the transgressors

MATTHEW 27:38 Two robbers were crucified with him, one on his right and one on his left.

ISAIAH 59:16 He saw that there was no one, he was appalled that there was no one to intervene; so his own arm worked salvation for him, and his own righteousness sustained him.

ROMANS 5:18 Consequently, just as the result of one tresspass was condemnation for all men, so also the result of one act of righteousness was justification that brings life for all men.

ISAIAH 61:1 The Spirit of the Sovereign LORD is on me, because the LORD has anointed me to preach good news to the poor. He has sent me to bind up the brokenhearted, to proclaim freedom for the captives and release from darkness for the prisoners.

MATTHEW 11:4 Jesus replied, "Go back and report to John what you hear and see: the blind receive sight, the lame walk, those who have leprosy are cured, the deaf hear, the dead are raised, and the good news is preached to the poor.

ISAIAH 63:1 Who is this coming from Edom, from Bozrah, with his garments stained crimson? Who is this, robed in splendor, striding forward in the greatness of his strength? "It is I, speaking in righteousness, mighty to save."

HEBREWS 9:14 How much more, then, will the blood of Christ, who through the eternal Spirit offered himself unblemished to God, cleanse our consciences from acts that lead to death, so that we may serve the living God!

JEREMIAH 23:5 "The days are coming," declares the LORD, "when I will raise up to David a righteous Branch, a King who will reign wisely and do what is just and right in the land."

JEREMIAH 31:15 This is what the LORD says: "A voice is heard in Ramah, mourning and great weeping, Rachel weeping for her children and refusing to be comforted, because her children are no more."

DANIEL 9:25 Know and understand this: From the issuing of the decree to restore and rebuild Jerusalem until the Anointed One, the ruler, comes, there will be seven 'sevens,' and sixty-two 'sevens.' It will be rebuilt with streets and a trench, but in times of trouble.

HOSEA 11:1 When Israel was a child, I loved him, and out of Egypt I called my son.

MICAH 5:2 But you, Bethlehem Ephrathah, though you are small among the clans of Judah, out of you will come for me one who will be ruler over Israel, whose origins are from of old, from ancient times.

HAGGAI 2:7 "I will shake all nations, and the desired of all nations will come, and I will fill this house with glory," says the LORD Almighty.

REVELATION 11:15 The kingdom of the world has become the kingdom of our Lord and of his Christ, and he will reign for ever and ever.

MATTHEW 2:16 When Herod realized that he had been outwitted by the Magi, he was furious, and he gave orders to kill all the boys in Bethlehem and its vicinity who were two years old and under, in accordance with the time he had learned from the Magi.

LUKE 2:1-2 In those days Caesar Augustus issued a decree that a census should be taken of the entire Roman world. (This was the first census that took place while Quirinius was governor of Syria.)

MATTHEW 2:14 So he got up, took the child and his mother during the night and left for Egypt.

MATTHEW 2:1 After Jesus was born in Bethlehem in Judea, during the time of King Herod, Magi from the east came to Jerusalem.

MATTHEW 12:6 I tell you that one greater than the Temple is here.

ZECHARIAH 3:8 Listen, O high priest Joshua and your associates seated before you, who are men symbolic of things to come: I am going to bring my servant, the Branch.

ZECHARIAH 9:9 Rejoice greatly, O Daughter of Zion! Shout, Daughter of Jerusalem! See, your king comes to you, righteous and having salvation, gentle and riding on a donkey, on a colt, the foal of a donkey.

ZECHARIAH 11:12-13 I told them, "If you think it best, give me my pay; but if not, keep it." So they paid me thirty pieces of silver. And the LORD said to me, "Throw it to the potter"-- the handsome price at which they priced me! So I took the thirty pieces of silver and threw them into the house of the LORD to the potter.

ZECHARIAH 12:10 And I will pour out on the house of David and the inhabitants of Jerusalem a spirit of grace and supplication. They will look on me, the one they have pierced, and they will mourn for him as one mourns for an only child, and grieve bitterly for him as one grieves for a firstborn son.

ZECHARIAH 13:7 "Awake, O sword, against my shepherd, against the man who is close to me!" declares the LORD Almighty. "Strike the shepherd, and the sheep will be scattered, and I will turn my hand against the little ones."

HEBREWS 5:5 So Christ also did not take upon himself the glory of becoming a high priest. But God said to him, "You are my Son; today I have become your Father."

JOHN 12:13-14 They took palm branches and went out to meet him, shouting, "Hosanna!" "Blessed is he who comes in the Name of the Lord!" "Blessed is the King of Israel!" Jesus found a young donkey and sat upon it, as it is written.

MATTHEW 26:15 And [he] asked, "What are you willing to give me if I hand him over to you?" So they counted out for him thirty silver coins. **MATTHEW 27:6-7** The chief priests picked up the coins and said, "It is against the Law to put this into the treasury, since it is blood money." So they decided to use the money to buy the potter's field as a burial place for foreigners.

JOHN 19:18 Here they crucified him, and with him two others -- one on each side and Jesus in the middle.

MARK 14:50 Then everyone deserted him and fled.

MALACHI 3:1 "See, I will send my messenger, who will prepare the way before me. Then suddenly the Lord you are seeking will come to his temple; the messenger of the covenant, whom you desire, will come," says the LORD Almighty.

JOHN 1:29 The next day John saw Jesus coming toward him and said, "Look, the Lamb of God, who takes away the sin of the world!"

Types of Christ

The purpose of types in the Old Testament is to teach us spiritual truths in pictures – using the things of this world to illustrate the things of God's world. I hope you realize that the realities of Heaven are not made up of what makes up our world! That would be a cheap victory, to get to Heaven only to discover that we have fought and hoped for the riches of this world warmed over. Christ died for something more permanent and valuable than what God has always intended to destroy at the end of time!

Nevertheless, the Lord uses impermanent things to illustrate truths about the permanent. Not only are types useful, they may be absolutely necessary to learn – the New Testament writers may feel that the type did the job so well that they simply won't go over the same ground twice. In order to learn this particular aspect of Christ or God's kingdom you must study the type; it won't be discussed again in the New Testament!

Following are some of the types of the Old Testament and how they illustrate God's spiritual world.

The Tree of Life	To eat of this tree meant to live forever. In Revelation 2:7 and 22:14 we read that all who enter into God's eternal city will eat of the Tree of Life. Christ himself points out that he is the vine that gives life and we are the branches. (John 15) Paul spoke of the Jews being cut off the Tree of Life and the Gentiles being grafted in. (Romans 11)
The marriage relationship	Paul teaches that the union between man and woman is a lesson on the union between Christ and his Church. (Ephesians 5:22-33)
The cherubim and flaming sword	Man was denied access to the Tree of Life. People throughout history have looked for and not found the life in Christ until God was pleased to open the way in his incarnation. Even now, only those who approach with faith will find him; (John 6:40) only those whom the Father draws will come to Life. (John 6:44)

The blood of Abel	Innocent blood shed on the ground still speaks its powerful message to a God who hears and will act on it. (Hebrews 12:24)
The life of Enoch	Enoch walked with God, and for his faith was taken to Heaven without dying. Our life of faith has a powerful reward in God's eternal life, and in avoiding the second death. (Revelation 2:11; 20:6)
The Flood	God intends to do away with the world and make a new world, and save his special people to live in it. (Revelation 21:1-5)
The Seed of promise	The seed promised to Abraham was actually Christ. (Galatians 3:16)
The land of Canaan	Canaan was a lesson about the land that God intends to give to all the descendants of Abraham – Heaven. (Hebrews 11:13-16)

The people of God	The Covenant people, a nation of priests, those with whom God plans to live forever. (1 Peter 2:9)
Melchizedek	He was a priest without birth or death, to whom Abraham gave tithes and honor. (Hebrews 7)
Joseph	There were prophecies of his exaltation, but he had to go through humiliation first. (Philippians 2:1-11)
Deliverance from Egypt	The troubles that the Israelites went through, under whom, and who led them out and by what means – all this is a picture of our deliverance in Christ. (Ephesians 2:1-10)
Manna	The bread from Heaven tells us how Christ is food for his people. (John 6)
Water from the Rock	The rock in the desert that refreshes the Lord's people. (1 Corinthians 10:4)
The Tabernacle	The Tabernacle was built after the Heavenly pattern and resembles the salvation we have in Jesus' work. (Hebrews 8:1 - 9:5)

The system of sacrificial worship	The sacrifices, the way they were done, and the forgiveness they got – all portrayed an idea of the power in Jesus' sacrifice. (Hebrews 9:6 - 10:39)
The Sabbath	The Lord required his people to rest on the Sabbath, as a picture of the rest of faith in Christ that he requires. (Hebrews 3:7 - 4:11)
Joshua the conqueror	Joshua led the people of God into the Promised Land, clearing out the inhabitants and dividing up the land for the tribes. Jesus leads his people too into the Kingdom of God through warfare. (1 Corinthians 15:12-34)
King David	In his duties, his character, and his experiences, David was a picture of the perfect King to come. (Luke 1:32-33)
The history of Israel	The successes and failures, the events and enemies, the benefits and punishments, all reflect the experiences of the Church universal. (1 Peter 2:10)

Joshua the High Priest

A priest of Israel is also the king. (Hebrews 8:1; Revelation 17:14)

The Old In The New

The Old Testament is critical to the New Testament's message. Aside from the outright prophecies of Christ, there are many ideas and principles from the Old that the New uses in its stories and teachings.

The apostles were astute students of their Bibles – which, by the way, was the Old Testament! They read and thought about and prayed about the Scriptures so much that they had a deep pool of knowledge to draw from when they wrote their letters. They did the same thing that modern writers do: they quoted Old Testament passages to support and illustrate their own point (though they didn't often give the reference and only gave the name of the prophet even then!).

The following is a listing of all the Old Testament Scriptures that are quoted in the New Testament, both Gospels and Epistles. The left column is the Old Testament passage, and the right column is the place in the New Testament where that passage is quoted. Notice that some OT passages are quoted several places in the New; the OT reference isn't printed more than once in these cases.

Also notice that some of the OT references are underlined. This means that the NT writer was using the Septuagint – a Greek translation of the OT – instead of the Hebrew Bible. As is true with all translations from the original, it often didn't read the same. This accounts for the fact that the quote that the NT writer gives us is different than the passage we find when we go back to the OT and look it up; our Old Testament comes from the Hebrew Bible, not the Septuagint. Don't worry about the differences, however; it is a bit technical, but what it boils down to is that the Hebrew Bible we have now isn't the original that the prophets wrote – there were older Hebrew Bibles then that we don't have. But the Septuagint translators had those older Bibles – which is why the Spirit wants that difference in the New Testament quote instead of the present version of the Hebrew. If that doesn't make sense, just trust the Lord that the version he wanted is what the apostles used!

Finally, you will notice that I italicized the Gospel references for easy location.

(This list is taken from The Greek New Testament, © 1983 by the United Bible Societies; edited by Aland, Black, Martini, Metzger and Wikgren; pp.897-8.)

OT Passage:	Quoted in:	OT Passage:	Quoted in:
Genesis 1:27	*Matthew 19:4*	Exodus 3:15	*Matthew 22:23*
	Mark 10:6		*Mark 12:26*
Genesis 2:2	Hebrews 4:4		Acts 3:13
Genesis 2:7	1 Cor.15:45	Exodus 9:16	Romans 9:17
Genesis 2:24	*Matthew 19:5*	Exodus 12:46	*John 19:36*
	Mark 10:7-8	Exodus 13:2	*Luke 2:23*
	1 Cor. 6:16	Exodus 13:12	*Luke 2:23*
	Ephesians 5:31	Exodus 13:15	*Luke 2:32*
Genesis 5:2	*Matthew 19:4*	Exodus 16:18	2 Cor. 8:15
	Mark 10:6	Exodus 19:6	1 Peter 2:9
Genesis 5:24	Hebrews 11:5	Ex. 19:12-13	Hebrews 12:20
Genesis 12:1	Acts 7:3	Ex. 20:12	*Matthew 15:4*
Genesis 12:3	Galatians 3:8		*Mark 7:10*
Genesis 12:7	Galatians 3:16		Ephesians 6:2-3
Gen.14:17-20	Hebrews 7:1-2	Ex. 20:12-16	*Matt. 19:18-19*
Genesis 15:5	Romans 4:18		*Mark 10:19*
Genesis 15:6	Rom.4:3,9,22		*Luke 18:20*
	Galatians 3:6	Exodus 20:13	*Matthew 5:21*
	James 2:23		James 2:11
Gen.15:13-14	Acts 7:6-7	Ex. 20:13-15,17	Romans 13:9
Genesis 17:5	Rom.4:17,18	Exodus 20:14	*Matthew 5:27*
Genesis 17:8	Acts 7:5		James 2:11
Genesis 18:10	Romans 9:9	Exodus 20:17	Romans 7:7
Genesis 18:14	Romans 9:9	Exodus 21:17	*Matthew 15:4*
Genesis 18:18	Galatians 3:8		*Mark 7:10*
Genesis 21:10	Galatians 4:30	Exodus 21:24	*Matthew 5:38*
Genesis 21:12	Romans 9:7	Exodus 22:28	Acts 23:5
	Hebrews 11:18	Exodus 24:8	Hebrews 9:20
Gen.22:16-17	Hebr.6:13-14	Exodus 25:40	Hebrews 8:5
Genesis 22:18	Acts 3:25	Exodus 32:1	Acts 7:40
Genesis 25:23	Romans 9:12	Exodus 32:6	1 Cor. 10:7
Genesis 26:4	Acts 3:25	Exodus 32:23	Acts 7:40
Genesis 47:31	Hebrews 11:21	Exodus 33:19	Romans 9:15
Genesis 48:4	Acts 7:5	Leviticus 12:8	*Luke 2:24*
		Leviticus 18:5	Romans 10:5
Exodus 1:8	Acts 7:18		Galatians 3:12
Exodus 2:14	Acts 7:27-28	Leviticus 19:2	1 Peter 1:16
	Acts 7:35	Leviticus 19:12	*Matthew 5:33*
Exodus 3:2	Acts 7:30	Leviticus 19:18	*Matthew 5:43*
Exodus 3:5-10	Acts 7:33-34		*Matthew 19:19*
Exodus 3:6	*Matthew 22:32*		*Matthew 22:39*
	Mark 12:26		*Mark 12:31*
	Luke 20:37		*Mark 12:33*
	Acts 3:13		*Luke 10:27*
	Acts 7:32		Romans 13:9
Exodus 3:12	Acts 7:7		Galatians 5:14

OT Passage:	Quoted in:	OT Passage:	Quoted in:
Leviticus 19:18	James 2:8		1 Timothy 5:18
Leviticus 23:29	Acts 3:23	Deut. 25:5	*Matthew 22:24*
Leviticus 24:20	*Matthew 5:38*		*Mark 12:19*
Leviticus 26:12	2 Cor. 6:16		*Luke 20:28*
		Deut. 27:26	Galatians 3:10
Numbers 9:12	*John 19:36*	Deut. 29:4	Romans 11:8
Numbers 16:5	2 Timothy 2:19	Deut. 30:12-14	Romans 10:6-8
Numbers 30:2	*Matthew 5:33*	Deut. 31:6,8	Hebrews 13:5
		Deut. 32:21	Romans 10:19
Deut. 4:35	*Mark 12:32*	Deut. 32:35	Romans 12:19
Deut. 5:16	*Matthew 15:4*	Deut. 32:35-36	Hebrews 10:30
	Mark 7:10	Deut. 32:43	Romans 15:10
	Ephesians 6:2-3	Deut. 32:43	Hebrews 1:6
Deut. 5:16-20	*Matt. 19:18-19*		
	Mark 10:19	1 Samuel 13:14	Acts 13:22
	Luke 18:20		
Deut. 5:17	*Matthew 5:21*	2 Samuel 7:8	2 Cor. 6:18
	James 2:11	2 Samuel 7:14	2 Cor. 6:18
Dt. 5:17-19, 21	Romans 13:9		Hebrews 1:5
Deut. 5:18	*Matthew 5:27*	2 Samuel 22:50	Romans 15:9
Deut. 5:21	Romans 7:7		
Deut. 6:4	*Mark 12:32*	1 Kgs 19:10,14	Romans 11:3
Deut. 6:4-5	*Mark 12:29-30*	1 Kings 19:18	Romans 11:4
Deut. 6:5	*Matthew 22:37*	Job 5:13	1 Cor. 3:19
	Mark 12:33	Job 41:11	Romans 11:35
	Luke 10:27		
Deut. 6:13	*Matthew 4:10*	Psalm 2:1-2	Acts 4:25-26
	Luke 4:8	Psalm 2:7	Acts 13:33
Deut. 6:16	*Matthew 4:7*		Hebrews 1:5
	Luke 4:12		Hebrews 5:5
Deut. 8:3	*Matthew 4:4*	Psalm 4:4	Ephesians 4:26
	Luke 4:4	Psalm 5:9	Romans 3:13
Deut. 9:4	Romans 10:6	Psalm 8:3	*Matthew 21:16*
Deut. 9:19	Hebrews 12:21	Psalm 8:4-6	Hebrews 2:6-8
Deut. 17:7	1 Cor. 5:13	Psalm 8:6	1 Cor. 15:27
Deut. 18:15	Acts 7:37	Psalm 10:7	Romans 3:14
Deut. 18:15-16	Acts 3:22	Psalm 14:1-3	Rom. 3:10-12
Deut. 18:19	Acts 3:23	Psalm 16:8-11	Acts 2:25-28
Deut. 19:15	*Matthew 18:16*	Psalm 16:10	Acts 2:31
	2 Cor. 13:1	Psalm 16:10	Acts 13:35
Deut. 19:21	*Matthew 5:38*	Psalm 18:49	Romans 15:9
Deut. 21:23	Galatians 3:13	Psalm 19:4	Romans 10:18
Deut. 24:1	*Matthew 5:31*	Psalm 22:1	*Matthew 27:46*
	Matthew 19:7		*Mark 15:34*
Deut. 24:1,3	*Mark 10:4*	Psalm 22:18	*John 19:24*
Deut. 25:4	1 Cor. 9:9	Psalm 22:22	Hebrews 2:12

OT Passage:	Quoted in:	OT Passage:	Quoted in:
Psalm 24:1	1 Cor. 10:26	Psalm 118:22	Luke 20:17
Psalm 31:5	Luke 23:46		Acts 4:11
Psalm 32:1-2	Romans 4:7-8		1 Peter 2:7
Psalm 34:12-16	1 Peter 3:10-12	Ps. 118:22-23	Matthew 21:42
Psalm 35:19	John 15:2		Mark 12:10-11
Psalm 36:1	Romans 3:18	Ps. 118:25-26	Matthew 21:9
Psalm 40:6-8	Hebrews 10:5-7		Mark 11:9-10
Psalm 41:9	John 13:18		John 12:13
Psalm 44:22	Romans 8:36	Psalm 118:26	Matthew 23:39
Psalm 45:6-7	Hebrews 1:8-9		Luke 13:35
Psalm 51:4	Romans 3:4		Luke 19:38
Psalm 53:1-3	Rom. 3:10-12	Psalm 132:11	Acts 2:30
Psalm 68:18	Ephesians 4:8	Psalm 140:3	Romans 3:13
Psalm 69:4	John 15:25		
Psalm 69:9	John 2:17	Prov. 3:11-12	Hebrews 12:5-6
	Romans 15:3	Proverbs 3:34	James 4:6
Psalm 69:22-23	Rom. 11:9-10		1 Peter 5:5
Psalm 69:25	Acts 1:20	Proverbs 11:31	1 Peter 4:18
Psalm 78:2	Matthew 13:35	Prov. 25:21-22	Romans 12:20
Psalm 78:24	John 6:31	Proverbs 26:11	2 Peter 2:22
Psalm 82:6	John 10:34		
Psalm 89:20	Acts 13:22	Isaiah 1:9	Romans 9:29
Psalm 91:11-12	Matthew 4:6	Isaiah 6:9	Luke 8:10
	Luke 4:10-11	Isaiah 6:9-10	Matt. 13:14-15
Psalm 94:11	1 Cor. 3:20		Mark 4:12
Psalm 95:7-8	Hebrews 3:15	Isaiah 6:9-10	Acts 28:26-27
	Hebrews 4:7	Isaiah 6:10	John 12:40
Psalm 95:7-11	Hebrews 3:7-11	Isaiah 7:14	Matthew 1:23
Psalm 95:11	Hebrews 4:3,5	Isaiah 8:8,10	Matthew 1:23
Ps. 102:25-27	Heb. 1:10-12	Isaiah 8:14	Romans 9:33
Psalm 104:4	Hebrews 1:7		1 Peter 2:8
Psalm 109:8	Acts 1:20	Isaiah 8:17	Hebrews 2:13
Psalm 110:1	Matthew 22:44	Isaiah 8:18	Hebrews 2:13
	Matthew 26:64	Isaiah 9:1-2	Matt. 4:15-16
	Mark 12:36	Isaiah 10:22-23	Rom. 9:27-28
	Mark 14:62	Isaiah 11:10	Romans 15:12
	Luke 20:42-43	Isaiah 22:13	1 Cor. 15:32
	Luke 22:69	Isaiah 25:8	1 Cor. 15:54
	Acts 2:34-35	Isaiah 27:9	Romans 11:27b
	Hebrews 1:13	Isaiah 28:11-12	1 Cor. 14:21
Psalm 110:4	Hebrews 5:6	Isaiah 28:16	Romans 9:33
	Heb. 7:17,21		Romans 10:11
Psalm 112:9	2 Cor. 9:9		1 Peter 2:6
Psalm 116:10	2 Cor. 4:13	Isaiah 29:10	Romans 11:8
Psalm 117:1	Romans 15:11	Isaiah 29:13	Matthew 15:8-9
Psalm 118:6	Hebrews 13:6		Mark 7:6-7

OT Passage:	Quoted in:	OT Passage:	Quoted in:
Isaiah 29:14	1 Cor. 1:19	Jer.31:33-34	Heb. 10:16-17
Isaiah 40:3-5	*Luke 3:4-6*	Ezek. 20:34,41	2 Cor. 6:17
Isaiah 40:3	*Matthew 3:3*	Ezekiel 37:27	2 Cor. 6:16
	Mark 1:3		
	John 1:23	Daniel 7:13	*Matthew 24:30*
Isaiah 40:6-8	1 Peter 1:24-25		*Matthew 26:64*
Isaiah 40:13	Romans 11:34		*Mark 13:26*
	1 Cor. 2:16		*Mark 14:62*
Isaiah 42:1-3	*Matt. 12:18-20*		*Luke 21:27*
Isaiah 42:4	*Matthew 12:21*		
Isaiah 43:20	1 Peter 2:9	Hosea 1:10	Romans 9:26
Isaiah 43:21	1 Peter 2:9	Hosea 2:23	Romans 9:25
Isaiah 45:21	*Mark 12:32*	Hosea 6:6	*Matthew 9:13*
Isaiah 45:23	Romans 14:11		*Matthew 12:7*
Isaiah 49:6	Acts 13:47	Hosea 10:8	*Luke 23:30*
Isaiah 49:8	2 Cor. 6:2	Hosea 11:1	*Matthew 2:15*
Isaiah 49:18	Romans 14:11	Hosea 13:14	1 Cor. 15:55
Isaiah 52:5	Romans 2:24		
Isaiah 52:7	Romans 10:15	Joel 2:28-32	Acts 2:17-21
Isaiah 52:11	2 Cor. 6:17	Joel 2:32	Romans 10:13
Isaiah 52:15	Romans 15:21		
Isaiah 53:1	*John 12:38*	Amos 5:25-27	Acts 7:42-43
	Romans 10:16	Amos 9:11-12	Acts 15:16-17
Isaiah 53:4	*Matthew 8:17*	Jonah 1:17	*Matthew 12:40*
Isaiah 53:7-8	Acts 8:32-33		
Isaiah 53:9	1 Peter 2:22	Micah 5:2	*Matthew 2:6*
Isaiah 53:12	*Luke 22:37*	Micah 7:6	*Matt. 10:35-36*
Isaiah 54:1	Galatians 4:27		
Isaiah 54:13	*John 6:45*	Habakkuk 1:5	Acts 13:41
Isaiah 55:3	Acts 13:34	Hab. 2:3-4	Heb. 10:37-38
Isaiah 56:7	*Matthew 21:13*	Habakkuk 2:4	Romans 1:17
	Mark 11:17		Galatians 3:11
	Luke 19:46		
Isaiah 59:7-8	Rom. 3:15-17		
Isaiah 59:20-21	Rom. 11:26-27	Haggai 2:6	Hebrews 12:26
Isaiah 61:1-2	*Luke 4:18-19*		
Isaiah 62:11	*Matthew 21:5*	Zechariah 8:16	Ephesians 4:25
Isaiah 64:4	1 Cor. 2:9	Zechariah 9:9	*Matthew 21:5*
Isaiah 65:1	Romans 10:20		*John 12:15*
Isaiah 65:2	Romans 10:21	Zechariah	*Matt. 27:9-10*
Isaiah 66:1-2	Acts 7:49-50	11:12-13	*John 19:37*
		Zech. 12:10	*Matthew 26:31*
Jeremiah 9:24	1 Cor. 1:31	Zechariah 13:7	*Mark 14:27*
	2 Cor. 10:17		
Jeremiah 31:15	*Matthew 2:18*	Malachi 1:2-3	Romans 9:13
Jer. 31:31-34	Hebrews 8:8-12	Malachi 3:1	*Matthew 11:10*

OT Passage:	Quoted in:
Malachi 3:1	*Mark 1:2* *Luke 7:27*

Christ in Ephesians

I once read the book of Ephesians with the purpose of marking all the places where Paul mentions Christ in some way. I was getting the feeling that modern preachers didn't understand Jesus as much as they thought they did, because they never seemed to talk about Christ; it was always about duties of Christians, or our sins, or social issues. Sometimes they would drop his Name around in their sermons but without any purpose -- only to sanctify, it would seem, what they were talking about. One could easily have taken Christ's Name out of their sermon and it would still make sense! What I wanted to see was if that held true of Paul's letter as well.

I found 100 places where Paul refers to Christ in some way. Examining each one I found that, far from simply using his Name to make the letter more "Christian," Paul was appealing to something in Christ to make his point. The letter would be nothing, in other words, if you took out the references to Christ. He *is* the argument of the letter.

This is all the more significant when one realizes that the letter to the Ephesians is the equivalent of a 20 minute sermon! For Paul to have used so many things about the Lord that many times in such a short span shows an amazing depth of knowledge of Jesus Christ. We simply are unequal to Paul's insight of the Lord; we are doing good when we form an entire sermon around one or two verses from his letter!

Here are the 100 occurrences of the references to Christ. I present them to show you that Jesus was constantly the theme for the apostles when they wrote the other books of the New Testament. Only if you get well-grounded in the Gospels will you begin to appreciate how the apostles founded their Church letters on the doctrine of Christ.

Eph. 1:1	Paul was an apostle of *Christ Jesus*
Eph. 1:1	the letter was written to those who were faithful in *Christ Jesus*
Eph. 1:2	Paul blesses them with grace and peace from the *Lord Jesus Christ*
Eph. 1:3	Paul praises the Father of the *Lord Jesus Christ* ...
Eph. 1:3	... for the spiritual blessings he gave us in *Christ*
Eph. 1:4	the Father chose us in *him* before the world
Eph. 1:5	he predestined us to be adopted as his sons in *Christ Jesus*
Eph. 1:6	he has freely given us grace in the *One* he loves
Eph. 1:7	in *him* we have redemption through his blood
Eph. 1:9	the mystery of his will, purposed in *Christ*
Eph. 1:10	he will bring all things under one head, even *Christ*
Eph. 1:11	in *him* we were also chosen
Eph. 1:12	the apostles were the first to hope in *Christ*
Eph. 1:13	and we also were included in *Christ* when we heard the gospel
Eph. 1:13	we were marked in *him* with a seal, the promised Holy Spirit
Eph. 1:15	Paul heard about their faith in the *Lord Jesus*
Eph. 1:17	Paul prayed that the God of our *Lord Jesus Christ* might give the Spirit
Eph. 1:20	the mighty power which God exerted in *Christ*
Eph. 1:20	he raised *him* from the dead ...
Eph. 1:20	... and seated *him* at his right hand
Eph. 1:22	God placed all things under *his* feet ...
Eph. 1:22	... and appointed *him* to be head over everything for the church
Eph. 1:23	the church is *his* body ...
Eph. 1:23	... the fullness of *him* who fills everything in every way
Eph. 2:5	God made us alive with *Christ*
Eph. 2:6	God raised us up with *Christ* ...
Eph. 2:6	in the heavenly realms in *Christ Jesus*
Eph. 2:7	his grace expressed in his kindness to us in *Christ Jesus*
Eph. 2:10	we were created in *Christ Jesus* to do good works
Eph. 2:12	once we were separate from *Christ*
Eph. 2:13	now in *Christ Jesus* we have been brought near ...
Eph. 2:13	... through the blood of *Christ*
Eph. 2:14	for *he himself* is our peace
Eph. 2:15	abolished the Law in *his* flesh
Eph. 2:15	*his* purpose was ...
Eph. 2:15	... to create in *himself* one new man out of the two

Eph. 2:16	*he* put to death their hostility
Eph. 2:17	*he* came and preached peace
Eph. 2:18	through *him* we both have access to the Father
Eph. 2:20	*Christ Jesus himself* is the chief cornerstone
Eph. 2:21	in *him* the whole building is joined together
Eph. 2:22	in *him* we too are being built together to become a dwelling
Eph. 3:1	Paul is a prisoner of *Christ Jesus* for the sake of the Gentiles
Eph. 3:4	Paul's insight into the mystery of *Christ*
Eph. 3:6	the Gentiles and Israel share in the promise in *Christ Jesus*
Eph. 3:8	Paul preaches to the Gentiles the unsearchable riches of *Christ*
Eph. 3:11	God accomplished his eternal purpose in *Christ Jesus our Lord*
Eph. 3:12	in *him* and ...
Eph. 3:12	... through faith in *him* we may approach God
Eph. 3:17	that *Christ* may dwell in our hearts through faith
Eph. 3:18	how wide and long and high and deep is the love of *Christ*
Eph. 3:21	to him be glory in the Church and in *Christ Jesus*
Eph. 4:1	Paul is a prisoner for the *Lord*
Eph. 4:5	there is one *Lord*
Eph. 4:7	each one of us has grace as *Christ* apportioned it
Eph. 4:8	when *he* ascended on high ...
Eph. 4:8	... *he* led captives in *his* train and gave gifts to men
Eph. 4:9	*he* also descended to the lower earthly regions
Eph. 4:10	*he* who descended is the very one who ascended higher than the heavens
Eph. 4:11	it was *he* who gave some to be apostles, etc.
Eph. 4:12	so that the body of *Christ* may be built up
Eph. 4:13	so that we reach unity in the knowledge of the *Son of God*
Eph. 4:13	attaining to the whole measure of the fullness of *Christ*
Eph. 4:15	we will grow up into the Head, that is, *Christ*
Eph. 4:16	from *him* the whole body grows and builds itself up
Eph. 4:17	Paul insists in the *Lord*
Eph. 4:20	we did not come to know *Christ* that way
Eph. 4:21	surely you heard of *him* and were taught in *him* ...
Eph. 4:21	... in accordance with the truth that is in *Jesus*
Eph. 4:32	just as in *Christ* God forgave you
Eph. 5:2	just as *Christ* loved us and gave *himself* up for us
Eph. 5:5	no idolaters have any inheritance in the kingdom of Christ and of God
Eph. 5:8	now we are light in the *Lord*
Eph. 5:10	find out what pleases the *Lord*
Eph. 5:14	wake up, O sleeper, and rise from the dead, and *Christ* will shine on you
Eph. 5:17	understand what the *Lord's* will is
Eph. 5:19	sing and make music in your heart to the *Lord*

Eph. 5:20	giving thanks for everything in the Name of our *Lord Jesus Christ*
Eph. 5:22	wives, submit to your husbands as to the *Lord*
Eph. 5:23	the husband is the head of the wife as *Christ* is the head of the Church
Eph. 5:24	the Church submits to *Christ*
Eph. 5:25	*Christ* loved the Church and ...
Eph. 5:25	... gave *himself* up for her
Eph. 5:27	*he* presented her to *himself* as a radiant Church
Eph. 5:29	*Christ* feeds and cares for the Church
Eph. 5:30	we are members of *his* body
Eph. 5:32	the union of *Christ* and the Church is a profound mystery
Eph. 6:1	children, obey your parents in the *Lord*
Eph. 6:4	bring your children up in the training and instruction of the *Lord*
Eph. 6:5	slaves, obey your masters just as you would obey *Christ*
Eph. 6:6	like slaves of *Christ*, doing the will of God from the heart
Eph. 6:7	serve wholeheartedly, as if you were serving the *Lord*
Eph. 6:8	the *Lord* will reward everyone for whatever good he does
Eph. 6:9	*he* who is both their Master and yours is in Heaven ...
Eph. 6:9	and there is no favoritism with *him*
Eph. 6:10	be strong in the *Lord* ...
Eph. 6:10	... and in *his* mighty power
Eph. 6:21	Tychicus, the faithful servant in the *Lord*
Eph. 6:23	Paul blesses with love and faith from the Father and the *Lord Jesus Christ*
Eph. 6:24	grace to all who love our *Lord Jesus Christ* with an undying love

The Tree of the Knowledge of Good and Evil

I have a strong feeling that the story in Genesis 3 has more importance in our lives than people usually give it credit for. The only reason why we *have* to struggle with sin and death, Judgment and Hell, and why we *must* find the Savior and salvation and true righteousness before we die, is because of what happened in the Garden of Eden. Something happened to us there that completely determined what life would be like for all mankind. If it had turned out differently we wouldn't be what we are today.

The Tree of the Knowledge of Good and Evil is a fascinating but perplexing part of the story of man's fall. What was that tree? Why is it called this? What did eating of its fruit do to us? If you look up the passage in most Bible commentaries, you will find that they either skirt the issue of the tree and focus on the fact that Adam and Eve disobeyed God's command to eat from it (which is what most of them will do), or they offer an inadequate explanation of the Tree. It seems that no two opinions from the scholars are the same!

And yet we know that this is an important part of the story. *First*, the Tree has a special name: the Tree of the Knowledge of Good and Evil. If it weren't important to know what that knowledge is, then it wouldn't have such a specific name attached to it. *Second*, God strictly forbade man to eat its fruit. If it were just a matter of testing man's obedience then God could have used anything; why this specific tree, however?

Third, it seems that we now have the knowledge of good and evil – we did eat from it, didn't we? *Fourth*, eating from it brought instant condemnation and death. It can be argued that disobedience brought death, which is true; but why did God keep us from eternal life? Only because we had this knowledge! (Genesis 3:22)

The reason I'm raising the issue here is that I think it has a lot to do with how children and adults relate to the Gospel. I believe I can show that, even though we all have this "ability" in us (the Knowledge of Good and Evil), children seem to lack the will to sit in judgment on the things of God. They simply hear the Bible and believe it; we adults can't. We pass judgment on God just as we do on everything else; we can't just believe what he tells us without being critical about it, or feeling that we have to approve of it (or change it!) before we are willing to accept it. When Jesus told us that we must become like little children if we want to enter Heaven, I think he was referring to the fact that children accept him at face value – no matter how far-fetched his teachings and miracles may seem.

If we at least know about the problem we have, we can better address the spiritual needs of children – that is, get the truths of the Bible into their heads and hearts before they grow up and start putting God to the test of reason and their senses.

THE PASSAGE ANALYZED

You will find this story in Genesis 2-3. Read it for yourself, and you will see that it was a deliberate act of rebellion against God's command. He told Adam and Eve not to eat of the fruit from the Tree of the Knowledge of Good and Evil; unfortunately, they did precisely that. And that, the Bible tells us, is the root of sin.

> Everyone who sins breaks the Law; in fact, sin is lawlessness. (1 John 3:4)

But actually there were two fatal events which happened in quick succession: *sin*, and *independence* from God. Let's slow down the action and examine how they came to be.

First, Eve listened to Satan's analysis of God's command. Satan very plainly cast doubt on God's wisdom, when he contradicted the command about eating the fruit. "You will not surely die," he lied. It was a subtle shift, but it was enough to get Eve to think that maybe God's wisdom wasn't what she thought it was. Perhaps God didn't mean to give her and her husband his best; another source – Satan, and the fruit of the Tree – offered her something better. That shift away from God was the critical step away from holiness, or God-centeredness, into a life consumed with pleasing one's senses apart from God. This was the *sin*.

Second, Eve took the fruit and ate it – and suddenly "the eyes of both of them were opened" and they now had the Knowledge of Good and Evil. Satan wasn't lying about this; even God admitted, later in the chapter, that now man had this ability. (Genesis 3:22) The reason this was fatal was that, instead of God deciding for man what was good and not good, man decides for himself what is good and not good. Instead of going to God and getting all good things from him, depending on God alone to make that decision for him, Adam judges for himself what he needs and wants. The problem is that he uses his own senses and desires as the standards of his judgment! This was the *independence* from God.

> When the woman saw that the fruit of the tree was good for food and pleasing to the eye, and also desirable for gaining wisdom, she took some and ate it. (Genesis 3:6)

Now the entire human race has this inclination to judge things, to select what they want instead of relying on God. (The fact that they ate the fruit means that it entered into our human nature; we all inherit this trait now.) We all choose what pleases us, and we reject what displeases us. And if we end up disagreeing with someone else's judgment about something, including God's judgment, there's going to be war.

Sin, therefore, was turning away from God. The disaster was that now we will never go back to God for anything, since we're independent agents now. The door was slammed shut on being holy, or God-centered.

This opens up a vital area that we have to understand if we want to cure our problem. Their act of disobedience led them away from God. Now they can't have God; they cut themselves off from their only good. They will have death now, not life.

Sin is disobeying God's command; it breaks the close relationship between us and God. It leads us away from God, by taking paths that he told us not to take; and when we wander out there in the world away from God then we're going to find death, not life. This is why the Bible lays so much emphasis on righteousness, or walking according to the Law of God, being the way to God's throne of life.

CATASTROPHE

Turning away from God, and picking up the character trait of judging for oneself (using one's own senses and reasoning as the standard) what is good or evil, is a toxic combination for life. It brought immediate death for the soul of man, and ultimate death on his physical side.

Cursed is the ground because of you; through
painful toil you will eat of it all the days of your life.

It will produce thorns and thistles for you, and you
will eat the plants of the field. By the sweat of your
brow you will eat your food until you return to the
ground, since from it you were taken; for dust you
are and to dust you will return. (Genesis 3:17-19)

Now instead of experiencing the blessings of God
through creation, man would suffer curses through that same
creation. The world was no longer a conduit to God but an
obstacle, a barrier that God would use to crush man in
punishment. The really fatal aspect of this situation is that man
lost his connection with God, and therefore with the goodness of
God. Instead of being our source of life, now God is our enemy
dealing out death. The result is that people haven't been able to
even figure out who God really is, let alone get in touch with
him; the doors to Heaven are shut. There have been uncounted
philosophies and religions throughout history that haven't done
us any good at all for solving our basic spiritual problems; we all
die in the end, cursed and lost. No matter how advanced and
civilized the world around us may get, we've never been able to
cross over that barrier that God set up between us. And
separation from Godis death; only in knowing God and getting
in touch with him will we find life. (John 17:3)

This situation between us and God has even worse
repercussions on earth. When nobody is in touch with God,
nobody can carry out their responsibilities on earth that God
gave us at Creation. So everyone is doing "what is right in their
own eyes." And when everyone is using themselves as the
standard of what is right and wrong, it's not surprising at all to
find everyone arguing with each other since nobody's version of
right and wrong is the same. There is war, murder, lust,
robbery, adultery, sexual perversions, rage, destruction and
much more as millions of independent agents struggle for "their
fair share" at the expense of everyone else around them. This
chaotic situation naturally happens when we lose touch with
God who alone is able to 1) decide what is good and right, and

2) orchestrate millions of humans to create a workable world. Without God, we end up fighting both God and man. We will never get along.

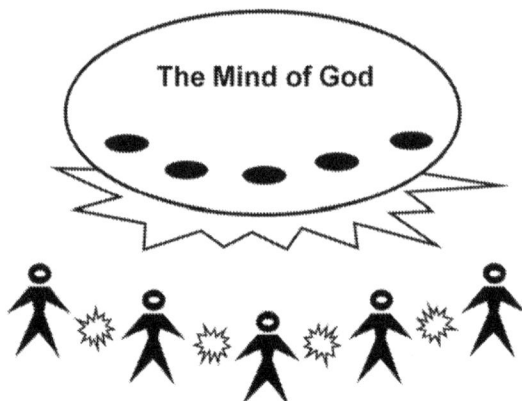

Out of touch with God and man

We can't agree on what the wise course of action should be in anything we do. We can't bring about law and order when everyone disagrees on what the standards should be. We can't make sure that everyone gets what they need to survive when we are so self-centered about our own desires. And even if we manage to put aside our differences for a time and cooperate, it won't be long till the project falls apart again. It's in our nature to look out for "number one" first.

> What causes fights and quarrels among you? Don't they come from your desires that battle within you? You want something but don't get it. You kill and covet, but you cannot have what you want. You quarrel and fight. You do not have, because you do not ask God. When you ask, you do not receive, because you ask with wrong motives, that you may spend what you get on your pleasures. (James 4:1-3)

When man found himself alone, with raging lusts that demanded to be satisfied, and no options for getting back to God and straightening this situation out, he started a new project: to re-create this world to fulfill his lusts and desires. If he can't have God's goodness, then he will create his own. And to this day humanity has been fanatically busy creating a world that gives them the satisfactions and thrills and riches and security that they want. We call it "the good life," or the American Dream, or Utopia. It's a life of wealth and power and lust and entertainment and, in many cases, vengeance and war and repression. We've replaced what God thought was "good" (Genesis 1:31) with what we think is good. And God hates it. It's actually idolatry, because we now worship the objects of our lusts instead of the Creator.

> Do not love the world or anything in the world. If anyone loves the world, the love of the Father is not in him. For everything in the world – the cravings of sinful man, the lust of his eyes and the boasting of what he has and does – comes not from the Father but from the world. (1 John 2:15-16)

> Put to death, therefore, whatever belongs to your earthly nature: sexual immorality, impurity, lust, evil desires and greed, which is idolatry. (Colossians 3:5)

Man doesn't have God's wisdom. God can create a universe with parts that fit together perfectly. Man, however, creates a disaster. He can't anticipate what will happen when he creates new machines and chemicals and governments and cultures, no matter what good intentions he may have. Notice that there is always a downside to man's works, for two reasons: first, God has a curse on this creation, which means he will make sure that we get hurt and frustrated working with it (see the story of Babel). He certainly isn't going to reward us in our rebellion! And second, we don't understand the materials we're working with well enough to avoid potential problems; we're always being surprised by hidden flaws. Just when we thought we found a miracle cure in penicillin, the germs found a way to get around it and become "superbugs." The poison we create to kill insects ends up polluting our neighborhood water sources. Today milk is good for us; tomorrow, the doctors decide that it's bad for us; the next week, it's "good" again. The automobile, a machine that solved so many of our problems of transportation, destroyed local communities and even families as people spread out across the nation.

In other words we have left the goodness of God (remember that he called what he made "very good") and are trying desperately to create another "good" out of the ingredients of this world without God's direction. But there's a problem in that: this world wasn't designed to fulfill the heart and life of man; only God can do that. So, as the wise man taught us, we will struggle to get what we want out of this world, fail, and die in the end anyway, having failed to achieve happiness.

So I hated life, because the work that is done under the sun was grievous to me. All of it is meaningless, a chasing after the wind. I hated all the things I had toiled for under the sun, because I must leave them to the one who comes after me. And who knows whether he will be a wise man or a fool? Yet he will have control over all the work into which I have poured my effort and skill under the sun. This too is meaningless. So my heart began to despair over all my toilsome labor under the sun. For a man may do his work with wisdom, knowledge and skill, and then he must leave all he owns to someone who has not worked for it. This too is meaningless and a great misfortune. What does a man get for all the toil and anxious striving with which he labors under the sun? All his days his work is pain and grief; even at night his mind does not rest. This too is meaningless. (Ecclesiastes 2:17-23)

> This too is a grievous evil: As a man comes, so he departs, and what does he gain, since he toils for the wind? All his days he eats in darkness, with great frustration, affliction and anger. (Ecclesiastes 5:16-17)

Not only have we cut ourselves off from our only good and replaced it with emptiness, we've settled for a lifestyle below the animals. We're following a progression from life to death; it's a deadly recipe for the "good life" that will only result in disaster. We turn our backs on God, and look for something else to fill our lives with. And since nothing will keep us alive like God can, our souls dry up in lawlessness and helplessness. As a result, man's character goes from bad to worse; and our relationships with each other turn into a putrid mass of reprobation, selfishness, materialism, and general, all-around nastiness. Paul, for example, describes a world without God.

> Furthermore, since they did not think it worthwhile to retain the knowledge of God, he gave them over to a depraved mind, to do what ought not to be done. They have become filled with every kind of wickedness, evil, greed and depravity. They are full of envy, murder, strife, deceit and malice. They are gossips, slanderers, God-haters, insolent, arrogant and boastful; they invent ways of doing evil; they disobey their parents; they are senseless, faithless, heartless, ruthless. Although they know God's righteous decree that those who do such things deserve death, they not only continue to do these very things but also approve of those who practice them. (Romans 1:28-32)

This is not the world that God created! This is the world that rebellious man created. And our answers and solutions to these kinds of problems have proved powerless, no matter how much law and coercion and reasoning we've tried to apply to them. God dropped us down into an inescapable prison where our wicked and perverse natures are destroying us, and we have no hope of getting out of this situation on our own.

INDEPENDENCE FROM GOD

This all came about, remember, from our deciding that God was not worth seeking out. We didn't want God; we wanted something other than God. Our lives now are in complete independence from God. The norm in our world is to treat God as if he's a fringe idea, a "help" only when we get into some kind of trouble that we can't get ourselves out of. God is only for those "religious fanatics" who need a "crutch" because they can't take care of themselves. The average person is too busy working and enjoying life and creating his own little nest to bother taking God seriously. Life without God is normal to us.

This isn't to say that many people totally ignore God. Many still go to church (let's deal with "Christians" at this point; pagan religions have their own special problem!) and "worship God." But that usually consists of thinking about God, and talking about God, without actually meeting with God himself. Listening to a sermon, and singing a hymn, is not the same as coming into God's presence and touching him.

This is a profound and shocking insult to God who alone is glorious. When we're looking for wisdom, we don't turn to God and his Word. When we need power, we look to some other power than God. When we need solutions to the disaster that sin is creating among us, we make up our own rules and try to fix it our own way instead of following God's directions out of the mess. In short, we don't think that God is the only good for us; in fact, we don't even consider him an option.

This is in spite of the fact that God is the Creator and can do anything! He still raises up nations and tears others down.

He keeps the planet running, he feeds all of us every day, he directs our steps even when we can't see him, he forbears punishing us with the hope that we will listen to him and change. Even though he's doing all of this and more on a daily basis, we give him no credit at all for knowing what he's doing. We refuse to include him in our plans.

It's an insult to God to be shoved aside like this. Is there any other god or power or wisdom that is better than Israel's God?

> Who among the gods is like you, O LORD?
> Who is like you – majestic in holiness, awesome in
> glory, working wonders? (Exodus 15:11)

Are we insane, that we have burned our bridges with God like this and are determined to live without him, come what may? Don't we realize that cutting ourselves off from him like this will be just as fatal as cutting off our own heads? It's moral and physical suicide.

To God, this shows a deep-seated hatred toward him in the heart of man. You may have reasons for not liking God, but you have no justification in avoiding him. Independence from God in any way is an act of treason, a declaration of war, a proclamation that you have found this God wanting. He doesn't give you what you want, and so you're looking elsewhere for your joy and purpose in life. In other words, the ruler of God's creation has declared independence and is leading a revolution against God's rule over him. God cannot allow such a situation to go unanswered; there's too much at stake.

IS THIS WHAT MAN DOES?

Does the rest of the Bible agree with this interpretation? Can we find this doctrine in other Scriptures? *Is this what God doesn't want us to do – to judge things for ourselves?* Is this, as a matter of fact, exactly what man does and God disapproves of?

Do not judge, or you too will be judged. For in the same way you judge others, you will be judged, and with the measure you use, it will be measured against you. (Matthew 7:1-2)

Do not judge, and you will not be judged. Do not condemn, and you will not be condemned. (Luke 6:37)

You judge by human standards; I pass judgment on no one. (John 8:15)

You, therefore, have no excuse, you who pass judgment on someone else, for at whatever point you judge the other, you are condemning yourself. (Romans 2:1)

Who are you to judge someone else's servant? To his own master he stands or falls. (Romans 14:4)

You, then, why do you judge your brother? Or why do you look down on your brother? For we will all stand before God's judgment seat. (Romans 14:10)

Therefore do not let anyone judge you by what you eat or drink, or with regard to a religious festival, a New Moon celebration or a Sabbath day. (Colossians 2:16)

Brothers, do not slander one another. Anyone who speaks against his brother or judges him, speaks against the Law and judges it. When you judge the Law, you are not keeping it, but sitting in

*judgment on it. There is only one Lawgiver and
Judge, the one who is able to save and destroy.
But you – who are you to judge your neighbor?
(James 4:11-12)*

Not all judgment is bad. Jesus claimed that he has the
authority to judge (John 5:27) – which implies that others do *not*
have the authority to judge, though they might attempt it. The
authority comes from God, not man. The reason that Jesus can
judge correctly is because, being the Son of God, he has the
fullness of the mind of God. He can't go wrong.

Paul once accused a high priest of judging him (Acts
23:3), and he revealed a double-standard in the priest's heart.
The reason why our judgment of things is often wrong is
because we don't use the same standards on ourselves that we
do on others. If we condemn others for the very sins that we're
guilty of, how can we dare to use our standards (our own lusts
and desires, in other words!) to judge others? We call this using
a "double standard" and everyone knows that's not fair.

In another place Paul teaches us something else about the
reason for our poor judgment:

*Therefore judge nothing before the appointed
time; wait until the Lord comes. He will bring to
light what is hidden in darkness and will expose
the motives of men's hearts. (1 Corinthians 4:5)*

We can't know all the facts about a case or person to
make a right judgment! We will always be blind to something
important; only God who knows all things can make a correct
judgment.   For example, we may think that someone is
wonderful and we want to be just like them (teenagers are
always doing this with their Hollywood heroes!), when actually
that person's heart may be a cesspool of immorality and death.
They are careful, however, to hide their private lives from us so

that we will follow them. Unfortunatley their feet "lead to the grave."

The reason we want the right to judge things is because we want to satisfy our senses, just as Eve did. We have our own agenda, our own purposes that we want to accomplish; rather than turn over judgment to someone else, then, and risk losing what *we* want to see happen, we assume the role of judge so that events will turn out to *our* liking.

But the root of the problem is that we don't want God to rule over us. That's why we've taken the function of judgment away from him. And often it's not that we think we know everything, it's the *authority* that we claim for ourselves. We are saying that we can, and have the right to, make our own judgements on things. We are, by that bold statement, challenging God's will and wisdom, and his position as King over us.

CAN WE SEE IT?

If this doctrine of the Tree of the Knowledge of Good and Evil is true, then we ought to be able to see it all around us. In fact, if it's as important as it seems to be, it ought to be *very* plain to see!

As a matter of fact, we find that we do this *all the time*. We constantly sit in judgment on everything and everybody around us. We judge others and their behavior based on our own standards of what is right or wrong. Need an example? Don't we often condemn somebody for the way they are raising their children? What standards do we use to do that? By the ways *we* raise *our* children! For some reason we think that everything we did was right, and if anybody else does something differently then *they* must be wrong.

When we talk to someone we are always passing judgment on what they're saying to us. Do we agree with them, or do we secretly despise them while smiling and pretending to agree? What standards do we use to decide whether they're right or not? Our own standards, or God's?

> The wicked … those who do evil, who speak cordially with their neighbors but harbor malice in their hearts. (Psalm 28:3)

Adults are good at this business of judging everything. We claim that we *need* to judge things because otherwise we will be tricked or hurt or deceived if we naïvely accept everything at face value. Well, yes, for some things. The problem is that our *immediate* reaction (which shows just how deep-rooted the act of judgment is for us) to *anything* we come across is judgment; we pass everything by the bar of our own opinions and feelings to see if we like it, whether it suits us, or whether it's interfering with what we want, without even realizing that we are doing it. This is our inheritance from Adam and Eve. We sit in the seat of judgment above the whole world.

The Scripture does talk about "judging a tree by its fruits" and "stop judging by mere appearances, and make a right judgment." (John 7:24) But this, I believe, assumes that you "have the mind of Christ" (1 Corinthians 2:15-16) and are able to see things as God sees them. This is a learned behavior that only mature Christians can claim; it takes many years of studying the Bible.

> In fact, though by this time you ought to be teachers, you need someone to teach you the elementary truths of God's word all over again. You need milk, not solid food! Anyone who lives on milk, being still an infant, is not acquainted with

the teaching about righteousness. But solid food is for the mature, who by constant use have trained themselves to distinguish good from evil. (Hebrews 5:12-14)

You can tell when you meet a Christian's mature judgment: they use the Word to judge things, checking for the hand of God in the situation, and their judgment agrees with God's judgment and with others who have spiritual insight.

Most people, however, judge not by the Word of God but by their own lusts and ignorance. They're looking out for their own interests; they accept others, and believe principles, only if it helps them achieve the immoral and rebellious lifestyle that they want. They don't even think about checking with God about anything.

You are judging *me* right now! You may be saying in your mind, "Is this right? I don't like the sound of that, because it makes me look bad or it makes me out to be a sinner." Or you may be saying, "He doesn't know me; who does he think he is? I don't have to listen to him." Or you may be saying, "He's a nobody. I've never heard that before; I won't believe it until three experts agree with it!" Or you may be saying, "If you want to get anywhere with me, you have to impress me!" (or flatter me, or please me) For whatever reason, you may be resisting the truth of the Bible with your own standards of what is right or wrong.

We started judging things when we got up this morning and we will end the day doing it. We set our own schedules and goals. We decide what we will work on, what we will enjoy, and who we will hang around with, using as a standard whatever pleases us. And if we can't actually control the events of the day and things don't go our way, we will pout and make someone miserable for not giving us what we want. Someone is going to pay if I have to suffer in any way!

Now I'm not referring to those things in which we *have* to judge – like whether a bridge is solid enough to drive over, or whether a dollar bill is genuine or not. What I'm talking about is judging about the things that *God alone* has the right to make a judgment about. There are certain things that we are not allowed to have our own opinions on! The Bible makes these issues very plain; we do not need to guess about what they are.

> We are *not allowed* to make our own judgment on the value of earthly treasures and whether they are worth living for; God alone tells us what to think of them and how to use them. (Matthew 6:19-21)

> We are *not allowed* to judge whether someone is worth our love and time; God alone tells us how to relate to them. (Matthew 22:39)

> We are *not allowed* to listen to the lusts in our heart and live in hatred, murder, robbery, and sexual perversion; God alone sets the laws for our behavior. (Colossians 3:8-10)

> We are *not allowed* to use the weapons of this world to bring about the kingdom of God, no matter how reasonable they seem; God alone gives us the spiritual resources to build his Kingdom in his way. (2 Corinthians 10:3-5))

What I'm saying is that there are many issues like these in which we cannot make a correct judgment on our own – not without God's total perspective and infinite truth and righteousness, found only in his Word. If we dare to judge the issues of life by what *we* feel or think, we will always go wrong and end up having to deal with God's condemnation as a result – as Eve did.

I mentioned above that you may be judging me right now. Actually that's allowed under one circumstance: you are allowed – it is your *duty* – to judge if what I am saying matches what God himself teaches in the Bible. Church leaders don't always teach us the truth; teachers too often substitute what they judge to be truth for the Word of God, and expect their students to believe them. God forbid! You must check everything a teacher says against God's eternal standards, because teachers are sinners too and liable to faulty judgment. The Bereans were careful to check the words of the apostle Paul himself! "Now the Bereans were of more noble character than the Thessalonians, for they received the message with great eagerness and examined the Scriptures every day *to see if what Paul said was true.*" (Acts 17:11) The point is that you are not allowed to judge my teaching against your opinions or feelings, only with God's Word. But do you know enough about God's Word to make a good judgment?

CHILDREN AND ADULTS

The reason I'm bringing up this issue is because children are an interesting exception in this matter of the Knowledge of Good and Evil. It's true that they too fall prey to the same temptation – to judge what to do, and what is good, by their own desires – but at first they are only concerned with physical matters. They plot how they can get more dessert or take someone's favorite toy away, and then justify their action!

But when it comes to spiritual matters they seem to be completely innocent of the charge. They just sit there and soak it all up, without a twinge of judgment, without any need to critically tear apart what you are teaching them. If you were teaching adults, you know that you would have a battle on your hands over many issues; with children, however, they simply listen and believe it. No problem! For this reason it's refreshing to teach children the Bible.

It appears that children are completely willing to accept God's authority over them. In their minority, they follow the leader. Just as they follow their parents without question, they follow God without question. If God says it in his Word, they believe it.

I'm not saying that the Knowledge of Good and Evil isn't in a child's heart; otherwise how could we explain its inevitable appearance later in life? Where could it have come from except deep in the heart? But they don't start questioning spiritual matters until the beginning of the teen years. Psychologists tell us that children below the teen years are unable to grapple with conceptual issues; between 12 and 14 years old, however, a switch turns on in their minds and they begin putting things together from an adult point of view, along with a fierce desire for independence. The change is dramatic and real. You have seen, most likely, how teenagers suddenly develop this attitude. They aren't willing to follow an adult's lead anymore; suddenly they know more than their parents know! (Adults, on the other hand, generally have learned how to be judgmental without being so obnoxious about it!) Teens want to chart their own course and be independent. Unfortunately, that often means trying out a lifestyle that will ruin them – because they're throwing off God's restraints on them as well as parental restraints.

What this means, then, is that you can slide the truth into a child's head much easier than you can an adult's. A child simply will not put your teaching through a test to see whether he wants to believe it or not – it goes right into his world view and becomes part of what he "knows" about the world. You are his or her authority; so is God. An adult, on the other hand, presents your teaching to a mental barrage of tests, like the old

Indian trial called "running the gauntlet" – if it survives what the person *wants to hear*, he will believe it! It's not without reason that Paul complained that some people "will not put up with sound doctrine. Instead, to suit their own desires [*reminds us of Genesis 3, doesn't it?*], they will gather around them a great number of teachers to say what their itching ears want to hear." (2 Timothy 4:3)

So, this is what we learn from all this: *first*, become like a child yourself and believe what the Bible says and teach no less than what it says. *Second*, don't worry that the children won't believe you – they will. *Third*, the problem will be with the adults; that's why we need to train these children in the way they should think and live before that switch turns on in their hearts and they begin submitting God himself to their own corrupt standards.

www.ingramcontent.com/pod-product-compliance
Lightning Source LLC
Chambersburg PA
CBHW031235090426
42742CB00007B/204